EXAMKRACKERS MCAT®

BIOLOGY 1 MOLECULES: BIOCHEMISTRY

10TH EDITION

JONATHAN ORSAY

OSOTE
PUBLISHING

Major Contributors:
Joshua Albrecht, M.D., Ph.D.
Jennifer Birk-Goldschmidt, M.S.
Kaitlyn Barkley
Stephanie Blatch, M.A.
Austin Mattox
Lauren Nadler
Mark Pedersen, M.D.
Colleen Moran Shannon

Contributors:
Mark Alshak
Leena Asfour
Jacob Ball
Kristin Bater
Ankush Chandra, M.S.
David Collins
Claudia Goodsett
Spenser Hayward
Jay Li
Xintong Li, M.D.
Laura Neubauer
Christina Snider
Chris Stewart
Darren Sultan
Richmond Woodward

Art Director:
Erin Daniel

Designers:
Dana Kelley
Charles Yuen

Illustrators:
Stephen Halker
Kellie Holoski

Published in the United States of America by Osote Publishing, New Jersey.

ISBN 10: 1-893858-84-7 (Volume 1)
ISBN 13: 978-1-893858-84-8 (6 Volume Set)
10th Edition

To purchase additional copies of this book or the rest of the 6 volume set, call 1-888-572-2536 or fax orders to 1-859-305-6464.

Examkrackers.com
Osote.com

PHOTOCOPYING & DISTRIBUTION POLICY

Acknowledgements

Although I am the author, the hard work and expertise of many individuals contributed to this book. The idea of writing in two voices, a science voice and an MCAT® voice, was the creative brainchild of my imaginative friend Jordan Zaretsky. I would like to thank Jerry Johnson for lending his science talent and exceptional science skills to this project. I would like to thank nineteen years worth of Examkrackers students for doggedly questioning every explanation, every sentence, every diagram, and every punctuation mark in the book, and for providing the creative inspiration that helped me find new ways to approach and teach biochemistry. Finally, I wish to thank my wife, Silvia, for her support during the difficult times in the past and those that lie ahead.

Introduction to the Examkrackers Manuals

The Examkrackers manuals are designed to give you exactly the information you need to do well on the MCAT® while limiting extraneous information that will not be tested. This manual organizes all of the information on the molecular biology tested on the MCAT® conceptually. Concepts make the content both simple and portable for optimal application to MCAT® questions. Mastery of the biological and biomolecular material covered in this manual will increase your confidence and allow you to succeed with seemingly difficult passages that are designed to intimidate. The MCAT® rewards your ability to read complex passages and questions through the lens of basic science concepts.

An in-depth introduction to the MCAT® is located in the Reasoning Skills manual. Read this introduction first to start thinking like the MCAT® and to learn critical mathematical skills. The second lecture of the Reasoning Skills manual addresses the research methods needed for success on 20% of questions on the science and psychology sections of the MCAT®. Research questions are the most difficult on the MCAT® and are the questions that help students beat the mean and get a high score. Once you have read those lectures, return to this manual to begin your review of the biology you will need to excel on the MCAT®.

How to Use This Manual

Examkrackers MCAT® manuals can be used with the Examkrackers Comprehensive MCAT® Course or as a tool for independent MCAT® study. Examkrackers MCAT® preparation experience has shown that you will get the most out of these manuals when you structure your studying as follows. If you are taking the Examkrackers Comprehensive MCAT® Course, read each lecture twice before the class lecture. During the first reading, you should not write in the book. Instead, read purely for enjoyment. During the second reading, highlight and take notes in the margins. Complete the twenty-four questions in each lecture during the second reading before coming to class. Do not look at the In-Class Exams before class. Immediately after class, read the lecture again, slowly and thoroughly.

If you are studying independently, read each lecture twice (as described above), completing the in-lecture questions during the second reading. Take the In-Class Exam, then read the lecture once more, slowly and thoroughly.

The In-Class Exams are designed to educate. They are similar to an MCAT® section, but are shortened and have most of the easy questions removed. We believe that you can answer most of the easy questions without too much help from us, so the best way to raise your score is to focus on the more difficult questions. The In-Class Exams are designed to help you prepare for test day when you will be faced with an intensity that is difficult to simulate. Technically, the Examkrackers In-Class Exams are timed to take as long as 35 minutes to complete. By practicing with a few minutes less, you will be ready for the pressure and pace of the real exam, and MCAT® day will feel more manageable. These methods are some of the reasons for the rapid and celebrated success of the Examkrackers prep course and products.

With each In-Class Exam you should see the number of questions you answer correctly increase. Do not be discouraged by poor performance on these exams; they are not meant to predict your performance on the real MCAT®. **The questions that you get wrong (or even guess correctly) are the most important ones. They represent your potential score increase.** When you get a question wrong or have to guess, determine why. If content was the problem, target those areas for review. If the issue was your approach to the question, make a commitment to a different approach for the next practice test. As you learn to think like the MCAT®, you will see your score increase.

In order to study most efficiently, it is essential to know what topics are and are not tested directly in MCAT® questions. This manual uses the following conventions to make the distinction. Any topic listed in the AAMC's guide to the MCAT® is printed in **red, bold type**. You must thoroughly understand all topics printed in **red, bold type**. Any formula that must be memorized is also printed in **red, bold type**.

If a topic is not printed in **bold and red**, it may still be important. Understanding these topics may be helpful for putting other terms in context. Topics and equations that are not explicitly tested but are still useful to know are printed in *italics*. Knowledge of content printed in *italics* will enhance your ability to answer passage-based MCAT® questions, as MCAT® passages may cover topics beyond the AAMC's list of tested topics on the MCAT®.

Features of the Examkrackers Manuals

The Examkrackers manuals include several features to help you retain and integrate information for the MCAT®. Take advantage of these features to get the most out of your study time.

- **The 3 Keys** – The Three Keys unlock the material and the MCAT® by highlighting the most important things to remember from each chapter. The Three Keys are listed at the beginning and end of each lecture with reminders from Salty throughout the text. Examine the Three Keys before and after reading a lecture to make sure you have absorbed the most important messages. As you read, continue to develop your own key concepts that will guide your studying and performance.

- **Signposts** – The MCAT® is fully integrated, asking you to apply the biological, physical, and social sciences simultaneously. The signposts alongside the text in this manual will help you build mental connections between topics and disciplines. This mental map will lead you to a high score on the MCAT®. The post of each sign "brackets" the paragraph to which it refers. When you see a signpost next to a topic, stop and consider how the topics are related. Soon you will begin making your own connections between concepts and topics within and between disciplines. This is an MCAT® skill that will improve your score. When answering questions, these connections give you multiple routes to find your way to the answer.

- **MCAT® Think** – These sidebars invite deeper consideration of certain topics. They provide helpful context for topics that are tested and will challenge you just like tough MCAT® passages. While MCAT® Think topics and their level of detail may not be explicitly tested on the MCAT®, read and consider each MCAT® Think to sharpen your MCAT® skills. The MCAT® Think sidebars provide essential practice in managing seemingly complex and unfamiliar content, as you will need to do for passages on MCAT® day.

I'm Salty the Kracker. Where you see purple text, that's me. I will show you why the content makes sense and help you develop your MCAT® intuition. My job is to make sure you 1. stay awake and 2. really understand and remember what you're reading. If you think I am funny, tell the boss. I could use a raise. If you get the munchies, reconsider... you'll want me around.

Additional Resources

If you find yourself struggling with the science or you want more practice, take advantage of the additional Examkrackers resources that are available.

Examkrackers offers a 9-week Comprehensive MCAT® Course to help you achieve a high score on the MCAT®. Whether in person or online, the course includes up to 120 hours with expert instructors, a unique course format, and regular full-length MCAT® exams. Each class includes lecture, a practice exam, and review, designed to help you develop essential MCAT® skills. For locations and registration please visit Examkrackers.com or call 1.888.KRACKEM.

EK-Tests® are Examkrackers full-length, online simulated MCAT® exams that match the AAMC MCAT® in style, content, and skills tested. Written by educators, high-scoring medical students, and physicians, EK-Tests® provide the best MCAT® practice available. To purchase EK-Tests®, please visit Examkrackers.com.

Your purchase of this book new will also give you access to the **Examkrackers Forums** at Examkrackers.com/mcat/forum. These bulletin boards allow you to discuss any MCAT® question with an MCAT® expert at Examkrackers. All discussions are kept on file so you can refer back to previous discussions on any question in this book. Once you have purchased the books you can take advantage of this resource by calling 1.888.KRACKEM to register for the forums.

Although we make every effort to ensure the accuracy of our books, the occasional error does occur. Corrections are posted on the Examkrackers Books Errata Forum, also at Examkrackers.com/mcat/forum. If you believe that you have found a mistake, please post an inquiry on the Study with Examkrackers MCAT® Books Forum, which is likewise found at Examkrackers.com/mcat/forum. As the leaders in MCAT® preparation, we are committed to providing you with the most up-to-date, accurate information possible.

Study diligently, trust this book to guide you, and you will reach your MCAT® goals.

Table of Contents

LECTURE 1 Biological Molecules and Enzymes 1

LECTURE 2 Genetics 31

LECTURE 3   Metabolism   69

LECTURE 4   Laboratory Techniques   95

30-Minute In-Class Exams   125

Answers & Explanations to In-Class Exams   159

Answers & Explanations to Questions in the Lectures   177

Photo Credits   191

Index   193

BIOLOGICAL SCIENCES

DIRECTIONS. Most questions in the Biological Sciences test are organized into groups, each preceded by a descriptive passage. After studying the passage, select the one best answer to each question in the group. Some questions are not based on a descriptive passage and are also independent of each other. You must also select the one best answer to these questions. If you are not certain of an answer, eliminate the alternatives that you know to be incorrect and then select an answer from the remaining alternatives. A periodic table is provided for your use. You may consult it whenever you wish.

PERIODIC TABLE OF THE ELEMENTS

1 **H** 1.0																	2 **He** 4.0
3 **Li** 6.9	4 **Be** 9.0											5 **B** 10.8	6 **C** 12.0	7 **N** 14.0	8 **O** 16.0	9 **F** 19.0	10 **Ne** 20.2
11 **Na** 23.0	12 **Mg** 24.3											13 **Al** 27.0	14 **Si** 28.1	15 **P** 31.0	16 **S** 32.1	17 **Cl** 35.5	18 **Ar** 39.9
19 **K** 39.1	20 **Ca** 40.1	21 **Sc** 45.0	22 **Ti** 47.9	23 **V** 50.9	24 **Cr** 52.0	25 **Mn** 54.9	26 **Fe** 55.8	27 **Co** 58.9	28 **Ni** 58.7	29 **Cu** 63.5	30 **Zn** 65.4	31 **Ga** 69.7	32 **Ge** 72.6	33 **As** 74.9	34 **Se** 79.0	35 **Br** 79.9	36 **Kr** 83.8
37 **Rb** 85.5	38 **Sr** 87.6	39 **Y** 88.9	40 **Zr** 91.2	41 **Nb** 92.9	42 **Mo** 95.9	43 **Tc** (98)	44 **Ru** 101.1	45 **Rh** 102.9	46 **Pd** 106.4	47 **Ag** 107.9	48 **Cd** 112.4	49 **In** 114.8	50 **Sn** 118.7	51 **Sb** 121.8	52 **Te** 127.6	53 **I** 126.9	54 **Xe** 131.3
55 **Cs** 132.9	56 **Ba** 137.3	57 **La*** 138.9	72 **Hf** 178.5	73 **Ta** 180.9	74 **W** 183.9	75 **Re** 186.2	76 **Os** 190.2	77 **Ir** 192.2	78 **Pt** 195.1	79 **Au** 197.0	80 **Hg** 200.6	81 **Tl** 204.4	82 **Pb** 207.2	83 **Bi** 209.0	84 **Po** (209)	85 **At** (210)	86 **Rn** (222)
87 **Fr** (223)	88 **Ra** 226.0	89 **Ac**⁼ 227.0	104 **Unq** (261)	105 **Unp** (262)	106 **Unh** (263)	107 **Uns** (262)	108 **Uno** (265)	109 **Une** (267)									

	58 **Ce** 140.1	59 **Pr** 140.9	60 **Nd** 144.2	61 **Pm** (145)	62 **Sm** 150.4	63 **Eu** 152.0	64 **Gd** 157.3	65 **Tb** 158.9	66 **Dy** 162.5	67 **Ho** 164.9	68 **Er** 167.3	69 **Tm** 168.9	70 **Yb** 173.0	71 **Lu** 175.0
⁼	90 **Th** 232.0	91 **Pa** (231)	92 **U** 238.0	93 **Np** (237)	94 **Pu** (244)	95 **Am** (243)	96 **Cm** (247)	97 **Bk** (247)	98 **Cf** (251)	99 **Es** (252)	100 **Fm** (257)	101 **Md** (258)	102 **No** (259)	103 **Lr** (260)

For your convenience, a periodic table is also inserted in the back of the book.

Biological Molecules and Enzymes

1.1 Introduction

This lecture discusses the structure and basic functions of the major chemical components of living cells and their surroundings. Most biological molecules can be classified as lipids, proteins, carbohydrates, or nucleotide derivatives. Each of these types of molecules possesses a carbon skeleton. Together with water and minerals, they form living cells and their environments. The unique features of these molecules, combined with the ways they are employed, help to explain their functions. Knowledge of these biological molecules and their roles in the cellular environment provides a strong base from which to understand the biology and biochemistry required for the MCAT®.

The Examkrackers Approach

Learning biochemistry and molecular biology for the MCAT® may seem to be an insurmountable task, but the Examkrackers approach will help you master the content you need to recognize on test day. More importantly, it will teach you how to reason through biochemistry and molecular biology passages and questions. Because the MCAT® will present situations you have never seen before, memorizing every reactant, product, and enzyme is not a good use of your time. Instead, master the information covered in the pages that follow, and sharpen your reasoning skills with the passages and questions associated with each chapter. Our approach to biochemistry covers the main macromolecules involved in maintaining human homeostasis, as well as the laboratory techniques that allow scientists and physicians to understand these pathways. Certain information is worth having at your fingertips, so focus on our notes about what to memorize, and aim to integrate that knowledge into your broader understanding of these subjects.

THE 3 KEYS

1. Each category of biological molecule has a "personality" - think structure and polarity - that matches its practical uses in living organisms.

2. Enzyme-substrate fit correlates with enzyme effectiveness and a lower K_m.

3. Competitive inhibitors block the active site; noncompetitive inhibitors bind to a separate site, changing the shape of the active site; uncompetitive inhibitors bind the enzyme-substrate complex, decreasing the concentration of substrate that can react.

Nucleotide: ATP

Protein: collagen

Carbohydrate: amylose

Lipid: phospholipid

1.2 Water

Water is the solvent in which the chemical reactions of living cells take place. 70 to 80 percent of a cell's mass is made up of water. Water is a small polar molecule that can participate in **hydrogen bonding** (intermolecular bonding between H and F, O, or N; Figure 1.1). Most compounds as light as water would exist as a gas at typical cell temperatures. The ability of water molecules to form hydrogen bonds with each other elevates the boiling point; as a result, water remains in a liquid state in the cellular environment. Hydrogen bonding also provides strong cohesive forces between water molecules, "squeezing" **hydrophobic** (Greek: hydros → water, phobos → fear) molecules away from water and causing them to aggregate. By contrast, **hydrophilic** (Greek: philos → love) molecules or ionic compounds dissolve easily in water because their negatively charged ends are attracted to the partial positive charge of water's hydrogens while their positively charged ends are attracted to the partial negative charge of the oxygen (Figure 1.2). Water molecules surround (solvate) a hydrophilic molecule or ion.

Besides acting as a solvent, water often acts as a reactant or product. Most macromolecules of living cells are broken apart via **hydrolysis** (Greek: lysis → separation) and are formed via dehydration. In a hydrolysis reaction, a macromolecule, such as a protein, is broken into two smaller molecules through the addition of water. The hydrolysis of ATP molecules provides the body's major source of energy. Digestion is primarily the hydrolysis of macromolecules, breaking a bond by adding the H and OH of water to either end. **Dehydration** is the reverse reaction of hydrolysis, where two molecules are combined to form a larger molecule and water is formed as a byproduct. As will be described later in this lecture, a dehydration reaction allows the formation of the bonds that make up biological molecules, such as the peptide bonds that make up proteins and the ester bonds that are essential to triglycerides.

When you think about water, think polarity. The polarity of water is what makes it a perfect solvent for chemical reactions in the body. As you read this lecture, consider how the polar and nonpolar regions of biological molecules affect their interactions with water. Due to polarity and hydrogen bonding, water molecules pull apart polar molecules or ions and form ordered networks around them. On the other hand, water molecules force nonpolar molecules to congregate together. These interactions play an important role in biological reactions.

Remember that in an ATP hydrolysis reaction, water serves as a nucleophile and attacks the electrophilic phosphoanhydride bond between the β and γ phosphates of the ATP molecule. The freed γ phosphate can then be used by a kinase enzyme to phosphorylate target proteins.

FIGURE 1.2 | Water as a Solvent

Ionic compound: sodium chloride NaCl

FIGURE 1.1 | Hydrogen Bonds

Hydrogen bonding between individual water molecules creates cohesive forces that are strong enough to support this raft spider.

Polar molecules or ionic compounds are readily solvated by water; nonpolar molecules are not. This is an example of how "like dissolves like."

1.3 | Lipids

Lipids are essential to life and perform a variety of functions in the body. While the types of lipids are characterized by a variety of structures and functional groups, they all share the same defining characteristics: low solubility in water and high solubility in nonpolar organic solvents. In other words, lipids are nonpolar and therefore hydrophobic. This property determines the behavior of lipids in the watery environment of the cell.

The roles played by lipids in an organism can be divided into three categories: 1. energy storage, 2. cellular organization and structure, particularly in the membrane, and 3. provision of precursor molecules for vitamins and hormones. The structural features of different lipids make them ideally suited for these cellular functions.

The major groups of lipids include fatty acids, triacylglycerols, phospholipids, glycolipids, steroids, terpenes, and waxes.

Omega-3 fatty acids are lipids. They are found in fish and other seafood including algae and krill, some plants, and nut oils.

FIGURE 1.3 | Types of Lipids

As you read about the following types of fats, relate each of them back to the three major functions of lipids. Remember that long carbon chains allow energy storage; that fats assemble into barriers separating aqueous environments because they are hydrophobic; and that lipids are useful as precursors for signaling molecules because they can pass through cellular membranes.

Consider Key 1: Think about how the different functional groups of lipids, carbohydrates, nucleotides, and proteins allow them to catalyze specific chemistry or maintain specific functions in the cell.

Each fat cell or adipocyte consists of a large central lipid droplet (yellow) surrounded by a thin layer of cytoplasm (red) containing the nucleus (blue). Fat cells store energy as an insulating layer of fat under the skin.

The simplest phosphoglyceride is phosphatidic acid. All other phosphoglycerides except one type, *plasmalogens*, have a phosphatidic acid backbone, which is just another way of describing the glycerol backbone with a phosphate group attached. They can be referred to as **phosphatids**.

Besides being lipids themselves, **fatty acids** are the building blocks for most complex lipids. They act as fuel for the body and are components of the cell membranes, as described below. Fatty acids are composed of long chains of carbons truncated at one end by a carboxylic acid. They usually contain an even number of carbons. In humans, the maximum number of carbons in a fatty acid is 24. Fatty acids can be saturated or unsaturated. **Saturated fatty acids** possess only single carbon-carbon bonds. **Unsaturated fatty acids** contain one or more carbon-carbon double bonds. (See the Metabolism Lecture for more about the differences between saturated and unsaturated fats.) Oxidation of fatty acids liberates large amounts of chemical energy for a cell, up to 9 kcal for every mole of fatty acid oxidized. Fatty acids can also be used for long-term energy storage. The high concentration of carbon-hydrogen bonds in fatty acids allows them to store more energy per gram than any other macromolecule in the body. Most fats reach the cell in the form of free fatty acids, meaning fatty acid chains not attached to a backbone, rather than as triacylglycerols.

Triacylglycerols, phospholipids, and glycolipids are sometimes referred to as fatty acids. **Triacylglycerols** (Latin: tri → three), commonly called **triglycerides** or simply **fats** and *oils*, are constructed from a three-carbon backbone called **glycerol**, which is attached to three fatty acid chains (as shown in Figure 1.3). Their function in a cell is to store energy. They can also provide thermal insulation and padding to an organism. **Adipocytes** (Latin: adips → fat, Greek: kytos → cell), also called fat cells, are specialized cells whose cytoplasm contains almost nothing but triglycerides.

Phospholipids are lipids with a phosphate group attached. For the purposes of the MCAT®, the most important phospholipids are phosphoglycerides. Like triglycerides, phosphoglycerides are built from a glycerol backbone, but a polar phosphate group replaces one of the fatty acids. The phosphate group lies on the opposite side of the glycerol from the fatty acids, making the phospholipid polar at the phosphate end and nonpolar at the fatty acid end. Molecules that have a polar and nonpolar end are referred to as **amphipathic** (Latin: ambo → both), and this quality makes phospholipids especially well suited as the major component of biological membranes. When forming bilayer membranes, the polar heads of phospholipids are able to face toward the watery environment within and outside the cell, while the tails create a nonpolar inner layer within the membrane, forming a barrier to polar molecules that allows the regulation of their passage in and out of the cell.

Glycolipids (Greek: glucus → sweet) are similar to phosphoglycerides, except that glycolipids have one or more carbohydrates attached to the three-carbon glycerol backbone instead of the phosphate group. Glycolipids are also amphipathic. They are found in abundance in the membranes of myelinated cells in the human nervous system.

Sphingolipids are also similar to phosphoglycerides, in that they have a long chain fatty acid and a polar head group, but the backbone molecule is an amino alcohol called a sphingosine rather than a glycerol. (One type of sphingolipid, *sphingomyelin*, has a phosphate group attached to the sphingosine backbone and is therefore a phospholipid, although it is not a phosphoglyceride.) Like phospholipids, glycolipids, and steroids, sphingolipids make up part of the cell membrane.

Steroids are four-ringed structures. They include some hormones, *vitamin D,* and cholesterol, an important membrane component. Cholesterol is particularly important for maintaining membrane stability and fluidity, and it also serves as the precursor for steroid hormones. See the Endocrine System Lecture in *Biology 2: Systems* to learn about the steroid class of hormones, and see the Cell Lecture in the same manual for how steroids affect the characteristics of the cellular membrane.

Terpenes are a sixth class of lipids that are often part of pigments in the body. They include *vitamin A,* which is important for vision.

Waxes are formed by an ester linkage between a long-chain alcohol and a long-chain fatty acid. They have a variety of functions in different types of organisms, determined by their characteristic water-repellent texture. Ear wax is an example of a wax in the human body.

Another class of lipids (not shown in Figure 1.3 but often listed as a fatty acid) are the 20 carbon *eicosanoids* (Greek: eikosi → twenty). Eicosanoids include **prostaglandins**, thromboxanes, and leukotrienes. Eicosanoids are released from cell membranes as local hormones that regulate, among other things, blood pressure, body temperature, and smooth muscle contraction. Aspirin is a commonly used inhibitor of the synthesis of prostaglandins.

Because lipids are insoluble in aqueous solution, they are transported in the blood via *lipoproteins.* A lipoprotein contains a lipid core surrounded by phospholipids and *apoproteins.* The lipoprotein is able to dissolve lipids in its hydrophobic core and move freely through the aqueous solution due to its hydrophilic shell. Lipoproteins are classified by their density. The greater the ratio of lipid to protein, the lower the density, because lipids are less dense than proteins of similar size. The major classes of lipoproteins in humans are chylomicrons, *very low density lipoproteins (VLDL), low density lipoproteins (LDL),* and *high density lipoproteins (HDL).* (For more on lipoproteins, see the Digestive and Excretory Systems Lecture in *Biology 2: Systems.*)

Vitamins are a particular type of organic molecule that are essential, meaning they cannot be produced by the body. Vitamin A and Vitamin D are examples of **fat-soluble vitamins**. Fat-soluble vitamins are transported in the body along with fats obtained from the diet, and also assist in the absorption of these fats.

When the ratio of protein to lipid is larger, the density of a lipoprotein is greater. Think about a solidly built athlete and remember that the proteins comprising muscles weigh more than an equivalent volume of fat. Because proteins are more dense than lipids, the greater the ratio of protein to fat in a lipoprotein, the denser the lipoprotein will be.

Know these major functions of lipids:

1. phospholipids serve as a structural component of membranes,

2. triacylglycerols store metabolic energy and provide thermal insulation and padding,

3. steroids regulate metabolic activities,

4. some fatty acids (eicosanoids) even serve as local hormones.

Apoprotein

Phospholipids

Cholesterol

Triglyceride

See the Oxygen Containing
Reactions Lecture in the Chemistry
manual for more on carbohydrates,
including the chemistry behind the
formation of polysaccharides.

FIGURE 1.4 | Glucose and Fructose

Glucose   Fructose

In the absence of insulin, only the
brain and the liver continue to
absorb glucose.

Liver cells contain large amounts of
glycogen. This helps the liver regulate
blood glucose levels.

Large chloroplasts (found in plants)
contain starch granules made by
photosynthesis.

1.4 Carbohydrates

The primary biological importance of **carbohydrates** lies with their usefulness in energy storage and providing easily accessible energy to the body. As
with fats, the high concentration of C-H bonds in carbohydrates allows for the
storage of a large amount of energy, up to 4 kcal/mol, which is less than half
the energy content of fatty acids. Carbohydrates do not store as much energy
per gram as lipids simply because they do not have as high a concentration of
C-H bonds; alcohols are also present along the carbon chain. The consistent
structure of carbohydrates allows them to be easily stacked together in the
cell, which contributes to their usefulness for energy storage. The structure of
carbohydrates also makes it possible for them to join together through a dehydration reaction, forming long chains, **polysaccharides**, for energy storage.
The reverse hydrolysis reaction allows the release of single sugar molecules,
monosaccharides, which the tissues can use for energy.

Carbohydrates can be thought of as carbon and water in a fixed one-to-one
ratio. For each carbon atom there exists one oxygen atom and two hydrogen
atoms. The formula for any carbohydrate is:

$$C_n(H_2O)_n$$

The carbohydrates most likely to appear on the MCAT® are fructose and
glucose. Both are six carbon carbohydrates called **hexoses**. **Glucose** (Greek:
glucus → sweet) is the most commonly occurring six-carbon carbohydrate.
The Fischer projections of fructose and glucose are shown in Figure 1.4, while
the cyclic forms of glucose are shown in Figure 1.5. Glucose normally accounts
for 80% of the carbohydrates absorbed by humans. Almost all digested carbohydrates reaching body cells have been converted to glucose by the liver or
enterocytes (intestinal cells).

The cell can oxidize glucose to transfer its chemical energy to a more readily usable form, ATP. If the cell already has sufficient ATP, glucose is polym-
erized to the polysaccharide form, glycogen, or converted to fat. As shown
in Figure 1.5, **glycogen** is a branched glucose polymer with alpha linkages.
Glycogen is found in all animal cells, but especially large amounts are found
in muscle and liver cells. The liver regulates the blood glucose level, so liver
cells are one of the few cell types capable of reforming glucose from glycogen
and releasing it back into the bloodstream when needed. Only certain epithelial cells in the digestive tract and the proximal tubule of the kidney are
capable of absorbing glucose against a concentration gradient. This is done via
a secondary active transport mechanism down the concentration gradient of
sodium. All other cells absorb glucose via facilitated diffusion. Insulin increases the rate of facilitated diffusion for glucose and other monosaccharides. In
the absence of insulin, only neural and hepatic cells are capable of absorbing
sufficient amounts of glucose via the facilitated transport system.

Just like animals, plants join glucose molecules to form polysaccharides.
Plants use **starch** for long-term storage instead of glycogen. Starch comes in
two forms: *amylose* and *amylopectin*. Amylose may be branched or unbranched
and has the same alpha linkages as glycogen. Amylopectin resembles glycogen
but has a different branching structure.

Plants also use glucose molecules to form **cellulose**. Cellulose is used as a
structural material rather than for energy storage, and in contrast to starch and
glycogen, it is composed of beta linkages. Like most animals, humans have
enzymes to digest the alpha linkages of starch and glycogen but do not have
enzymes that can digest the beta linkages of cellulose. Some animals such as
cows have bacteria in their digestive systems that release an enzyme to digest
the beta linkages in cellulose. Recent research suggests that certain insects do
produce an enzyme to digest the beta linkages of cellulose.

FIGURE 1.5 Glucose and Glucose Polymers

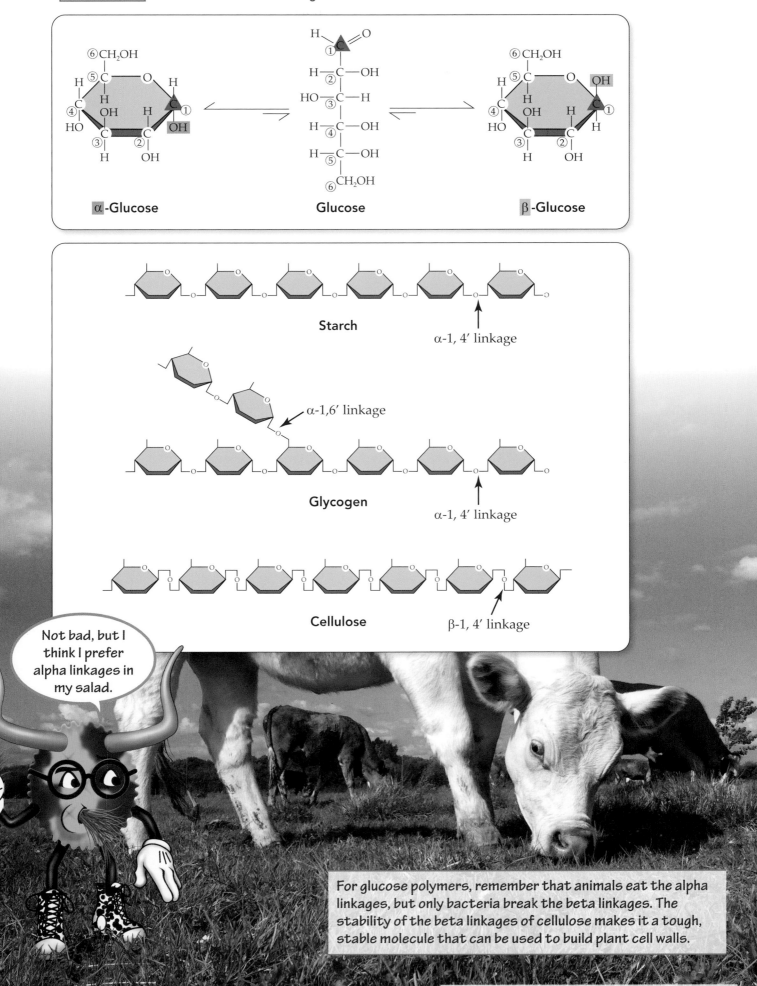

α-Glucose

Glucose

β-Glucose

Starch

α-1, 4' linkage

α-1,6' linkage

Glycogen

α-1, 4' linkage

Cellulose

β-1, 4' linkage

Not bad, but I think I prefer alpha linkages in my salad.

For glucose polymers, remember that animals eat the alpha linkages, but only bacteria break the beta linkages. The stability of the beta linkages of cellulose makes it a tough, stable molecule that can be used to build plant cell walls.

1.5 | Nucleotides

Nucleotides are an important class of molecules that comprise the building blocks of every organism's genetic material and are involved in the cell's use of energy. They are made up of three components:

1. a five carbon (pentose) sugar,

2. a nitrogenous base, and

3. a phosphate group.

The three components of nucleotides allow them to form the characteristic structure of DNA. The highly stable sugars, along with the phosphate groups, are able to link together to form a stable and organized backbone. Both are polar and can face outward into the watery solvent of the cell. Meanwhile, the nitrogenous bases can form weak hydrogen bonds with each other that stabilize the double-stranded structure of DNA but can also be separated to allow the replication of genetic material. Two hydrogen bonds form between A and T, while three hydrogen bonds form between C and G. The AT connection is weaker and easier to separate than the CG connection because there are fewer hydrogen bonds holding the bases together. More heat is required to separate the bond between G and C due to the extra hydrogen bond.

A **nucleoside** consists of a pentose sugar attached to a nitrogenous base. Nucleotides are formed by the addition of one or more phosphate groups to a nucleoside. Nucleotides form polymers to create the **nucleic acids**, DNA and RNA, which allow for the expression of genetic traits by specifying the production of proteins (see the Genetics Lecture).

In nucleic acids, nucleotides are joined together into long strands by **phosphodiester bonds** between the phosphate group of one nucleotide and the third carbon of the pentose sugar of the next nucleotide, forming a **sugar-phosphate backbone**. By convention, a strand of nucleotides in a nucleic acid is written as a list of its nitrogenous bases. A nucleotide attached to the number 3 carbon (3') of its neighbor follows that neighbor in the list. In other words, strands of nucleotides are synthesized by DNA polymerases in the 5' to 3' direction (5'→ 3'). By convention, DNA sequences are written so that the top strand runs 5'→ 3' and the bottom runs 3'→ 5'.

Four nitrogenous bases exist in **DNA (deoxyribonucleic acid): adenine (A), guanine (G), cytosine (C), and thymine (T)**. Adenine and guanine are two-ring structures called **purines**, while cytosine and thymine are single ring structures called **pyrimidines**. DNA usually exists in a particular form described by the **Watson-Crick model**, named for the scientists who are credited with first theorizing the structure of DNA. In this typical structure, also known as the B form, the two strands lie side by side in opposite 3´ → 5´ directions (**antiparallel**) bound together by hydrogen bonds between nitrogenous bases, forming a **double stranded** structure. This hydrogen bonding is commonly referred to as **base-pairing**. The length of a DNA strand is measured in **base-pairs (bp)**. Under normal circumstances, the hydrogen bonds form only between specific purine-pyrimidine pairs; adenine forms 2 hydrogen bonds with thymine, and guanine forms 3 hydrogen bonds with cytosine. In order for two strands to bind together, their bases must match up in the correct order. Two strands that match in such a fashion are called **complementary strands**. When complementary strands bind together, they curl into a **double helix** (Figure 1.7). The double helix contains two distinct grooves called the major groove and the minor groove. Each groove spirals once around the double helix for every ten base-pairs. This structure of DNA is stable in the cellular environment and allows for replication of genetic material.

Watson and Crick discovered the double helix structure of DNA.

FIGURE 1.6 | NADH

NADH is an example of a dinucleotide. Notice that a phosphomonoester linkage joins the two nucleotides.

FIGURE 1.7 DNA Double Helix

Hydrogen bond

5' end

3' end

Phosphodiester bond

Purines	Pyrimidines
Guanine (G)	Cytosine (C)
Adenine (A)	Thymine (T)

Major Groove

Minor Groove

3' end

5' enc

Remember that DNA is a polymer of nucleotides, and each nucleotide is made up of three parts: the phosphate group, the 5-carbon sugar, and the nitrogenous base. Know the names of the purines (adenine and guanine) and the pyrimidines (cytosine and thymine). A good way to remember this is: "pyrimidine" contains a "y," and so do "cytosine" and "thymine." Uracil, a nitrogenous base in RNA, is also a pyrimidine. This is easy to remember since it replaces the pyrimidine thymine. Know the pairings (AT, GC) and the number of H-bonds between each pair. Two hydrogen bonds hold together AT, while three hold together GC. This means that more energy is required to separate GC bonds.

RNA (ribonucleic acid) is identical to DNA in structure except that:

1. carbon number 2 on the pentose is not "deoxygenated" (it has a hydroxyl group attached),

2. RNA is almost always single stranded, and

3. RNA contains the pyrimidine uracil (U) instead of thymine.

Unlike DNA, RNA can move through the nuclear pores and is not confined to the nucleus. Three important types of RNA, which will be described further in the Genetics Lecture, are mRNA (messenger RNA), rRNA (ribosomal RNA), and tRNA (transfer RNA). Notice the similarity in structure between uracil and thymine. This is a common cause of mutations in DNA.

In addition to forming genetic material, nucleotides also serve other purposes in the cell. Important nucleotides include ATP (adenosine triphosphate: Figure 1.8), the main source of readily available energy for the cell; cyclic AMP (cAMP), an important component in many second messenger systems; and NADH and $FADH_2$, the coenzymes involved in the Krebs cycle and the electron transport chain.

Thymine (T)   **Uracil (U)**

FIGURE 1.8   ATP

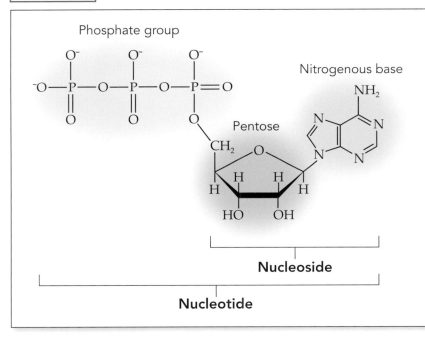

You will learn much more about the role of ATP as an energy source in Metabolism and Muscle, Bone, and Skin, about second messenger systems in Endocrine, and about NADH and $FADH_2$ in Metabolism.

Question 1

The most common catabolic reaction in the human body is:

○ **A.** dehydration.
○ **B.** hydrolysis.
○ **C.** condensation.
○ **D.** elimination.

Question 2

A molecule of DNA contains all of the following EXCEPT:

○ **A.** deoxyribose sugars.
○ **B.** polypeptide bonds.
○ **C.** phosphodiester bonds.
○ **D.** nitrogenous bases.

Question 3

Which of the following contribute to structural stability in both proteins and DNA?

   I. Van der Waals forces
  II. Disulfide bonds
 III. Hydrogen bonds

○ **A.** I only
○ **B.** II only
○ **C.** I and III only
○ **D.** I, II, and III only

Question 4

Metabolism of carbohydrate and fat spares protein tissue. All of the following are true of fats EXCEPT:

○ **A.** Fats may be used in cell structure.
○ **B.** Fats may be used as hormones.
○ **C.** Fats are a more efficient form of energy storage than proteins.
○ **D.** Fats are a less efficient form of energy storage than carbohydrates.

Question 5

Which of the following is found in the RNA but not the DNA of a living cell?

○ **A.** Thymine
○ **B.** A double helix
○ **C.** An additional hydroxyl group
○ **D.** Hydrogen bonds

Question 6

Like cellulose, chitin is a polysaccharide that cannot be digested by animals. Chitin differs from cellulose in that it possesses an acetyl-amino group at the second carbon. What molecule is a reactant in the breaking of the β-1,4 glycoside linkages of cellulose and chitin?

○ **A.** Water
○ **B.** Oxygen
○ **C.** α-1,4-glucosidase
○ **D.** β-1,4-glucosidase

Question 7

Which of the following is always true concerning the base composition of DNA?

○ **A.** In each single strand, the number of adenine residues equals the number of thymine residues.
○ **B.** In each single strand, the number of adenine residues equals the number of guanine residues.
○ **C.** In a molecule of double stranded DNA, the ratio of adenine residues to thymine residues equals the ratio of cytosine residues to guanine residues.
○ **D.** In a molecule of double stranded DNA, the number of adenine residues plus thymine residues equals the number of cytosine residues plus guanine residues.

Question 8

All of the following types of lipids can be found in cell membranes EXCEPT:

○ **A.** glycolipids.
○ **B.** steroids.
○ **C.** prostaglandins.
○ **D.** sphingolipids.

Peanuts are a source of protein.

1.6 | Amino Acids and Proteins

Amino acids are the building blocks of proteins. As described below, amino acids contain side groups with varying physical and chemical properties. The large number of possible combinations of amino acids with different properties allows proteins to have a wide variety of structures, contributing to the multitude of functions that proteins carry out in the body. A single protein is built from a chain of amino acids linked together by peptide bonds; proteins are sometimes referred to as polypeptides (Greek: polys → many).

It is important to be able to recognize the general structure of an amino acid and a polypeptide. A peptide bond creates the functional group known as an **amide**, an amine connected to a carbonyl carbon. It is formed via a dehydration reaction of two amino acids. The reverse reaction is the hydrolysis of a peptide bond.

FIGURE 1.9 | Hydrolysis of a Peptide Bond

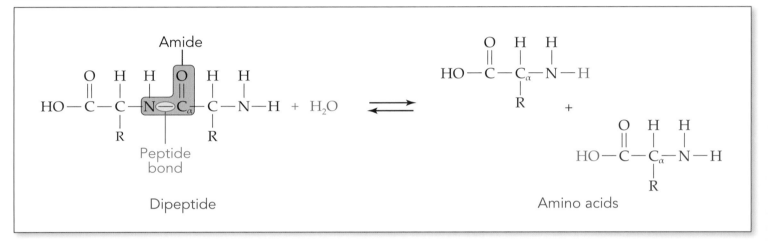

Since nitrogen is most stable with four bonds and oxygen attracts electron density, resulting in a partial negative charge, electrons delocalize to give the peptide bond a partial double bond character. This double bond character prevents the bond from rotating freely and affects the secondary and, to some extent, the tertiary structure of the polypeptide (these types of protein structure are described later in this section).

Nearly all proteins in all species are built from the same 20 α-amino acids. They are called alpha amino acids because the amine is attached to the carbon in the alpha position to the carbonyl. In humans, nine of the amino acids are essential, meaning that they cannot be manufactured by the body and must be ingested directly. Digested proteins reach the cells of the human body as single amino acids.

Notice the R group on each amino acid. The R group is called the **side chain** of the amino acid. Each amino acid differs only in its R group. Like the amino group, the side chain is attached to the α-carbon. The R groups can be divided into four categories based on distinct chemical properties: 1. acidic, 2. basic, 3. polar, and 4. nonpolar. All acidic and basic R groups are also polar. Generally, if the side chain contains carboxylic acids, then it is acidic; if it contains amines, then it is basic. These properties of the side chains affect the overall structure of the protein. The R groups inside an enzyme's active site determine the chemical events that can occur. Acidic or basic amino acids may facilitate an acid-base reaction. Polar amino acids can stabilize polar substrates with hydrogen bonds, while nonpolar amino acids can stabilize nonpolar substrates through Van der Waals interactions.

Mutations that change the amino acids inside a protein can greatly affect function. In Sickle Cell Disease, an acidic glutamate is replaced with a nonpolar valine. This substitution changes the structure of the hemoglobin chain and causes hemoglobin to polymerize, which can bend the cell into a sickle-shape under conditions of low oxygen. This effect would be considerably diminished if the acidic glutamate were instead replaced with an acidic aspartate.

Notice that the α-carbon has four chemically distinct groups attached to it, meaning that it will be chiral for all amino acids except Glycine. Glycine is achiral because it has two chemically identical hydrogen atoms attached to the α-carbon. Because most amino acids are chiral, they will rotate plane polarized light. For more information about chirality, see the Introduction to Organic Chemistry Lecture in *Chemistry*.

You need to memorize the three letter and one letter abbreviations for each amino acid.

FIGURE 1.10 The 20 Common Amino Acids

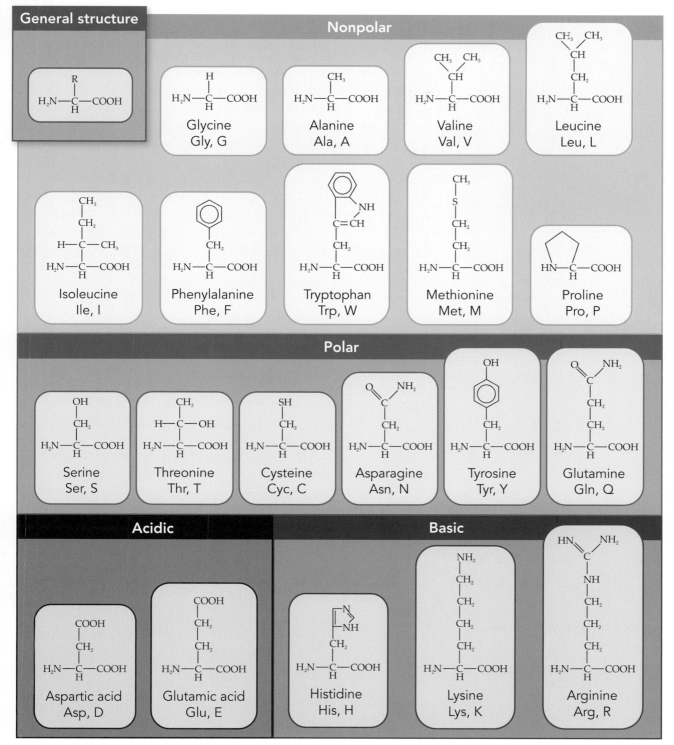

The amino acid structures shown in this figure are artificial representations. Amino acids in solution, such as in the biological environment, will always carry one or more charges. The position and nature of the charges will depend upon the pH of the solution. For more on pI and determining the charge of a protein at various pH, see the Acids and Bases Lecture in *Chemistry*.

FIGURE 1.11 Protein Structure

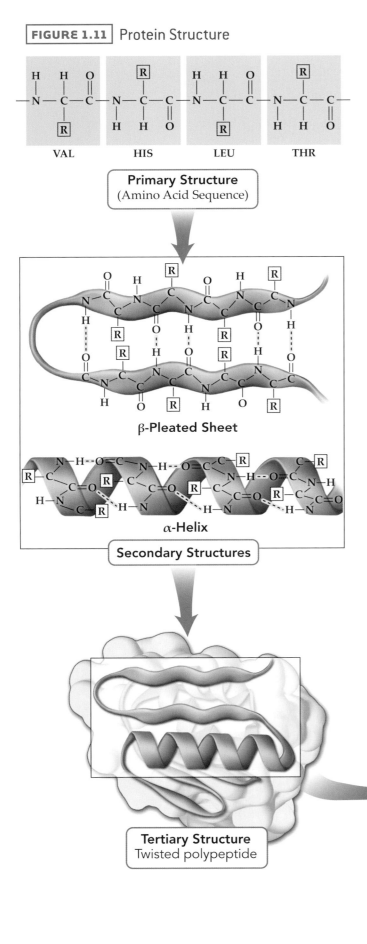

VAL   HIS   LEU   THR

Primary Structure
(Amino Acid Sequence)

β-Pleated Sheet

α-Helix

Secondary Structures

Tertiary Structure
Twisted polypeptide

Quaternary Structure
Several polypeptides bonded together

You need to memorize the categories of functional groups on each amino acid. For example, know that aspartic acid has a carboxylic acid functional group, so it can participate in acid-base reactions. It is also useful to be able to tell whether an active site is negatively or positively charged. If you notice a predominance of acidic amino acids, such as glutamate or aspartate, the active site is probably negatively charged. If you see more basic amino acids, such as histidine, lysine, or arginine, expect it to be positively charged.

The structure of a protein comes from several levels of organization. The number and sequence of amino acids in a polypeptide is called the **primary structure**. Once the primary structure is formed, the single chain can form into distinct shapes known as the **secondary structure** of the protein. The polypeptide can twist into an α-helix, or lie alongside itself and form a β-pleated sheet. With β-pleated sheets, the connecting segments of the two strands can lie in the same direction or in opposite directions. Both α-helices and β-pleated sheets are reinforced by hydrogen bonds between the carbonyl oxygen of one amino acid and the hydrogen on the amino group of another. A single protein usually contains both structures at various locations along its chain. These areas of secondary structure contribute to the **conformation**, or overall shape, of the protein.

All proteins have a primary structure and most have areas of secondary structure. Larger proteins can have a tertiary and quaternary structure. The **tertiary structure** refers to the three dimensional shape formed by curls and folds of the peptide chain. Five forces contribute to the tertiary structure: 1. covalent disulfide bonds between two **cysteine** amino acids on separate parts of the chain, creating the dimer **cystine**, 2. electrostatic (ionic) interactions, mostly between acidic and basic side chains, 3. hydrogen bonds, 4. van der Waals forces, and 5. hydrophobic, or nonpolar, side chains pushed away from water toward the center of the protein (**hydrophobic bonding**). In addition to these forces, turns that disrupt both α-helix and β-pleated sheet formation are induced by the amino acid proline due to its physical structure: the R group binds to the amine group, causing proline to be more rigid than a typical amino acid. This binding prevents proline from acting as a hydrogen bond donor, causing the formation of kinks that disrupt both α-helices and β-pleated sheets.

When two or more polypeptide chains bind together, they form the **quaternary structure** of the protein. The same five forces at work in the tertiary structure can also act to form the quaternary structure.

Although many different conformations are possible for any one protein, it will generally exist in one of a few possible conformations that have the highest stability and allow the protein to carry out its necessary functions. As described above, the water surrounding proteins in the biological environment helps stabilize these *native* conformations. Due to the presence of hydrophobic R groups on the protein, surrounding molecules assemble into an organized structure known as a **solvation layer** that forces these hydrophobic groups towards the inner area of the protein. The gathering of hydrophobic R groups away from the surrounding water is highly favorable because it allows a decrease in the size of the highly ordered solvation layer, increasing the **entropy** of the system (see the Thermodynamics Lecture of the *Chemistry* manual for more on entropy).

When the native conformation is disrupted, the protein is said to be **denatured**. A denatured protein has lost most of its secondary, tertiary, and quaternary

Protein is found in nearly all unprocessed foods.

FIGURE 1.12 Six Factors that Contribute to Tertiary Structure

1. Covalent **disulfide bonds** between two cystine amino acids on different parts of the chain

2. Electrostatic (ionic) interactions mostly between acidic and basic side chains

3. Hydrogen bonds

4. Van der Waals forces

5. Hydrophobic side chains pushed away from water (toward center of protein)

6. R group of proline causes kinks

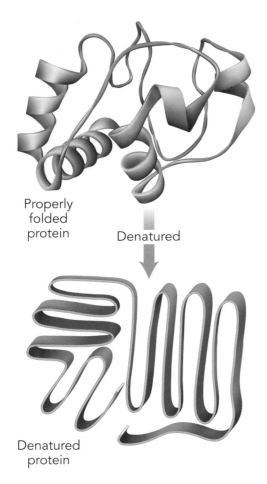

Properly
folded
protein

Denatured

Denatured
protein

structure. Some denaturing agents and the forces that they disrupt are given in Table 1.1. Very often, once the denaturing agent is removed, the protein will spontaneously refold to its original conformation. This suggests that the amino acid sequence plays a key role in the conformation of a protein.

There are two types of proteins: *globular* and *structural*. There are more types of globular proteins than there are types of structural proteins. Globular proteins function as enzymes (e.g. pepsin), hormones (e.g. insulin), membrane pumps

TABLE 1.1 > Denaturing Agents

Denaturing Agents	Forces Disrupted
Urea	Hydrogen bonds
Salt or change in pH	Electrostatic bonds
Mercaptoethanol	Disulfide bonds
Organic solvents	Hydrophobic forces
Heat	All forces

Heat, salt, and changes in pH can cause a protein to lose its higher-level conformation. Notice, for example, that the denatured form of the protein does not contain any of the α-helices that the properly folded protein has. Denaturing agents rarely affect the primary structure of a protein, which contains the essential information for conformation. Mildly denatured proteins can often spontaneously return to their original conformation.

Later in this lecture, proteins' function as enzymes will be discussed extensively, but proteins have MANY additional roles in the body that will be covered throughout *Biology 1: Molecules* and *Biology 2: Systems*. Remember that the large array of possible functions is made possible by the numerous possible combinations of amino acids that have different physical properties. See the immune section of Lecture 4 in *Biology 2: Systems* for proteins that are involved in the immune system; the Muscle, Bone and Skin Lecture in the same manual for motor proteins that enable the movement of muscles; and the Genetics Lecture for DNA binding proteins.

and channels (e.g. Na^+/K^+ pump and voltage gated sodium channels), membrane receptors (e.g. nicotinic receptors on a post-synaptic neuron), intercellular and intracellular transport and storage (e.g. hemoglobin and myoglobin), osmotic regulators (e.g. albumin), in the immune response (e.g. antibodies), and more.

Structural proteins are made from long polymers. They maintain and add strength to cellular and matrix structure. *Collagen*, a structural protein made from a unique type of helix, is the most abundant protein in the body. Collagen fibers add great strength to skin, tendons, ligaments, and bone, among other structures. Microtubules, which make up eukaryotic flagella and cilia, are made from globular tubulin, which polymerizes under the right conditions to become a structural protein.

Glycoproteins are proteins with carbohydrate groups attached. The AB antigens on red blood cells that determine an individual's blood type are examples of glycoproteins. These are a component of cellular plasma membranes and are generally more than 50% protein. *Proteoglycans* are also a mixture of proteins and carbohydrates, but they generally consist of more than 50% carbohydrates. Proteoglycans are the major component of the extracellular matrix.

Cytochromes (Greek: kytos → cell, chroma → color or pigment) are proteins which require a *prosthetic* (nonproteinaceous) *heme* (Greek: haima → blood) group in order to function. Cytochromes get their name from the color that they add to the cell. Examples of cytochromes are hemoglobin and the cytochromes of the electron transport chain in the inner membrane of mitochondria. Proteins containing nonproteinaceous components are called *conjugated proteins*.

> Remember to think "sugar" when you see "glyco-." Just as glycolipids are lipids with sugars attached, glycoproteins are proteins with sugars attached.

> Proteins are important. Understand the different levels of structures, 1°, 2°, 3°, and 4°, and the bonding involved. You need to know the forces that contribute to the stability of protein conformations and what denaturation means. You should be familiar with the chemical structure of the various amino acids. Focus on knowing which chemical functional groups make an amino acid nonpolar, polar, basic, or acidic. Although nucleic acids, some lipids, and even some carbohydrates contain nitrogen, when you see nitrogen on the MCAT®, think protein.

Cytochrome proteins carry out electron transport via oxidation and reduction of the heme group.

This fractured surface of a bone consists of an organic matrix of collagen fibers and mineral-based molecules such as hydroxyapatite and chondroitin sulfate.

1.7 | Minerals

Minerals are the dissolved inorganic ions inside and outside the cell. By creating electrochemical gradients across membranes, they assist in the transport of substances entering and exiting the cell. They can combine and solidify to give strength to a matrix, such as *hydroxyapatite* in bone. Minerals also act as cofactors (discussed later in this lecture) assisting enzyme or protein function. For instance, iron is a mineral found in *heme*, the prosthetic group of *cytochromes*.

This completes an overview of the major chemicals acting in the body. Your emphasis should be on understanding functions, not memorizing details. That doesn't mean breezing right through this section. A large portion of your success on biology and biochemistry questions on the MCAT® depends on reading comprehension. Since it is impossible to know the exact topic of the passages ahead of time, you can't do well just by memorizing facts. Instead, it is helpful to become familiar with the terms and dialect in which the passages are written. Try to see the big picture and how each little piece fits into the big picture. Be certain that you thoroughly understand all the terms that are bolded and red! Your goal by the time you finish *Biology 1: Molecules* and *Biology 2: Systems* is to attain a general overview of how the body functions on each level of organization (i.e. molecular, cellular, tissue, organ, system, organism), and to know the specific contribution of any bold and red term or concept.

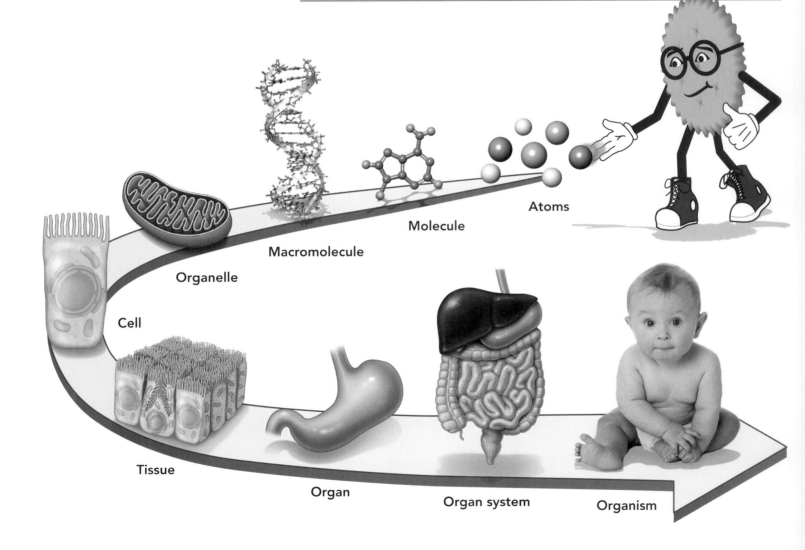

Atoms

Molecule

Macromolecule

Organelle

Cell

Tissue

Organ

Organ system

Organism

1.8 | Features of Enzymes

Virtually all biological reactions are regulated and made possible by **enzymes**. Enzymes are typically globular proteins, although there are a few nucleic acids that act as enzymes. Just as the variability in structure of proteins makes them well-suited for many different biological functions, this variability also facilitates their action as enzymes. The differing characteristics of enzymatic R groups accounts for the specificity of enzymes for certain substrates.

The function of any enzyme is to act as a **catalyst**, lowering the energy of activation (also called E_a) for a biological reaction, thus increasing the rate of that reaction. Enzymes increase reaction rates by magnitudes of as much as thousands of trillions. This is a much greater increase than typical lab catalysts. Such extreme control over reaction rates gives enzymes the ability to pick and choose which reactions will or will not occur inside a cell. Without the catalytic effect of enzymes, the energy of activation of essential biological reactions would be impossibly high. Enzymes have a regulatory ability, making the body's chemical reactions possible, but ensuring that they occur only when needed. Enzymes, like any catalysts, are neither consumed nor permanently altered by the reactions they catalyze. Only a small amount of catalyst is required for any reaction. Also like other catalysts, enzymes do not alter the equilibrium of a reaction; in other words, they do not alter the relative amount of reactants and products at equilibrium. This means that enzymes also do not alter the overall ΔG of the reaction.

The reactant or reactants upon which an enzyme works are called the **substrates**. Substrates are generally smaller than the enzyme. The substrate binds to the enzyme at a particular location called the **active site**, usually with numerous noncovalent bonds. The enzyme and substrate bind together to form the **enzyme-substrate complex**.

Normally, enzymes are designed to work only on a specific substrate or group of closely related substrates, a property called **enzyme specificity**. The **lock and key model** is an example of enzyme specificity. In this model, the active site of the enzyme has a specific shape like a lock that only fits a specific substrate, the key. The lock and key model explains some but not all enzymes. A second theory called the **induced fit model** says that the shapes of both the enzyme and the substrate are altered upon binding. Besides increasing specificity, the alteration actually helps the reaction to proceed by destabilizing the substrate. In reactions with more than one substrate, the enzyme may also orient the substrates relative to each other, creating optimal conditions for a reaction to take place.

Hexokinase lowers the activation energy for the phosphorylation of glucose.

Enzyme lowers activation energy by this amount

Without enzyme

With enzyme

Energy

Reactant

Progress of reaction

Product

FIGURE 1.13 | Enzyme-Catalyzed Reaction

Saturation kinetics are analogous to assembly line workers. When there are more workers (more enzymes), the rate of production (V_{max}) increases. However, there comes a point when there is just too much starting material (substrate) and the workers cannot go any faster. At this point, the workers, or enzymes, are saturated and have reached V_{max}.

Glucokinase and hexokinase both add a phosphate to glucose, forming glucose-6-phosphate, which is trapped inside the cell. Glucokinase has a significantly higher K_m, meaning that it has lower affinity for glucose compared to hexokinase. Glucokinase acts in the liver, so high levels of blood glucose would be required to begin phosphorylating glucose in the hepatocyte cytosol. This lower affinity allows glucose to be phosphorylated in other cells, which use hexokinase. Only when glucose concentrations become high will the liver begin storing it as glycogen and fatty acids.

Understand Key 2: How well a substrate fits in the active site of an enzyme correlates with its effectiveness. A lower K_m represents a tight fit.

Enzymes exhibit **saturation kinetics**; as the relative concentration of substrate increases, the rate of the reaction also increases, but to a lesser and lesser degree until a maximum rate, the V_{max}, has been achieved. This occurs because as more substrate is added, individual substrates must begin to wait in line for an unoccupied enzyme. V_{max} is therefore proportional to enzyme concentration. Turnover number, also called k_{cat}, is the number of substrate molecules one active site can convert to product in a given unit of time when an enzyme solution is saturated with substrate. k_{cat} provides a rough estimate of the catalytic efficiency of an enzyme. If the V_{max} and concentration of enzyme are known, it can be calculated by the equation, $k_{cat} = V_{max}/[E]_t$.

Related to V_{max} is the **Michaelis constant**, also known as the K_m. The K_m is the substrate concentration at which the reaction rate is equal to $\frac{1}{2}V_{max}$. The value of the Michaelis constant indicates how highly concentrated the substrate must be to speed up the reaction. If a higher concentration of substrate is needed, the enzyme must have a lower affinity for the substrate. K_m is inversely proportional to enzyme-substrate affinity. Unlike V_{max}, K_m does not vary when the enzyme concentration is changed; in other words, it is a characteristic of the intrinsic fit between the enzyme and substrate, rather than reflecting the amount of substrate present. The value of K_m can be altered by certain types of enzyme inhibition, which will be covered in the next section.

Michaelis–Menten curves plot reaction velocity as a function of substrate concentration and show an enzyme's V_{max} and K_m (Figure 1.14). They are valuable tools for recalling and understanding the types of enzyme inhibition, as will be discussed later in this lecture.

FIGURE 1.14 | Michaelis-Menten Curves at Different Enzyme Concentrations

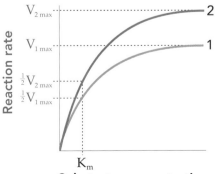

Temperature and pH also affect the rates of enzymatic reactions. As temperature increases, the reaction rate initially goes up. Since enzymes are generally proteins, at some point the enzyme denatures and the rate of the reaction drops off precipitously. For enzymes in the human body, the optimal temperature is most often around 37° C. Enzymes also function within specific pH ranges. The optimal pH varies depending upon the enzyme. For instance, pepsin, which is active in the stomach, prefers a pH below 2, while trypsin, which is active in the small intestine, works best at a pH between 6 and 7.

In order to reach their optimal activity, many enzymes require a non–protein component called a **cofactor** (Latin: co- → with or together). Cofactors can be coenzymes or metal ions.

Coenzymes are cofactors that are organic molecules. They often need to be present in stoichiometric quantities or in excess, depending on whether the molecule is consumed or permanently altered in the processes they help to catalyze. Many types of **water-soluble vitamins** serve as coenzymes or their precursors. Coenzymes are divided into two types: *cosubstrates* and *prosthetic* groups.

Cosubstrates reversibly bind to a specific enzyme, and transfer some chemical group to another substrate. The cosubstrate then reverts to its original form via another enzymatic reaction. This reversion to original form is what distinguishes a cosubstrate from normal substrates. ATP is an example of the cosubstrate type of coenzyme.

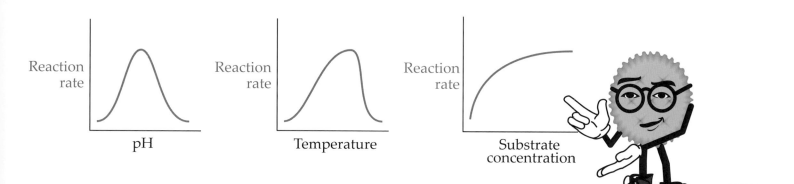

Prosthetic groups remain covalently bound to the enzyme throughout the reaction, and, like the enzyme, emerge from the reaction unchanged. As mentioned previously, *heme* is a prosthetic group. Heme binds with *catalase* in peroxisomes to degrade hydrogen peroxide.

Metal ions are the second type of cofactor. These are inorganic small molecules required for some enzyme activities. They can act alone or with a prosthetic group and often need to be present in stoichiometric amounts because they are not consumed in the processes they help catalyze. Typical metal ions that function as cofactors in the human body are iron, copper, manganese, magnesium, calcium, and zinc.

An enzyme without its cofactor is called an *apoenzyme* (Greek: apo- → away from) and is completely nonfunctional. An enzyme with its cofactor is called a *holoenzyme* (Greek: holos → whole, entire, complete).

The important relationships between enzymes and their environment are represented by these three graphs. Memorize the basic shapes of the graphs and understand how to use them to predict relative rates of enzymatic reactions under different environmental conditions.

Just know that some enzymes need cofactors to function, and that cofactors are either minerals or coenzymes. Also remember that many coenzymes are vitamins or their derivatives.

Question 9

Excessive amounts of nitrogen are found in the urine of an individual who has experienced a period of extended fasting. This is most likely due to:

- **A.** glycogenolysis in the liver.
- **B.** the breakdown of body proteins.
- **C.** lipolysis in adipose tissue.
- **D.** a tumor on the posterior pituitary causing excessive ADH secretion.

Question 10

Proline is not technically an α-amino acid. Due to the ring structure of proline, it cannot conform to the geometry of the α-helix and creates a bend in the polypeptide chain. This phenomenon assists in the creation of what level of protein structure?

- **A.** Primary
- **B.** Secondary
- **C.** Tertiary
- **D.** Quaternary

Question 11

Prosthetic groups that contribute to the holoenzyme act most similarly to a(n):

- **A.** catalyst.
- **B.** intermediate.
- **C.** reactant.
- **D.** co-factor.

Question 12

All of the following must change the rate of an enzyme catalyzed reaction EXCEPT:

- **A.** changing the pH.
- **B.** lowering the temperature.
- **C.** decreasing the concentration of substrate.
- **D.** adding a noncompetitive inhibitor.

Question 13

Since an increase in temperature increases the reaction rate, why is the elevation of temperature not a method normally used to accelerate enzyme-catalyzed reactions?

- **A.** Raising the temperature causes the reaction to occur too quickly.
- **B.** Raising the temperature does not sufficiently surmount the activation energy barrier.
- **C.** Heat changes the configuration of proteins.
- **D.** Heat does not increase the probability of molecular collision.

Question 14

The partial double bond character of a peptide bond has its greatest effect in which level of structure of an enzyme?

- **A.** Primary
- **B.** Secondary
- **C.** Tertiary
- **D.** Quaternary

Question 15

In the final step of the clotting cascade, thrombin catalyzes a reaction that cleaves fibrinogen to the active fibrin enzyme. This means that fibrinogen and thrombin are:

- **A.** a zymogen and a restriction enzyme, respectively.
- **B.** a protease and a zymogen, respectively.
- **C.** a restriction enzyme and a protease, respectively.
- **D.** a zymogen and a protease, respectively.

Question 16

All of the following are true of enzymes EXCEPT:

- **A.** the active site of an enzyme can destabilize bonds in the substrate.
- **B.** enzymes increase the amount of product at equilibrium.
- **C.** some enzymes change shape after binding to the substrate.
- **D.** enzymes have a greater catalytic effect than lab catalysts.

1.9 | Enzyme Regulation

Enzymes select which reactions take place within a cell, so the cell must regulate them. Catalytic activity is desirable only when it is needed. While a lack of certain enzymatic products could inhibit cellular functions, unnecessary activity can be wasteful or even harmful. Enzymes are regulated by four primary means:

1. *Proteolytic cleavage (irreversible covalent modification)*—Many enzymes are released into their environment in an inactive form called a **zymogen** or *proenzyme* (Greek: pro → before). When specific peptide bonds on zymogens are cleaved, the zymogens become irreversibly activated. Activation of zymogens may be instigated by other enzymes, or by a change in environment. For instance, pepsinogen (notice the "−ogen" at the end indicating zymogen status) is the zymogen of pepsin and is activated by low pH.

2. *Reversible covalent modification*—Some enzymes are activated or deactivated by phosphorylation or the addition of some other modifier such as AMP (adenosine monophosphate). The removal of the modifier is almost always accomplished by hydrolysis. Phosphorylation typically occurs in the presence of a *protein kinase*, a type of catalytic enzyme.

3. *Control proteins*—Control proteins are protein subunits that associate with certain enzymes to activate or inhibit their activity. *Calmodulin* and *G-proteins* are typical examples of control proteins.

4. **Allosteric interactions**—Allosteric regulation is the modification of an enzyme's configuration through the binding of an activator or inhibitor at a specific binding site on the enzyme.

This acinar cell produces digestive enzymes in zymogen granules (purple). These enzymes are excreted into the pancreatic ducts and carried to the small intestine, where they are activated and aid in the breakdown of carbohydrates, fats, and proteins.

Think about why the body would release an enzyme in an inactive form. You will learn about the function of pepsin in digestion, but for now it's enough to know that it digests proteins. The release of pepsin as a zymogen that is activated only by low pH ensures that pepsin only digests proteins where it is supposed to—in the stomach!

FIGURE 1.15 | Enzymatic Regulation

Hold on! Don't go overboard here. You will not be asked to distinguish allosteric inhibition from noncompetitive inhibition. Many good biology texts don't distinguish them, and the MCAT® certainly won't. However, it is crucial to understand negative feedback. Negative feedback will be tested on the MCAT®.

$$A + B \xrightarrow{E_1} C + D \xrightarrow{E_2} G$$

Negative Feedback

Hemoglobin's oxygen dissociation curve is similar to the Michaelis-Menten curves that you have seen throughout this lecture. The axes are analogous to those of a Michaelis-Menten curve: instead of reaction velocity there is oxygen saturation, and instead of substrate concentration there is partial pressure of oxygen. Just as reaction velocity levels off to a maximum as high concentrations of substrate are reached, the oxygen saturation of hemoglobin levels off at high partial pressures of oxygen. Expect that the MCAT® may ask you to apply your understanding of K_m and V_{max} to situations that are more complex than the typical Michaelis-Menten curve.

An enzyme normally governs just one reaction in a series of reactions. In a phenomenon called **negative feedback** or **feedback inhibition**, one of the products downstream in a reaction series comes back and inhibits the enzymatic activity of an earlier reaction. Negative feedback provides a shutdown mechanism for a series of enzymatic reactions when that series has produced a sufficient amount of product. Most enzymes work within some type of negative feedback cycle. Positive feedback also occurs, where the product returns to an earlier step to activate the associated enzyme. **Positive feedback** occurs less often than negative feedback. Positive and negative feedback work in a complementary fashion to ensure that a reaction series leads to the right amount of product.

Negative feedback inhibition is typical in many amino acid synthesis pathways. It is wasteful and unnecessary to synthesize amino acids that are readily available in the environment. Upstream enzymes involved in a particular synthetic metabolic pathway typically have allosteric inhibitory sites that bind the final amino acid product. If the final product is present in the environment, it acts as an allosteric inhibitor in a negative feedback loop, preventing synthesis of additional product.

Products that exert negative feedback inhibition do not resemble the substrates of the enzymes that they inhibit and do not bind to the active site. Instead, they bind to the enzyme and cause a conformational change. This process is called **allosteric regulation** (Greek: allos → different or other, stereos → solid), which can be exerted by both **allosteric inhibitors** and **allosteric activators**. Not all allosteric inhibitors and activators are necessarily noncompetitive inhibitors (discussed in the next section), because many alter K_m without affecting V_{max}. Allosteric enzymes, meaning enzymes that have sites for allosteric regulation, do not exhibit typical kinetics because they normally have several binding sites for different inhibitors, activators, and even substrates. At low concentrations of substrate, small increases in concentration increase enzyme efficiency as well as reaction rate. The first substrate changes the shape of the enzyme, allowing other substrates to bind more easily. This phenomenon is called **positive cooperativity**. The opposite phenomenon, **negative cooperativity**, occurs as well. Cooperativity in the presence of the allosteric inhibitor is what gives the oxygen dissociation curve of hemoglobin its sigmoidal shape.

Remember Key 3: Make sure you know the types of inhibition. A competitive inhibitor blocks the active site, while a noncompetitive inhibitor changes the shape of the protein by binding to an allosteric site. Uncompetitive inhibitors bind the enzyme-substrate complex to decrease the concentration of substrate that can react.

MCAT® THINK

Sometimes the effects of feedback inhibition can seem counterintuitive. Glycolysis (described in the Metabolism Lecture) provides an example of negative inhibition. When there is a buildup of ATP, it exerts negative feedback on an enzyme earlier in the glycolytic pathway. This may seem strange because ATP is also a required reactant for the reaction to occur in the first place! However, as with all regulatory feedback, the point is to ensure that the amount of product created is the amount that the cell needs to function. If the cell has too little ATP it will not have enough energy; however, producing too much ATP would be a waste of cellular resources.

Enzyme Inhibition

Enzyme inhibitors provide an important mechanism for regulation of enzymatic activity in the body. Some inhibitors bind to the active site, blocking the substrate from binding. Others bind elsewhere on the enzyme and cause a change in its shape, disrupting its specific affinity for the substrate. Remember that enzyme inhibitors affect the rates of both the forward and reverse reactions. These general mechanisms for altering enzymatic activity make regulation by positive and negative feedback possible.

Enzyme inhibitors can be broadly classified as either irreversible or reversible. Agents that bind irreversibly to enzymes and disrupt their function are **irreversible inhibitors**. Most inhibitors of this type bind to enzymes via covalent bonds, but a few bind noncovalently. Irreversible inhibitors tend to be highly toxic. Any of the following types of inhibitors can be irreversible if covalent modification occurs.

Competitive inhibitors compete with the substrate by binding reversibly with noncovalent bonds to the active site. They are the only type of reversible inhibitor that binds directly to the active site rather than binding to a different site on the enzyme. They typically bind directly to the active site for only a fraction of a second, blocking the substrate from binding during that time. The reverse is also true; if the substrate binds first, it blocks the inhibitor from binding. Competitive inhibitors raise the apparent K_m but do not change V_{max}. In the presence of a competitive inhibitor, the rate of the reaction can be increased to the original, uninhibited V_{max} by increasing the concentration of the substrate. Since an increased concentration of substrate is required to reach V_{max}, an increased concentration is also required to reach $\frac{1}{2} V_{max}$. The K_m is raised, reflecting the lowered affinity of the enzyme for the substrate. The ability to overcome inhibition by increasing substrate concentration is the classic indication of a competitive inhibitor.

> You need to memorize the specific types of inhibition and their effects on enzyme kinetics.

> In order to identify each of the four inhibitors, think first about where on the enzyme the inhibitor binds. If the inhibitor binds to the enzyme's active site when the substrate is not bound, it is a competitive inhibitor. If it binds to an allosteric site or to the E-S complex, it is one of the other three types. Next, ask whether it binds to the enzyme or to the enzyme-substrate complex. An inhibitor that binds only to the E-S complex is uncompetitive. If it can bind to either the enzyme alone or the E-S complex, it is a mixed inhibitor. A noncompetitive inhibitor is a special type of mixed inhibitor that binds with the same affinity whether to the enzyme alone or to the E-S complex.

FIGURE 1.16 Types of Enzyme Inhibition

> Irreversible and reversible inhibition are broad categories that include the four major types. For example, a competitive inhibitor can be reversible or irreversible.

FIGURE 1.17 Effect of Inhibition on V_{max} and K_m

Competitive inhibition ($K_m \uparrow$, V_{max} constant)

Noncompetitive inhibition ($V_{max} \downarrow$, K_m constant)

Recognize and reason through the graphs for each inhibitor type. Use the above Lineweaver-Burk plots to read the effects of inhibition on V_{max} and K_m. Remember that, in a Lineweaver-Burk plot, the x-intercept represents $1/K_m$ and correlates with the enzyme-substrate fit. The y-intercept is $1/V_{max}$, where V_{max} for any enzyme is its maximum rate of catalysis. If you see the linear graph, you may need to extend the lines to find their intersections with the axes. Think... the lines of competitors cross like swords.

Competitive inhibitors often resemble the substrate. *Sulfanilamide* is an antibiotic which competitively inhibits a bacterial enzyme that manufactures folic acid, leading to the death of bacterial cells. Although humans require folic acid, sulfanilamide does not harm humans because we use a different enzymatic pathway to manufacture folic acid.

Unlike competitive inhibitors, **uncompetitive inhibitors** bind at a site other than the active site. Regulatory molecules can also bind to a site other than the active site and exert a positive feedback effect, rather than an inhibitory effect. Uncompetitive inhibitors do not bind to the enzyme until it has associated with the substrate to form the enzyme-substrate complex. Once the uncompetitive inhibitor has bound, the substrate remains associated with the enzyme. The apparent affinity of the enzyme for the substrate increases, meaning that K_m decreases. Because the uncompetitive inhibitor only affects enzymes that have already bound substrate, adding more substrate does not overcome the effect of the inhibitor. The V_{max} is lowered because the substrate stays bound to the enzyme for a longer period of time.

Like uncompetitive inhibitors, **mixed inhibitors** bind at a site on the enzyme other than the active site, so they do not prevent the substrate from binding. Their name comes from the fact that they can bind to either the enzyme alone or the enzyme-substrate complex. Most types of mixed inhibitors have a preference for one or the other, which dictates the effect on K_m and V_{max}. Mixed inhibitors that act like competitive inhibitors by binding primarily to the enzyme before the substrate is associated increase K_m, just as competitive inhibitors do. In contrast, mixed inhibitors that act more like uncompetitive inhibitors by preferring to bind to the enzyme-substrate complex lower K_m. All mixed inhibitors lower V_{max} to some extent.

Noncompetitive inhibitors are a special type of mixed inhibitors. They bind just as readily to enzymes with a substrate as to those without. Like other mixed inhibitors, noncompetitive inhibitors bind noncovalently to an enzyme at a spot other than the active site and change the conformation of the enzyme. Because noncompetitive inhibitors do not resemble the substrate, they commonly act on more than one type of enzyme. Unlike competitive inhibitors, they cannot be overcome by excess substrate, so they lower V_{max}. They do not, however, lower the enzyme's affinity for the substrate because they bind to a site other than the active site, so K_m remains the same.

TABLE 1.2 ▸ Characteristics of Enzyme Inhibitors

Type of inhibitor	Binding site	Inhibits binding of substrate?	Effect on K_m	Effect on V_{max}
Competitive	Enzyme (active site)	Yes	Increase	No change
Uncompetitive	E-S complex	No	Decrease	Decrease
Mixed	E-S complex or enzyme	No	Increase or decrease	Decrease
Noncompetitive	E-S complex or enzyme	No	No change	Decrease

Know the distinct characteristics of each of the inhibitor types shown in Table 1.2: where the inhibitor binds (active site or other site), to what the inhibitor binds (enzyme or E-S complex), whether and how it affects the fit of enzyme bound to substrate (fit is inverse to K_m), and how the kinetic features of the enzyme-catalyzed reaction are affected (V_{max}). Remember: NOncompetitive inhibitors have NO preference between the enzyme and enzyme-substrate complex. As enzyme-substrate fit decreases, K_m increases, and vice versa.

1.10 Enzyme Classification

Enzymes are named according to the reactions that they catalyze. Very often, the suffix "-ase" is simply added to the end of the substrate upon which the enzyme acts. For instance, acetylcholinesterase acts upon the ester group in acetylcholine.

According to systematic naming conventions, enzymes are classified into six categories:

1. Oxidoreductases catalyze the transfer of electrons or hydrogen ions, i.e. oxidation–reduction reactions,

2. Transferases catalyze reactions in which groups are transferred from one location to another,

3. Hydrolases regulate hydrolysis reactions,

4. Lyases catalyze reactions in which functional groups are added to double bonds or, conversely, double bonds are formed via the removal of functional groups,

5. Isomerases catalyze the transfer of groups within a molecule, with the effect of producing isomers (discussed in the *Chemistry* manual),

6. Ligases catalyze condensation reactions coupled with the hydrolysis of high energy molecules.

One major distinction between classifications occurs between lyases and ligases. The particular type of lyase that catalyzes the addition of one substrate to the double bond of a second substrate is sometimes called a *synthase*. ATP synthase is an example of a lyase. Ligase enzymes require energy input from ATP or some other nucleotide. Ligases are sometimes called *synthetases*. Notice that synthases and synthetases are two distinct types of enzymes. Synthases do not require ATP to catalyze their reactions, while synthetases do.

Kinases and *phosphatases* may also come up on the MCAT®. A kinase is an enzyme that phosphorylates a molecule, while a phosphatase is an enzyme that dephosphorylates a molecule. Often a kinase phosphorylates another enzyme in order to activate or deactivate it. *Hexokinase* is the enzyme that phosphorylates glucose as soon as it enters a cell (see the Metabolism Lecture to learn how this phosphorylation assists metabolic processes).

Look for the "-ase" ending. Often a seemingly complicated question about a complex chemical will depend upon the simple fact that the chemical is an enzyme, and the only clue is the "-ase" at the end of the name. Once you recognize that the chemical is an enzyme, you know that it contains nitrogen and that it is subject to denaturation. Similarly, many carbohydrates are easy to recognize by their "-ose" ending.

Oxygen Containing Reactions
CHEMISTRY

As you learn more about the types of reactions described above in later lectures and other manuals, look back to refresh your memory on which reaction types are catalyzed by which enzymes.

The best way to remember the structures of different types of biological molecules is to think back from their functions. Carbohydrates need to be stable, uniform molecules so that they can be used for energy storage and release by all cells. Similarly, nucleotides have to be stable and highly organized molecules (including the carbohydrate component) in order to create a stable structure for genetic material. Carbohydrates and lipids are both used for energy storage, so they both must have a high density of C-H bonds. However, lipids are also used to construct membranes, so it makes sense for them to have a polar end and a nonpolar end. Finally, proteins are needed for many different functions in the cell, so they need to be able to have a wide array of possible structures. Therefore the building blocks of proteins, in contrast to nucleic acids and polysaccharides, need to have a large variety of possible structures. Amino acids meet the needs of proteins through their R groups that vary in polarity and other structural features.

Question 17

Which of the following is (are) true concerning feedback inhibition?

    I. It often acts by inhibiting enzyme activity.
    II. It works to prevent a buildup of excess nutrients.
    III. It only acts through enzymes.

- **A.** I only
- **B.** II only
- **C.** I and II only
- **D.** I, II, and III

Question 18

One mechanism of enzyme inhibition is to inhibit an enzyme without blocking the active site, but by altering the shape of the enzyme molecule. This mechanism is called:

- **A.** competitive inhibition.
- **B.** noncompetitive inhibition.
- **C.** feedback inhibition.
- **D.** positive inhibition.

Question 19

The continued production of progesterone caused by the release of HCG from the growing embryo is an example of:

- **A.** positive feedback.
- **B.** negative feedback.
- **C.** feedback inhibition.
- **D.** feedback enhancement.

Question 20

Peptidases that function in the stomach most likely:

- **A.** *increase* their function in the small intestine due to *increased* hydrogen ion concentration.
- **B.** *decrease* their function in the small intestine due to *increased* hydrogen ion concentration.
- **C.** *increase* their function in the small intestine due to *decreased* hydrogen ion concentration.
- **D.** *decrease* their function in the small intestine due to *decreased* hydrogen ion concentration.

Question 21

The rate of a reaction slows when the reaction is exposed to a competitive inhibitor. Which of the following might overcome the effects of the inhibitor?

- **A.** Decreasing enzyme concentration
- **B.** Increasing temperature
- **C.** Increasing substrate concentration
- **D.** The effects of competitive inhibition cannot be overcome.

Question 22

Suppose that an enzyme inhibitor lowers V_{max} and has no effect on K_m. This inhibitor is likely to be:

- **A.** Uncompetitive
- **B.** Proteolytic
- **C.** Noncompetitive
- **D.** Mixed

Question 23

Which of the following is necessary for an enzyme to exhibit positive and/or negative cooperativity?

- **A.** The presence of a mixed inhibitor
- **B.** Multiple binding sites on the enzyme
- **C.** A high concentration of substrate
- **D.** Positive and/or negative feedback

Question 24

Why do uncompetitive inhibitors cause a decrease in K_m?

- **A.** The enzyme's apparent affinity for the substrate is decreased.
- **B.** The enzyme's apparent affinity for the substrate is increased.
- **C.** Uncompetitive inhibitors bind to the enzyme only before it binds substrate.
- **D.** Uncompetitive inhibitors do not actually cause a decrease in K_m.

α-helix

β-pleated sheet

½ V_{max}

Active site

Adenine (A)

Adipocytes

Allosteric activators

Allosteric inhibitors

Allosteric interactions

Allosteric regulation

Amide

Amino acids

Amphipathic

Antiparallel

ATP (adenosine triphosphate)

Base-pairing

Base-pairs (bp)

Carbohydrates

Catalyst

Cellulose

Coenzymes

Cofactor

Competitive inhibitors

Complementary strands

Conformation

Cysteine

Cystine

Cytosine (C)

Dehydration

Denatured

DNA (deoxyribonucleic acid)

Double helix

Double stranded DNA

Entropy

Enzyme specificity

Enzyme-substrate complex

Enzymes

Fat-soluble vitamins

Fats

Fatty acids

Feedback inhibition

Glucose

Glycerol

Glycogen

Guanine (G)

Hexoses

Hydrogen bonding

Hydrolases

Hydrolysis

Hydrophilic

Hydrophobic

Hydrophobic bonding

Induced fit model

Irreversible inhibitors

Isomerases

K_m

Ligases

Lipids

Lock and key model

Lyases

Michaelis constant

Minerals

Mixed inhibitors

Monosaccharides

Negative cooperativity

Negative feedback

Noncompetitive inhibitors

Nucleic acids

Nucleoside

Nucleotides

Oxidoreductases

Phosphatids

Phosphodiester bonds

Phospholipids

Polypeptides

Polysaccharides

Positive cooperativity

Positive feedback

Primary structure

Proline

Prostaglandins

Purines

Pyrimidines

Quaternary structure

RNA (ribonucleic acid)

Saturated fatty acids

Saturation kinetics

Secondary structure

Side chain

Single stranded RNA

Solvation layer

Sphingolipids

Starch

Steroids

Substrates

Sugar-phosphate backbone

Tertiary structure

Thymine (T)

Transferases

Triacylglycerols

Triglycerides

Uncompetitive inhibitors

Unsaturated fatty acids

Uracil (U)

Vitamins

Water

Water-soluble vitamins

Watson-Crick model

Waxes

V_{max}

Zymogen

DON'T FORGET YOUR KEYS

1. Each category of biological molecule has a "personality" - think structure and polarity - that matches its practical uses in living organisms.

2. Enzyme-substrate fit correlates with enzyme effectiveness and a lower K_m.

3. Competitive inhibitors block the active site; noncompetitive inhibitors bind to a separate site, changing the shape of the active site; uncompetitive inhibitors bind the enzyme-substrate complex, decreasing the concentration of substrate that can react.

Genetics

2.1 Introduction

The study of genetics is central to understanding life forms: how they develop, how they function, how they reproduce, and how a species survives. Genes determine what proteins are created on a moment to moment basis for living organisms. The genome is, therefore, an essential contributor to both the regulation of processes within the body and to inheritance. This lecture will discuss the primary functions of genetic material, which include, 1. coding for products necessary within the lifetime of an organism, 2. passing information between cells, and 3. passing information from one generation to the next. While the genome contains a vast wealth of information, the way a cell uses this information to make products is flexible, varying with the environment and needs of the cell. When considering the processes that lead to gene expression, location is an important orienting tool. In eukaryotes, but not prokaryotes, the nuclear membrane separates the processes of transcription and translation in both space and time, which allows step-by-step regulation of gene expression.

This lecture will first introduce the basics of genetics, including the genome and the definition of a gene. It will then discuss the organization of genetic material and how that organization is involved in regulation. Next, the lecture will cover transcription and translation, the major processes involved in producing products based on the genome.

The passing of genetic information to new cells via cell division will be discussed, along with the errors that can occur. Finally, the lecture will address the passing of genetic information from one generation to the next. Throughout the lecture, environmental influences and regulation of genetic expression will be emphasized.

THE 3 KEYS

1. DNA is potential; RNA is regulation; protein is action.

2. Location matters – nucleus or cytoplasm?

3. See mitosis, think replication; see meiosis, think reproduction.

I look good in genes...

The Genome and Regulation

Genetic information is a mechanism of regulation; it provides the tools necessary for the immediate cellular processes that help cells survive in fluctuating environments. It also allows these processes and adaptations to be passed on to future generations. Genes are crucial for both the passing of hereditary traits and the cellular activities of an organism's lifetime.

Genetic information exhibits a remarkable amount of similarity among living organisms. Variation of the nucleotide sequence among humans is small; human DNA differs between individuals at approximately 1 nucleotide out of every 1200, or about 0.08%. Humans share about 98% of their nucleotide sequence with chimpanzees, about 60% with a fruit fly, and about 50% with a banana! These similarities exist because the genetic language necessary to carry out the basic processes of life is universal. The amount of uniformity found in genomes of living organisms also demonstrates that small changes in the DNA sequence can make a significant difference. Differences between organisms are caused not just by variation in their nucleotide sequences, but also differences in the regulation of how those sequences are expressed. In other words, the sequence of nucleotides alone does not determine what an organism is like; how and when a sequence is read is also important. There is an enormous amount of variability in how the genetic code of an organism can be expressed in response to its environment. Even if certain genes are present, they may never be expressed during an organism's lifetime. Understanding the regulation of gene expression is critical to the study of genetics.

The versatility of the genetic code is best understood by first distinguishing between genetics and epigenetics. The raw material of genetics, the **genome**, is the complete sequence of nucleotides of the genetic material. The genome is usually DNA but can be RNA in some viruses. (See the Biological Molecules and Enzymes Lecture for a review of DNA and RNA structure.) These sequences of nucleotides comprise a huge repository of information. By reading the genome, the cellular machinery is able to make all of the proteins and products that sustain life. This process is not like reading a book cover to cover. The cell can create distinct products and variable amounts of those products from the same single genetic code in response to the cellular environment. Changes in the kind or amount of gene products are not due to changes in the genome; instead, they depend on how the genome is read by the cellular machinery. The importance of being able to alter the expression of the genes in a genome is illustrated by considering how many types of cells there are in a human body. Each cell contains the same complete genome, yet some cells become bone while others become muscle, liver, etc. Regulation affects which genes from the genome are expressed, and the products of that gene expression affect the cell's function and identity.

The concept of epigenetics explains how some of these changes in gene expression take place. *Epigenetics* (Greek: epi → around) is a term used to describe changes that are made around the genome that do not alter the actual nucleotide sequence. These changes instruct the cellular machinery how to read the genome, thereby altering gene expression. Epigenetic changes do not change the genome itself. Epigenetics include changes such as the attachment of chemical markers to the genome, histone protein modification, and use of non-coding RNAs to influence gene expression. These topics will be discussed in greater detail later within this lecture. The purpose of epigenetic control is to provide a system of regulation that allows gene expression to adapt to the needs of the organism. Epigenetic control of gene expression changes continually, allowing gene expression to adapt to changes in the organism's internal and external environment. In addition to changing gene expression throughout the lifetime of an individual, epigenetic chemical markers and histone modifications can be passed down from one generation to the next.

The MCAT® will test your knowledge of genetics as a system of regulated gene expression. Keep in mind that gene expression is dynamic; it is constantly changing based on the environment and an organism's needs.

Epigenetic changes influence how the cellular machinery reads the genome. They can act like bookmarks saying "Read here!" or "Don't read here!" depending on the chemical signals present.

FIGURE 2.1 | Epigenetic Regulation

The genetic sequence is often thought of as a set of functional units called genes. For the MCAT® it is best to consider the definition of a gene in terms of its functions. A **gene** is a nucleotide sequence that can code for a certain product or set of products depending on factors such as alternative splicing and protein modification, which will be discussed later in this lecture. A gene is also a unit of heredity – a sequence of nucleotides that codes for a **trait**, meaning a genetically influenced characteristic.

Within a cell's lifetime, the function of the genome is to code for the products, usually proteins, that are necessary for cellular processes. The Central Dogma of gene expression is that DNA is transcribed to RNA, which is translated to amino acids to form a protein. All living organisms use this method to express their genes. Retroviruses (which are not living organisms) store their information as RNA and must first convert their RNA to DNA in order to express their genes.

This lecture discusses how the genetic code performs its three major functions: 1. coding for necessary products during the lifetime of a cell, 2. copying genetic information for the creation of new cells within an organism, and 3. passing on genetic information to the next generation. (For more information on retroviruses, see Lecture 1 of The Cell, *Biology 2*).

FIGURE 2.2 | The Central Dogma

FIGURE 2.3 Chromatin

Chromosomes

Supercoil within chromosome

Chromatin

Coiling within supercoil

Chromatin fiber

DNA

Core of 8 histones

Nucleosome

Double helix

2.3 Organization of Genetic Material

Knowledge of the general structure and vocabulary of genetic material provides a base for the study of genetics. The Biological Molecules and Enzymes Lecture discusses the general structure of DNA and RNA nucleotides, how those nucleotides are joined together through phosphodiester bonds to form single-stranded nucleic acid sequences, and how complementary sequences of single-stranded DNA join in an antiparallel fashion to form double-stranded DNA. All living organisms have double-stranded DNA as their genetic material.

Chromosomes as a System of Organization

In eukaryotic cells, double-stranded DNA sequences are arranged into **chromosomes** (Greek: chroma → color, soma → body). This compact organization is necessary because of the large size of eukaryotic genomes. If a double strand of all the DNA in a single human cell were stretched out straight, it would measure around 5 feet in length. The nucleus of the cell is of course much smaller than this! Chromosomes allow the genome to be compressed and organized

A chromosome consists of compactly wrapped DNA and protein in a hierarchy of organizational levels. The sections of DNA that are not in use are wrapped tightly around globular proteins called **histones**. Histones have basic functional groups that give these proteins a net positive charge at the normal pH of the cell (see the discussion of the isoelectric point in the Acids and Bases Lecture of the *Chemistry* manual). The net positive charge attracts the negatively charged DNA strands and assists in the wrapping process. Eight histones wrapped in DNA form a **nucleosome**. Nucleosomes, in turn, wrap into coils called *solenoids*, which wrap into **supercoils**. The entire DNA/protein complex (including a very small amount of RNA) is called **chromatin** (Greek: chroma → color). By mass, chromatin is about one third DNA, two thirds protein, and a small amount of RNA. Chromatin received its name because the large amount of basic amino acid content in histones allows chromatin to absorb basic dyes.

Not all chromatin is equally compact. The cellular machinery that "reads" the genetic code can only act on **euchromatin** (Greek: eu → well or properly), which is uncoiled. The nucleotide sequences found in euchromatin are usually accessible to the cell's translation machinery. Euchromatin is only coiled during nuclear division when translation has stopped. Chromatin that is tightly condensed is called **heterochromatin** (Greek: heteros → other). Heterochromatin is not accessible to the cellular machinery and will not be transcribed. Some chromatin, called constitutive heterochromatin, is permanently coiled. The structure of chromatin influences gene expression and is regulated by epigenetic modifications that are described on the next page.

Nucleotide sequences that code for protein products often contain **single copy DNA**, which are nucleotide sequences represented by only one copy of a nucleotide sequence, and are associated with regions of euchromatin that are being actively transcribed. Non-coding regions of DNA (found only in eukaryotes) often contain **repetitive DNA**, which has multiple consecutive copies of the same nucleotide sequence and remains tightly coiled in regions of heterochromatin.

In animals, DNA is found only in the nucleus and the mitochondria.

Regulation of Chromatin Structure

Because the structure of chromatin is important in determining which sequences of DNA are transcribed, the coiling and uncoiling of chromatin is highly regulated by epigenetic controls according to the needs of the cell.

Chemical changes to histone proteins help control which sections of DNA are tightly wound and which are accessible to cellular machinery. Chemical epigenetic changes can also control which coding sequences are unwound and transcribed. The most common example of epigenetic regulation through chemical change is **DNA methylation**, which involves the addition of an extra methyl group to particular cytosine nucleotides. Methylation causes DNA to be wound more tightly. Methylated sections are inaccessible to cellular machinery and cannot be transcribed, so the expression of genes in these sections is reduced. Histones can also be methylated or acetylated, which involves the addition of an acetyl group. Histone modification can have variable effects, though in general histone methylation reduces transcription, while acetylation increases transcription. Sections of RNA that do not code for protein products, called **non-coding RNA (ncRNA)**, contribute to the regulation of the chemical changes that affect chromatin structure.

Patterns of DNA methylation can be inherited from previous generations. There is increasing evidence that the life experiences of your ancestors can affect gene expression in your lifetime. Inherited epigenetic changes can make people more prone to conditions such as asthma, obesity, and anxiety.

Methylation Mutes transcription, while Acetylation Activates transcription.

FIGURE 2.4 | DNA Methylation

Chromosomes and nucleus stained to visualize individual chromosomes. The karyotype on the right can be used to detect large chromosomal deletions, insertions, and translocations but cannot show single nucleic acid changes. Trisomy 21, also known as Down Syndrome, would show three copies of chromosome 21.

Chromosomal Vocabulary

Inside the nucleus of a human somatic cell, there are 46 double-stranded DNA molecules. The chromatin associated with each one is wound into a chromosome. In human cells, each chromosome possesses a partner that codes for the same traits. Two such chromosomes are called **homologues** (Greek: homologein → to agree with, homo → same, logia → collection). Humans possess 23 homologous pairs of chromosomes. Although the traits are the same (e.g. eye color), the actual genes may code for different versions of the trait (e.g. blue vs. brown). Different forms of the same gene are called alleles, as will be discussed in greater detail later in this lecture. Any cell that contains homologous pairs of chromosomes is said to be **diploid** (Greek: di- → twice). Any cell that does not contain homologues is said to be **haploid** (Greek: haploos → single or simple). *Polyploidy* occurs when a cell has more than two copies of homologous chromosomes.

| **FIGURE 2.5** | Chromosomes

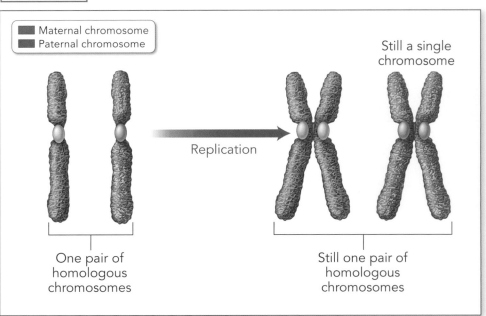

Diploid means that the cell has homologous pairs. It's that simple. Diploid = homologues.

The tricky question about chromosomes is, "How many are there?" In the nucleus of a human cell, there are 46 chromosomes before replication, and 46 chromosomes after replication. The replicated and un-replicated versions of a chromosome are each considered to be a single chromosome. The duplicates can be referred to separately as sister chromatids.

These questions are NOT related to a passage.

Question 25

Scientists perform an experiment evaluating the effects of a specific compound on DNA repair pathways during replication. Which of the following would serve as an effective experimental control?

- ○ **A.** Comparing the prevalence of mutations with non-dividing cells in the absence of the compound
- ○ **B.** Comparing the prevalence of mutations with dividing cells in the absence of the compound
- ○ **C.** Comparing the heterochromatin/euchromatin ratio with non-dividing cells in the absence of the compound
- ○ **D.** Comparing the heterochromatin/euchromatin ratio with dividing cells in the absence of the compound

Question 26

Which of the following best describes the relationship between genetic sequence and the environment?

- ○ **A.** Environmental factors affect gene expression only when they act at the level of translation.
- ○ **B.** Because genetic differences between living organisms are negligible, environmental effects play a large role in producing phenotypic differences.
- ○ **C.** Not all genes in the genome are expressed.
- ○ **D.** An organism can create different products or amounts of products in response to the environment.

Question 27

Which of the following statements about the genome is LEAST accurate?

- ○ **A.** The genome can be changed by environmental influence through epigenetic alterations.
- ○ **B.** The genome can be read in variable ways to produce different products.
- ○ **C.** The genome can be composed of DNA or RNA.
- ○ **D.** In multi-cellular organisms, different types of cells can read the genome differently.

Question 28

Epigenetic changes are one way the environment influences gene expression. Which of the following is NOT an example of an epigenetic change?

- ○ **A.** A methyl group is added to a cytosine residue in the DNA sequence.
- ○ **B.** A methyl group is added to a lysine within a histone protein.
- ○ **C.** ncRNAs influence chromatin structure.
- ○ **D.** Mutagens in the environment cause the creation of a new single nucleotide polymorphism.

Question 29

Scientists studying an autoimmune disease in mourning doves find that activation of a certain area of their genome (Section X) up-regulates the products of a gene (Gene Y) located downstream, and that the products of Gene Y caused increased symptoms of the disease examined. Increased DNA methylation of Section X would most likely result in which of the following?

- ○ **A.** Activation of Section X and decreased disease symptoms
- ○ **B.** Inactivation of Section X and decreased disease symptoms
- ○ **C.** Activation of Section X and increased disease symptoms
- ○ **D.** Inactivation of Section X and increased disease symptoms

Question 30

Which of the following correctly indicates increasing levels of complexity in the organization of genetic information around protein complexes?

- ○ **A.** Histones → Nucleosomes → Chromatin → Chromosomes
- ○ **B.** Nucleosomes → Histones → Chromatin → Chromosomes
- ○ **C.** Histones → Nucleosomes → Chromosomes → Chromatin
- ○ **D.** Nucleosomes → Histones → Chromosomes → Chromatin

Question 31

Which of the following is NOT true regarding nuclear DNA and its associated proteins?

- ○ **A.** Nucleosomes provide the structure for DNA to form into solenoids and supercoils.
- ○ **B.** Histones contain basic functional groups that result in a net positive charge.
- ○ **C.** Constitutive heterochromatin is transcribed by cellular machinery.
- ○ **D.** By mass, chromatin contains more protein than DNA.

Question 32

Which of the following is true regarding chromosomes?

- ○ **A.** The number of chromosomes in a human cell doubles during replication.
- ○ **B.** Diploid cells lack homologous chromosomes.
- ○ **C.** Homologous chromosomes can contain different alleles.
- ○ **D.** Chromosomes only form prior to transcription.

Transcribing DNA to RNA

A major function of the genome is to code for the products (usually proteins) that are necessary for cells to carry out the processes of life. Most cells spend the majority of their lives in the non-growing phase of G_0. Far from being a period of rest as the name implies, during G_0 cells are busy serving their various functions within the body and producing proteins for this purpose. Although cells manufacture protein products throughout the cell cycle, most production takes place during G_0 when the cell is not exerting energy in self-replication.

Genes undergo transcription and translation in order to make products. **Transcription** is the process by which RNA is manufactured from a DNA template. During transcription, an RNA transcript, which essentially copies the information in DNA, is created. Different genes can code for different types of RNA including ribosomal RNA (**rRNA**), transfer RNA (**tRNA**), small nuclear RNA (**snRNA**), and messenger RNA (**mRNA**). Some of these RNAs, such as rRNA, tRNA, and snRNA, are functional end products that serve important purposes in the cell. A large portion of the RNA transcribed is mRNA, which serves as the "message" that is translated for protein production.

FIGURE 2.6 | The Cell Life Cycle

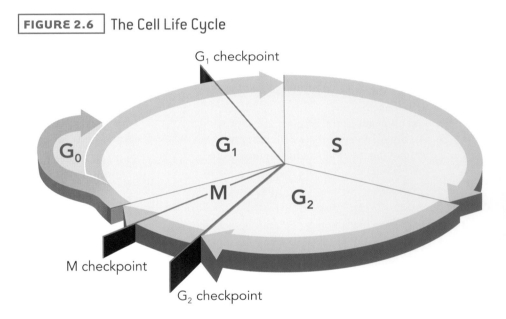

To produce proteins, transcribed mRNA must undergo the process of translation. **Translation** takes the nucleotide sequence of the RNA transcript and translates it into the language of amino acids, which are then strung together to form a functional protein. Recall from the Biological Molecules and Enzymes Lecture that proteins form the basis of many cell structures and regulate practically all cellular processes. Creating proteins through transcription and translation is essential to the processes of life.

Transcription

The purpose of transcription is to create an RNA copy of a DNA template. Transcription is itself a form of regulation of gene expression. If transcription did not exist, and instead the whole genome was translated directly into proteins, every cell in an organism would be the same. Only DNA which has first been transcribed into RNA and post-transcriptionally modified has the opportunity to be translated into a protein.

Transcription includes three main stages: initiation, elongation, and termination. The beginning of transcription is called **initiation**. In initiation, a group

In eukaryotes, nuclear DNA cannot leave the nucleus and mitochondrial DNA cannot leave the mitochondrial matrix. Eukaryotic transcription takes place only in these two places.

of DNA binding proteins called **transcription factors** identifies a promoter on the DNA strand. A **promoter** is a sequence of DNA nucleotides that designates a beginning point for transcription. At the promoter, the transcription factors assemble into a *transcription initiation complex*, which includes the major enzyme of transcription, **RNA polymerase**. Promoter sequences help regulate where on the genome transcription can take place and how often certain sequences are transcribed. Promoter regions of DNA have some sequence variability, which serves a regulatory function. The most commonly found promoter nucleotide sequence recognized by a given species of RNA polymerase is called the *consensus sequence*. Variation from the consensus sequence causes RNA polymerase to bond less tightly and less often to a given promoter, which leads to the associated genes being transcribed less frequently.

After binding to the promoter, RNA polymerase unzips the DNA double helix, creating a *transcription bubble*. Next the complex switches to **elongation** mode. In elongation, RNA polymerase transcribes only one strand of the DNA nucleotide sequence into a complementary RNA nucleotide sequence. The transcribed strand is called the *template strand* or (–) *antisense strand*. The other strand, called the *coding strand* or (+) *sense strand*, protects its partner against degradation. RNA polymerase moves along the DNA strand in the 3′ → 5′ direction, building the new RNA strand in the 5′ → 3′ direction. There is no proofreading mechanism that corrects for errors in the transcription process. (Errors in RNA are not called mutations, unlike errors in DNA.) Errors created in RNA are not transmitted to progeny. Most genes are transcribed many times in a cell's lifetime, so errors in individual instances of transcription are not generally harmful.

The end of transcription is called **termination**, which occurs when a specific sequence of nucleotides known as the termination sequence is reached. It can also

---

FIGURE 2.7 Transcription

① RNA polymerase looks for the promoter on DNA.

② RNA polymerase recognizes the promoter.

③ A transcription bubble is formed and elongation begins.

Only the template strand of the DNA double helix is transcribed. The sequence of the coding strand resembles the sequence of the newly synthesized mRNA. Recall from the Biological Molecules and Enzymes Lecture that one of the major differences between DNA and RNA is that DNA is double-stranded while RNA is single-stranded. Make sure you understand that both the coding strand and the mRNA are complementary to the template strand. You could see a question about this on the MCAT®.

involve special proteins, known as *Rho proteins*, which help to dissociate RNA polymerase from the DNA template.

Transcription is the main level of activation or deactivation of genes. In both prokaryotic and eukaryotic cells, regulation of gene expression occurs at the level of transcription via proteins called activators and repressors. **Activators** and **repressors** bind to DNA close to the promoter and either activate or repress the activity of RNA polymerase. Activators and repressors are often allosterically regulated by small molecules such as cAMP. Gene regulation in eukaryotes adds complexity through the interaction of many genes and other proteins called enhancers. Because of this, more room is required than is available near the promoter. *Enhancers* are short, non-coding regions of DNA found in eukaryotes. They function similarly to activators but act at a much greater distance from the promoter.

Regulation of Transcription in Prokaryotes

Although regulation of gene expression occurs in both prokaryotes and eukaryotes, it serves different purposes. The primary function of gene regulation in prokaryotes is to respond to changes in the environment, such as changes in the concentration of specific nutrients in and around the cell. In contrast, the maintenance of *homeostasis,* or a stable and unchanging state of the intracellular and extracellular compartments, is the hallmark of multicellular organisms. The primary function of gene regulation in multicellular organisms is to control the intra- and extracellular environments of the cell.

Prokaryotic mRNA typically includes several genes in a single transcript (*polycistronic*), whereas eukaryotic mRNA includes only one gene per transcript (*monocistronic*). In the **Jacob-Monod model** of prokaryotic genetic regulation, the genetic unit consisting of the operator, promoter, and genes that contribute to a single prokaryotic mRNA is called the **operon**. A well-studied and commonly used example of an operon is the **lac operon** in the species *E. coli. E. coli* generally prefer to use glucose as a fuel source when it is present in the environment. The lac operon codes for enzymes that allow *E. coli* to import and metabolize lactose when glucose is not present in sufficient quantities. The lac operon is activated only if both of two conditions are met: 1. glucose is scarce and 2. lactose is present. Low glucose levels lead to high cAMP levels. cAMP binds to and activates a *catabolite activator protein (CAP)*. The activated CAP protein binds to a CAP site located adjacent and upstream to the promoter on the lac operon. In an example of **positive control**, CAP activates the promotor, allowing the formation of an initiation complex and the subsequent transcription and translation of three proteins. A

Use the simpler model of the prokaryotic genome to gain a basic understanding of the actions of activators and repressors. Know that eukaryotes also have activators and repressors along with many other forms of regulation for gene expression.

Most genetic regulation occurs at the level of transcription. In other words, the amount of a given type of protein within a cell is likely to be related to how much of its mRNA is transcribed. One reason for this is that mRNA has a short half-life in the cytosol, so soon after transcription is completed, the mRNA is degraded and its protein is no longer translated. Also, many proteins can be transcribed from a single mRNA, creating an amplifying effect.

FIGURE 2.8 Structure of Lac Operon

second regulatory site on the lac operon, called the *operator*, is located adjacent and downstream to the promoter. When lactose is not present in the cell, a lac repressor protein binds to the operator site and prevents transcription of the lac genes, thereby preventing gene expression. This process is called **gene repression**. When lactose is available, it will bind to the lac repressor protein, making that protein unable to bind to the operator site. Without inhibition from the repressor protein, transcription of the lac genes can proceed. The presence of lactose can therefore *induce* the transcription of the lac operon only when glucose is not present. The promoter and gene for the lac repressor are located adjacent and upstream to the CAP binding site.

> An operon is a sequence of bacterial DNA containing an operator, a promoter, and related genes. The genes of an operon are transcribed on one mRNA. Genes outside the operon may code for activators and repressors.

2.5 | Modification of RNA

When transcription is complete, the RNA products of transcription are modified by the cell. In addition to epigenetic modifications, the post-transcriptional modification of RNA is one of the major means through which gene expression is regulated. Post-transcriptional processing of RNA occurs in both eukaryotic and prokaryotic cells. In eukaryotes, each type of RNA undergoes post-transcriptional processing. Modifications to RNA transcripts, particularly to mRNA strands prior to translation, allow the cell to employ additional methods of gene regulation, which will be further described below. In prokaryotes, rRNA and tRNA go through post-transcriptional processing, but almost all mRNA is translated directly to protein.

> Post-transcriptional modification of mRNA only occurs in the nucleus in eukaryotes. The bacterial genome does not contain introns.

Post-transcriptional Processing of mRNA in Eukaryotes

In eukaryotes, the initial mRNA nucleotide sequence arrived at through transcription is not ready to be translated into proteins until it has first been modified by the cell. The initial RNA nucleotide sequence arrived at through transcription is called the **primary transcript** (also called *pre-mRNA*, or *heterogeneous nuclear RNA [hnRNA]*). The modifications that change a primary transcript into a final, processed mRNA serve several purposes. These include: helping the molecules that initiate translation recognize the mRNA, protecting the mRNA from degradation, eliminating extraneous sequences of nucleotides from the transcript before translation, and providing a mechanism for variability in protein products produced from a single transcript. All of these modifications take place in the nucleus.

Post-transcriptional processing includes modification of both ends of an mRNA sequence. Even before the eukaryotic mRNA is completely transcribed, its 5′ end is capped in a process using GTP. The **5′ cap** serves as an attachment site in protein synthesis during translation and as a protection against degradation by enzymes that cleave nucleotides, called *exonucleases*. The 3′ end of the transcript is similarly protected from exonucleases by the addition of a long series of adenine nucleotides. When this **poly-A tail** has been added, the 3′ end is said to be *polyadenylated*. The poly-A tail also aids in the export of the mature RNA to the cytoplasm after splicing and serves a role in helping to initiate translation.

The primary transcript is much longer than the mRNA that will be translated into a protein. Before leaving the nucleus, portions of the primary transcript are excised and discarded through the process of **splicing**. The portions of transcript that are removed are called **introns**, while the portions that become part of the mature mRNA and will code for proteins are called **exons**. Introns are generally much longer than exons. They do not code for proteins and are degraded within the nucleus. The process of splicing removes introns from the primary transcript and joins the ends of the exons together to form one, uninterrupted coding sequence of mRNA. The mechanism of splicing involves several small nuclear ribonucleoproteins (**snRNPs**, "snurps"). Each snRNP contains both an assortment of proteins and snRNA. During the splicing process, snRNA acts as

Biological Molecules and Enzymes
≡ BIOLOGY 1

FIGURE 2.9 | Introns

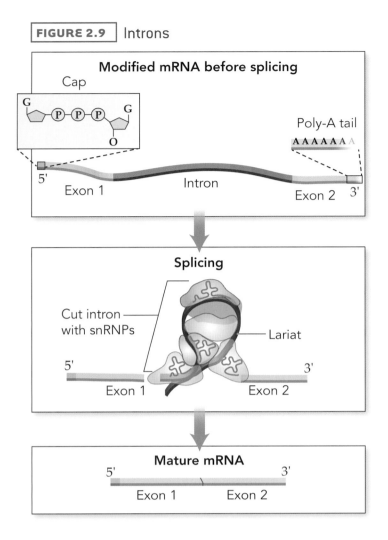

Modified mRNA before splicing

Cap

G
P P P
G
O

5'
Exon 1
Intron
Poly-A tail
A A A A A A
Exon 2   3'

Splicing

Cut intron
with snRNPs

Lariat

5'
Exon 1
Exon 2
3'

Mature mRNA

5'
3'
Exon 1   Exon 2

SPLICESOME SALTY

EXONS: TO CYTOPLASM

INTRONS

Introns play a role in determining possible splicing patterns and promoting protein production. Because of their functional significance, many introns are highly conserved between species.

a ribozyme – an RNA molecule capable of catalyzing specific chemical reactions. (Note that this is one of the few enzymes that is not a protein.) Splicing occurs when snRNPs recognize nucleotide sequences at the ends of the introns. The snRNPs pull the ends of the introns together, forming an intron loop or *lariat*. The complex formed from the association of the snRNPs and additional associate proteins is called a **spliceosome**. The spliceosome excises the introns and joins the ends of the exons together to form the single mRNA strand that ultimately codes for a polypeptide.

Remember that, in general, INtrons remain IN the nucleus, and EXons EXit the nucleus to be translated.

Eukaryotic cells exert control over gene expression and add to the variety of protein products possible through the process of alternative splicing, one of the major mechanisms in the regulation of eukaryotic gene expression. **Alternative splicing** allows the cell to incorporate different variable coding sequences into the mature mRNA. This highly regulated process can create a variety of mRNA molecules for translation from a single DNA coding sequence. The mechanisms for creating this variability include omitting certain exons, incorporating certain introns, and utilizing variable splicing sites. Increasing evidence indicates that introns play an important function in determining gene expression. The nucleotide sequences in both introns and exons determine the multiple ways a primary transcript may be spliced. Sequences that contain introns are associated with amplified protein production compared to sequences that lack introns. Alternative splicing, together with other eukaryotic techniques such as the use of alternative promoter sites or terminating transcription at different sites, allows the cell to create a vast variety of proteins from a relatively limited number of protein-coding nucleotide sequences. Although the human genome is estimated to contain only 20,000-25,000 protein-coding gene regions, it can code for more than 100,000 proteins. Alternative splicing is an important contributor to this diversity of protein products.

One reason there are more proteins than genes is that different splicing patterns of the same gene can create different polypeptides.

Transcription and post-transcriptional modifications take place in the nucleus of eukaryotes. The spatial separation between transcriptional and translational processes provided by the nuclear membrane is a form of regulation in eukaryotes. This separation allows the RNA transcript to be modified before it leaves the nucleus and before translation can begin. Prokaryotes have no nuclear membrane. The lack of spatial separation means that prokaryotes can carry out transcription and translation concurrently and that they do not modify RNA transcripts prior to the start of translation.

FIGURE 2.10 Alternative Splicing

2.6 Translating RNA to Protein

Making Sense of the Genetic Code

When post-transcriptional processing is finished, a mature mRNA is ready for translation. Translation is the process through which a cell creates the protein products that are necessary to carry out the processes of life. As described earlier in the lecture, it involves the "translation" of the nucleotide sequence of mRNA into the amino acid sequence of the corresponding protein.

During the process of translation, the information contained in mRNA is used as a set of instructions to create a specific polypeptide chain. mRNA nucleotides are strung together to form a **genetic code** consisting of four different nucleotides, as described in the Biological Molecules and Enzymes Lecture. In nature, there are approximately 20 different amino acids that commonly make up functional proteins. The four RNA nucleotides (adenine, guanine, cytosine, and uracil) together must create a language that unambiguously codes for each of these common amino acids. The genetic code of mRNA accomplishes this task by using a series of three nucleotides to code for each amino acid — a system known as the **triplet code**. Some quick math reveals why sets of three nucleotides are needed. Because there are only four kinds of nucleotides, if each nucleotide coded for a different amino acid, only four amino acids would be possible. The number of possible combinations from a set of two nucleotides, where each nucleotide might contain any one of the four nitrogenous bases, is $4^2 = 16$, which is still not enough to code for the 20 amino acids (see Table 2.1). Therefore, the code must use a combination of three nucleotides for each amino acid. The number of possible combinations of any three nucleotides gives $4^3 = 64$, which is greater than the number of amino

TABLE 2.1 > **Nucleotides in Pairs**

	A	C	G	T
A	AA	CA	GA	TA
C	AC	CC	GC	TC
G	AG	CG	GG	TG
T	AT	CT	GT	TT

acids. The genetic code is therefore said to be **degenerative**, which means that more than one series of three nucleotides may code for the same amino acid. Any single series of three nucleotides, however, will code for one and only one amino acid, so the code is also unambiguous. The use of three nucleotide series to code for a single amino acid works well and is highly conserved. The codes shown in Table 2.2 are almost universal; nearly every living organism uses these same codes to translate mRNA sequences into strings of amino acids.

Three consecutive nucleotides on a strand of mRNA comprise a codon. All but three possible codons code for amino acids. The remaining codons, UAA, UGA, and UAG, are stop codons (also called **termination codons**). Stop codons signal an end to protein synthesis. The start codon (also called the **initiation codon**), AUG, indicates where translation will begin. The start codon codes for the amino acid methionine, which is always the first amino acid incorporated into a polypeptide during protein synthesis. By convention, a sequence of RNA nucleotides is written $5' \rightarrow 3'$.

TABLE 2.2 > **The Genetic Code**

First position 5' end ↓	Second position				Third position 3' end ↓
	U	**C**	**A**	**G**	
U	Phe	Ser	Tyr	Cys	U
	Phe	Ser	Tyr	Cys	C
	Leu	Ser	STOP	STOP	A
	Leu	Ser	STOP	Trp	G
C	Leu	Pro	His	Arg	U
	Leu	Pro	His	Arg	C
	Leu	Pro	Gln	Arg	A
	Leu	Pro	Gln	Arg	G
A	Ile	Thr	Asn	Ser	U
	Ile	Thr	Asn	Ser	C
	Ile	Thr	Lys	Arg	A
	Met	Thr	Lys	Arg	G
G	Val	Ala	Asp	Gly	U
	Val	Ala	Asp	Gly	C
	Val	Ala	Glu	Gly	A
	Val	Ala	Glu	Gly	G

Translation

Translation is the process by which the cellular machinery "reads" the mRNA transcript and translates it into a polypeptide. Each of the three major types of RNA plays a unique role in translation. mRNA is the template which carries the genetic code from the nucleus to the cytosol in the form of codons. tRNA plays a vital role in actually rendering the triplet code of the mRNA into a specific amino acid sequence. Each tRNA molecule has two distinct ends. One end contains a series of three nucleotides, called an **anticodon**, which will bind to the complementary codon sequence on mRNA. The other end of the tRNA carries the amino acid that corresponds to that codon, which can be added to a growing polypeptide chain as tRNAs bind to the codons along the mRNA strand (Figure 2.12). The first two base pairs in the codon and anticodon must be strictly complementary (A with U and C with G). There is some flexibility in bonding at the third base pair position. This flexibility is called **wobble pairing** and helps explain why multiple codons can code for the same amino acid.

All translation takes place using a specialized organelle called a **ribosome**. Ribosomes may be free-floating in the cytosol or attached to the outer surface of the endoplasmic reticulum to form rough ER, as described in the Cell Lecture in *Biology 2: Systems*. A ribosome is composed of a **small subunit** and a **large subunit**, both made up of rRNA. These subunits function as the catalytic component of the ribosome, while many separate proteins contribute structural support. The ribosome and its subunits are measured in terms of *sedimentation coefficients* given in *Svedberg units (S)*. The sedimentation coefficient gives the speed of a particle in a centrifuge and is proportional to mass and related to shape and density. Prokaryotic ribosomes are smaller than eukaryotic ribosomes. Prokaryotic ribosomes are made from a 30S and a 50S subunit and have a combined sedimentary coefficient of 70S. Eukaryotic ribosomes are made of 40S and 60S subunits and have a combined sedimentary coefficient of 80S. The complex structure of ribosomes requires a special organelle called the **nucleolus** in which to manufacture them. (Prokaryotes do not possess a nucleolus, but synthesis of prokaryotic ribosomes is similar to that of eukaryotic ribosomes.) Although the ribosome is assembled in the nucleolus, the small and large subunits are exported separately to the cytosol.

Notice that the sedimentation coefficients don't add up: 40 + 60 ≠ 80. Eukaryotic ribosome sedimentation coefficients are Even (40S, 60S, 80S).

The process of translation is divided into the same three stages as transcription (initiation, elongation, and termination), but whereas transcription produces a strand of RNA, the product of translation is a chain of amino acids. After post-transcriptional processing in a eukaryote, mRNA leaves the nucleus through the nuclear pores and enters the cytosol. With the help of **initiation factors** (co-factor proteins), the 5′ end attaches to the small subunit of a ribosome. A tRNA containing the 5′-CAU-3′ anticodon sequesters the amino acid methionine and settles into the P site (peptidyl site). This is the signal for the large subunit to join and form the **initiation complex**. This process is termed **initiation**. Most of the regulation of translation occurs during the initiation stage through the recognition (or lack of recognition) between the ribosomal subunits and the secondary structure of the mRNA transcript.

Once the initiation complex is fully formed, **elongation** of the polypeptide begins. During elongation, the ribosome slides down the mRNA strand one codon at a time in the 5′ → 3′ direction while matching each codon to a complementary tRNA anticodon. The corresponding amino acids attached to these tRNAs are bound together using the rRNA-based peptidyl transferase, which catalyzes the reaction at the interface of the two ribosomal subunits. A growing polypeptide emerges as the process proceeds. The mechanism of elongation requires the input of energy. Once a methionine-bearing tRNA has attached to the P site, a new tRNA, with its corresponding amino acid, attaches to the neighboring A site (aminoacyl site). The amino acid attached to the tRNA in the A site becomes the second amino acid in the polypeptide sequence. The C-terminus (carboxyl end) of methionine attaches to the *N-terminus* (amine end) of the amino acid at the A site in a dehydration reaction, forming a peptide bond. The bond formation takes place through peptidyl transferase activity, which is catalyzed by rRNA in the ribosome, another example of ribozyme function. After lengthening the polypeptide by a single amino acid, the ribosome shifts 3 nucleotides toward the 3' end of the mRNA. The tRNA that carried methionine moves to the E site, from which it can exit the ribosome. The tRNA carrying the newly formed dipeptide moves

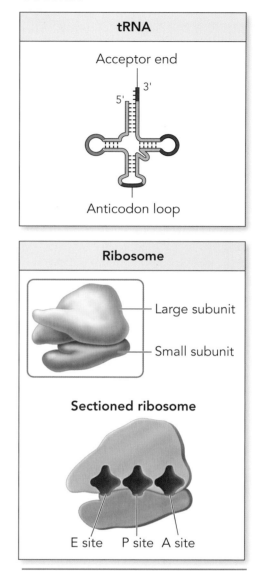

FIGURE 2.11 tRNA and Ribosome Structure

It is helpful to consider location when thinking about the differences between prokaryotic and eukaryotic transcription and translation. In eukaryotes, mRNA is transcribed in the nucleus, where the DNA is kept. The mRNA must then leave the nucleus to be translated in the cytoplasm. For this reason, in eukaryotes, transcription and translation are separated both in both space and time. This separation is one mechanism to regulate which sequences are converted to products and which are not. Because prokaryotes have no separate, membrane-bound nucleus, transcription and translation can occur simultaneously.

FIGURE 2.12 Translation

NH₃

Polypeptide

tRNA without amino acid

tRNA with amino acid

Ribosome

mRNA

3'

5'

Start sequence

Stop sequence

H₃N — MET GLN ILE CYS SER VAL

Newly formed polypeptide

Within each ribosome there are three sites where tRNA molecules can bind. At the A site, the Anticodon matches up with the codon, ensuring that the correct Amino Acid is chosen. At the P site, a Peptide bond between amino acids is formed, lengthening the Polypeptide chain. Finally, at the E site, the tRNA, which now lacks an amino acid, is free to Exit the ribosome.

Know the steps of translation: initiation, elongation, and termination. Know the role of each type of RNA.

Understand Key 2: The intracellular locations of biological processes play a major role in their functions. Make sure to think of whether a process, such as transcription or translation, occurs in the nucleus or cytoplasm. Cells often separate competing pathways, such as fatty acid oxidation and fatty acid synthesis, into two distinct compartments to regulate their activities more effectively. Fatty acid oxidation occurs in the mitochondria, while fatty acid synthesis occurs in the cytosol.

to the P site, leaving the A site open for the next tRNA. The elongation process is repeated until a stop codon reaches the P site.

Translation ends when the ribosome reaches a stop codon in a step called termination. When a stop codon (or **nonsense codon**) reaches the A site, proteins known as **release factors** (co-factor proteins) bind to the A site, allowing a water molecule to add to the end of the polypeptide chain. The polypeptide is freed from the tRNA and ribosome, and the ribosome breaks up into its subunits to be reused in later rounds of protein synthesis.

Even as the polypeptide is being translated, it begins folding. The amino acid sequence determines the folding conformation, and the folding process is assisted by proteins called *chaperones*. For further information on protein folding and structure, revisit the Biological Molecules and Enzymes Lecture.

After Translation: The Fates of Proteins

Once a protein is completely synthesized, it can still undergo post-translational modifications. These modifications are a mechanism for regulating gene expression by affecting which products of translation ultimately become functional proteins. Sugars, lipids, or phosphate groups may be added to amino acids to influence functionality. The polypeptide can be cleaved in one or more places. Separate polypeptides may join to form the quaternary structure of a protein.

The final destination of a protein is related to where it is translated. Proteins translated by free-floating ribosomes function in the cytosol, while proteins synthesized by ribosomes that attach to the rough ER during translation are injected into the ER lumen. Proteins injected into the ER lumen are destined to become membrane bound proteins of the nuclear envelope, ER, Golgi, lysosomes, or plasma membrane, or, often, to be secreted from the cell. Free floating ribosomes are identical in structure to ribosomes that attach to the ER. The growing polypeptide itself may or may not cause the ribosome to attach to the ER, depending upon the polypeptide. A 20 amino acid sequence called a **signal peptide** near the front of the polypeptide is recognized by a protein-RNA **signal-recognition particle (SRP)** that carries the entire ribosome complex to a receptor protein on the ER. There the protein grows across the membrane, where it is either released into the lumen or remains partially attached to the ER. The signal peptide is usually removed by an enzyme. Signal peptides may also be attached to polypeptides to target them to mitochondria, the nucleus, or other organelles. In this way, proteins end up in locations appropriate to their structures and functions, and one of the main purposes of the genome, production and delivery of the products the cell needs, is achieved.

Translation begins on a free-floating ribosome. A signal peptide at the beginning of the translated polypeptide may direct the ribosome to attach to the ER, in which case the polypeptide is injected into the ER lumen. Polypeptides injected into the lumen may be secreted from the cell via the Golgi body or may remain partially attached to the membrane.

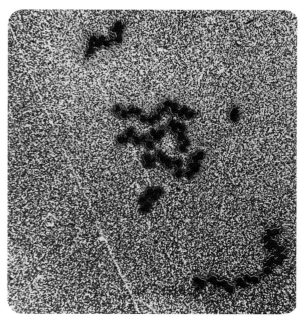

This false-color transmission electron micrograph (TEM) of a structural gene from the bacterium *Escherichia coli* shows the coupled transcription of DNA into mRNA and the simultaneous translation into protein molecules. The DNA fiber runs down the image (in yellow) from top left, with numerous ribosomes (in red) attached to each mRNA chain. The longest chairs (called polysomes) are furthest from the point of gene origin.

| FIGURE 2.13 | Polypeptide Synthesis

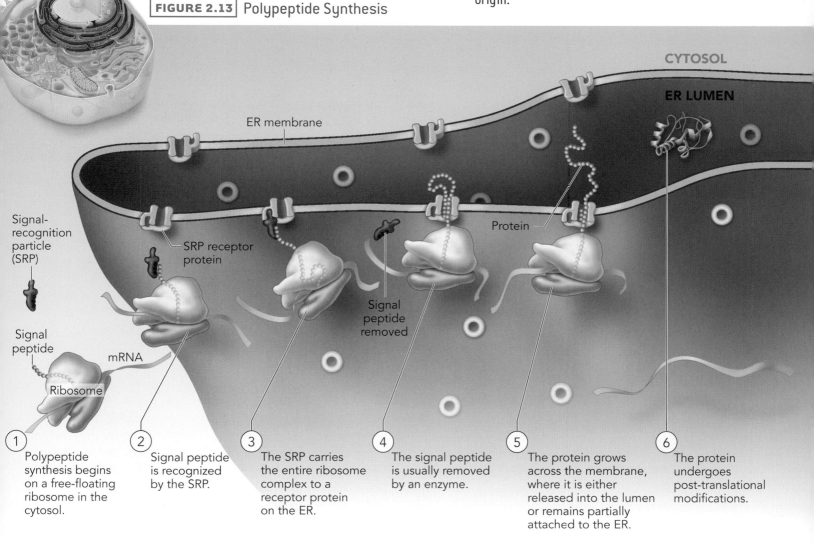

1. Polypeptide synthesis begins on a free-floating ribosome in the cytosol.

2. Signal peptide is recognized by the SRP.

3. The SRP carries the entire ribosome complex to a receptor protein on the ER.

4. The signal peptide is usually removed by an enzyme.

5. The protein grows across the membrane, where it is either released into the lumen or remains partially attached to the ER.

6. The protein undergoes post-translational modifications.

2.7 Genetic and Cellular Replication: Mitosis

Not all cell types in the body regularly undergo cell division. Fully differentiated neurons rarely divide to produce new cells. Neurons primarily remain in the G_0 phase of the cell cycle and devote their time and energy toward carrying out the normal functions of a neuron (producing neurotransmitters, maintaining the resting potential, etc.) rather than toward producing new neurons. Some cell types, such as skin and intestinal cells, have short lifespans or are lost to the environment and must regularly be replaced. To replace lost cells, some skin cell progenitors must routinely undergo cellular division to produce new cells. One of the major functions of the genome is directing the process of **DNA replication**, through which an exact copy of the genome is synthesized to be included in the newly created cell after division. As described in the Cell Lecture in *Biology 2: Systems*, cell division is a highly regulated series of phases. DNA replication takes place during the S phase of the interphase portion of the cell cycle. This allows two copies of the genome to be available during the M phase – one for each of the two resultant cells.

FIGURE 2.14 The Cell Life Cycle: S Phase

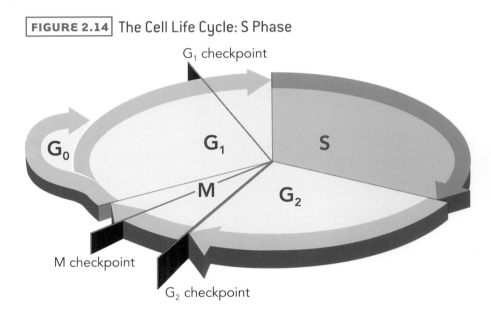

Replication of the Genome

The purpose of DNA replication is to produce two identical copies of the genome, each of which can be distributed to one of the cells created during division. This goal is accomplished by unwinding the DNA double helix and separating the two strands of DNA. Using the two single strands as templates, complementary nucleotides are matched along the lengths of each strand, resulting in two identical double-stranded copies of the same genome. Because each copy contains one strand from the original DNA and one newly synthesized strand, the process of DNA replication is said to be **semiconservative**.

The mechanism of DNA replication is governed by a group of proteins called a *replisome* (Figure 2.15). Replication does not begin at the end of a chromosome, but toward the middle at a site called the **origin of replication**. Replication in prokaryotes usually takes place from a single origin on the circular chromosome. Eukaryotic chromosomes are much larger, so they usually contain multiple origins of replication. Epigenetic markers designate the origins of replication and help regulate how and where replication begins. At the origin of replication, two replisomes proceed in opposite directions along the chromosome, making replication a **bidirectional** process. The point where a replisome is attached to the chromosome is called the replication fork. Each chromosome of eukaryotic DNA is replicated in many discrete segments called *replication units* or *replicons*.

Included in the replisome are several enzymes necessary for DNA replication. The first of these enzymes, **DNA helicase**, unwinds the double helix, separating the two strands. **DNA polymerase** synthesizes the new DNA strands by pairing complementary free-floating deoxynucleotides with the sequence of nucleotides on the exposed strands of DNA. DNA polymerase cannot initiate a new strand of nucleotides; it can only add nucleotides to an existing strand. **Primase**, an RNA polymerase, creates an **RNA primer** approximately 10 ribonucleotides in length to initiate the strand. DNA polymerase adds deoxynucleotides to the primer and moves along each DNA strand, creating a new complementary strand. DNA polymerase reads the parental strand in the $3' \to 5'$ direction, creating the new complementary strand in the $5' \to 3'$ direction. By convention, the nucleotide sequence in DNA is written $5' \to 3'$ as well. This direction is sometimes referred to as downstream and the $3' \to 5'$ direction as upstream.

Because DNA polymerase reads in only one direction, one strand of DNA is looped around the replisome, giving it the same orientation as the other strand. The single strand in the loop is prevented from folding back onto itself by *single strand binding (SSB) tetramer proteins* (also called *helix destabilizer proteins*). As is shown in Figure 2.15, at each replication fork, one of the separated strands is able to be read continuously in the $3' \to 5'$ direction while DNA polymerase continuously synthesizes a complementary strand in the $5' \to 3'$ direction. However, for the other original DNA strand, the polymerization of its new, complementary strand must be regularly interrupted and restarted with a new RNA primer so that the DNA may still be read $3' \to 5'$ as the replication fork is unzipped. The continuous strand is called the **leading strand**, while the interrupted strand is called the **lagging strand**. The lagging strand is formed from a series of disconnected strands called **Okazaki fragments**. Okazaki fragments are approximately 100 to 200 nucleotides long in eukaryotes and about 1000 to 2000 nucleotides long in prokaryotes. Because the formation of one strand is continuous and the other

Transcription requires a promoter, whereas replication requires a primer. The words are similar, but don't get confused. A promoter is a spot on the DNA that tells RNA polymerase where to begin transcription. A primer is a short piece of RNA that jump starts replication.

Replication proceeds in both directions from an origin. Each direction produces a leading and a lagging strand.

FIGURE 2.15 Prokaryotic Replisome

1 At the origin of replication, DNA helicase unwinds the double helix into a leading and lagging strand. Primase creates RNA primers to intiate the lagging strand. DNA polymerase synthesizes the new DNA strands by pairing the leading and lagging strands with complementary deoxynucleotides.

DNA polymerase III complex

Helicase

Parent DNA

Primase

DNA polymerase III complex

Leading strand

SSB tetramer

RNA primer

Lagging strand

Okazaki fragment (2) Okazaki fragment (1)

2 Because DNA polymerase reads in only one direction, the lagging strand is looped around the replisome, giving it the same orientation as the leading strand. DNA polymerase reads the parent DNA in the $3' \to 5'$ direction, creating the new complementary strand in the $5' \to 3'$ direction.

Fork movement

Parent DNA

Leading strand

DNA ligase (joining Okazaki fragments 1 & 2)

Lagging strand

Shown here are human chromosomes with their telomeres labeled in white. Telomeres are like the plastic tips on shoelaces that prevent them from fraying.

is fragmented, the process of replication is said to be **semidiscontinuous**. Once the new DNA strands are synthesized, the RNA primers are removed from the sequence by the enzyme RNAase H and the gaps created by the loss of the RNA primers are filled in with deoxynucleotides by DNA polymerase. In the final step of DNA replication, neighboring Okazaki fragments on the lagging strand are joined together by **DNA ligase** (Latin: ligare → to fasten or bind) to form a completed copy of the double-stranded DNA helix. Because the leading strand is continually synthesized, it does not require the action of DNA ligase.

In DNA replication, the ends of chromosomes are of special importance. The ends of eukaryotic chromosomal DNA possess telomeres. **Telomeres** are repeated six nucleotide units from 100 to 1,000 units long that protect the ends of chromosomes. Telomeres can become shortened through by repeated rounds of replication, a condition that has been linked to aging and disease. To somewhat counteract this shortening effect of replication on telomeres, *telomerase* catalyzes the lengthening of telomeres in eukaryotic organisms by adding many 5'-TTAGGG-3' nucleotide sequences to the ends of chromosomes.

In order to complete a copy of an entire genome in a reasonable period of time, replication must be fast. The DNA polymerase shown in Figure 2.15 moves at over 500 nucleotides per second. DNA polymerase in humans moves much more slowly, at around 50 nucleotides per second. Multiple origins of replication, however, allow the over 6 billion base pairs that make up the 46 human chromosomes to be replicated quite quickly. Replication in a human cell requires about 8 hours.

In addition to being fast, it is also important that DNA replication be accurate. DNA replication includes a mechanism to ensure that a faithful copy of the genome is produced. Besides being a polymerase, one of the subunits in DNA polymerase is an exonuclease that removes nucleotides from the strand. This enzyme automatically proofreads each new strand as it is synthesized and makes repairs when it discovers any mismatched nucleotides (e.g. thymine matched with guanine). DNA replication in eukaryotes is extremely accurate. Only one out of every 10^9–10^{11} base pairs is incorrectly incorporated.

Although there are some differences, replication in eukaryotes and prokaryotes is very similar. Except where specified, the process described above is accurate for both.

Mitosis

Mitosis is the process by which two cells are created that are identical to both each other and to the original cell. Once the genome is replicated, the copied chromosomes must be properly allocated to ensure that each daughter cell receives a complete copy of the genome during division. The large number of chromosomes

FIGURE 2.16 Mitosis

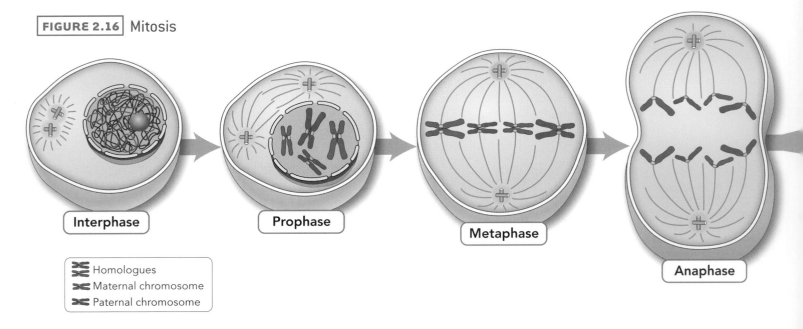

Interphase · Prophase · Metaphase · Anaphase

Homologues
Maternal chromosome
Paternal chromosome

in eukaryotic genomes makes the division of chromosomes between cells a potentially chaotic process. The cell requires a system of organization to divide the chromosomes evenly between daughter cells and uses the machinery of mitosis to accomplish this division efficiently and accurately. **Mitosis** (Greek: mitos → cell) is nuclear division without genetic change. It consists of a series of steps that organize and divide replicated chromosomes. The four main stages of mitosis are prophase, metaphase, anaphase, and telophase (Figure 2.16). These stages in turn are divided into sub-stages, but these categories are beyond the MCAT®. Mitosis varies among eukaryotes. The following stages describe mitosis in a typical animal cell.

Prophase is characterized by the condensation of chromatin into chromosomes. The tightly coiled chromatin limits transcription, down-regulating gene expression during mitosis. The two identical copies of duplicated chromosomes, called sister **chromatids**, are joined together at groups of proteins near their centers called **centromeres**. Structures called **centrioles**, located in the **centrosomes**, move to opposite poles of the cell. First the nucleolus and then the defined nucleus disappear as the nuclear envelope breaks down. The **spindle apparatus** begins to form, consisting of **asters** (microtubules radiating from the centrioles), *kinetochore microtubules* growing from the centromeres, and **spindle microtubules** connecting the two centrioles. (The **kinetochore** is a structure of protein and DNA located at the centromere of the joined chromatids of each chromosome.)

In **metaphase** (Greek: meta → between), chromosomes align along the equator of the cell. This orderly lining up of the chromosomes ensures that they will be separated such that each daughter cell receives one of each chromosome.

During **anaphase**, sister chromatids split at their attaching centromeres and segregate to opposite sides of the cell. Shortening of the kinetochore microtubules pulls the sister chromatids apart and moves them toward opposite poles. This split is termed *disjunction*. **Cytokinesis**, the actual separation of the cellular cytoplasm due to constriction of microfilaments around the center of the cell, may or may not commence toward the end of this phase.

In **telophase** (Greek: teleios → complete), the nuclear membrane reforms, followed by the reformation of the nucleolus. Chromosomes de-condense and become difficult to see under a light microscope. Cytokinesis continues, resulting in two identical daughter cells that each contain one complete copy of the parent cell's genome.

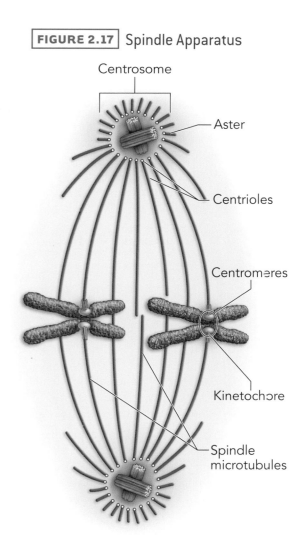

FIGURE 2.17 Spindle Apparatus

Centrosome

Aster

Centrioles

Centromeres

Kinetochore

Spindle microtubules

Telophase

Interphase

Remember the order of the stages of mitosis using the acronym PMAT.

Know the basic conditions that define each phase of mitosis. It is especially important to realize that mitosis results in genetically identical daughter cells.

These questions are NOT related to a passage.

Question 33

Researchers exploring the mechanism of eukaryotic transposition should be careful to screen for variables that may alter the results. Which of the following would NOT be a consideration?

- ○ **A.** The presence of bacteria in the samples
- ○ **B.** The use of primary spermatocytes
- ○ **C.** A nucleotide substitution next to the first gene of the transposon
- ○ **D.** The presence of stop codons inside the transposon

Question 34

Translation in a eukaryotic cell is associated with each of the following organelles or locations EXCEPT:

- ○ **A.** the mitochondrial matrix.
- ○ **B.** the cytosol.
- ○ **C.** the nucleus.
- ○ **D.** the rough endoplasmic reticulum.

Question 35

Sickle cell anemia is an autosomal recessive disorder that causes abnormal red blood cell formation and low life expectancy. In Western Africa where lethal bloodborne parasite infections by malaria are common, a high sickle cell anemia carrier population also persists. What best explains this phenomenon?

- ○ **A.** Sickle cell anemia exacerbates the malaria, further decreasing expected lifespan.
- ○ **B.** Malaria affects a different population of individuals independent of the sickle cell anemia population.
- ○ **C.** Sickle cell anemia genes may confer some resistance to malarial infection.
- ○ **D.** The population bears an inherent genetic predisposition to both anemia and malaria.

Question 36

One difference between prokaryotic and eukaryotic translation is that:

- ○ **A.** eukaryotic ribosomes are smaller.
- ○ **B.** prokaryotic translation may occur simultaneously with transcription, while eukaryotic translation cannot.
- ○ **C.** prokaryotes do not contain supra molecular complexes such as ribosomes.
- ○ **D.** prokaryotic DNA is circular so it does not require a termination sequence.

Question 37

An mRNA molecule being translated at the rough endoplasmic reticulum is typically shorter than the gene from which it was transcribed because:

- ○ **A.** the primary transcript was cut as it crossed the nuclear membrane.
- ○ **B.** normally multiple copies of the mRNA are produced and spliced.
- ○ **C.** introns in the primary transcript are excised.
- ○ **D.** several expressed regions of the primary transcript have equal numbers of base pairs.

Question 38

The gene for triose phosphate isomerase in maize (a corn plant) spans over 3400 base pairs of DNA and contains eight introns and nine exons. Which of the following would most likely represent the number of nucleotides found in the mature mRNA after post-transcriptional processing?

- ○ **A.** 1050
- ○ **B.** 3400
- ○ **C.** 6800
- ○ **D.** 13,600

Question 39

Eukaryotic mRNA production occurs in the following sequence:

- ○ **A.** transcription from DNA in the cytoplasm followed by post-transcriptional processing on the ribosome.
- ○ **B.** transcription from DNA in the nucleus followed by post-transcriptional processing in the nucleus.
- ○ **C.** translation from DNA in the nucleus followed by post-transcriptional processing in the nucleus.
- ○ **D.** translation from DNA in the cytoplasm followed by post-transcriptional processing on the ribosome.

Question 40

Which of the following statements regarding transcription is FALSE?

- ○ **A.** The mRNA produced is complementary to the coding strand.
- ○ **B.** Activators and repressors bind to DNA and affect the activity of RNA polymerase.
- ○ **C.** The nucleotide sequence of the promoter region affects how often a region of RNA is transcribed.
- ○ **D.** During transcription, RNA polymerase moves along the DNA strand in the 3' → 5' direction.

2.8 | Mutations

Although the processes of DNA replication and mitosis are extremely accurate and efficient, the huge number of repetitions of these processes throughout the body ensures that mistakes do happen and that changes to the genome can occur. Any alteration in the genome that is not due to genetic recombination (which takes place in meiosis, described below) is called a **mutation**. Mutations are important not only for the individual carrier, but as a crucial source of genetic variation within populations, without which evolution could not occur. Mutations can be *spontaneous* (occurring due to **random errors** in the natural process of replication and genetic recombination) or *induced* (occurring due to physical or chemical agents called **mutagens**, which can damage DNA and increase the frequency of mutation above the baseline frequency of spontaneous mutations). The effects on the cell are the same in either case. The effect of a mutation on an organism's fitness may be **advantageous** or **deleterious**, or there may be no effect at all. Mutations may occur at the level of the nucleotide or the level of the chromosome.

A **gene mutation** is the alteration in the sequence of DNA nucleotides in a single gene. A **chromosomal mutation** occurs when the structure of a chromosome is changed. In multicellular organisms, a mutation in a somatic cell (Greek: soma → body) is called a *somatic mutation*. A somatic mutation of a single cell may have very little effect on an organism with millions of cells. In contrast, a mutation in a germ cell, from which all other cells arise, can have large consequences for the offspring produced. Under normal conditions, mutations are rare. Only about one out of every million gametes will carry a mutation for a given gene. Different types of mutations are categorized both by the effect of the change on the structure of the genetic sequence and by the effect on the sequence's function.

Structural Changes to Genes

Mutations at the level of the gene most often change one nucleotide at a time. If a mutation changes a single nucleotide in a double strand of DNA, that mutation is called a **point mutation**. There are several known types of point mutations. One type, called a **base substitution mutation**, results when one nucleotide is swapped for another during DNA replication. A base substitution exchanging one purine for the other purine (A ↔ G) or one pyrimidine for the other pyrimidine (C ↔ T) is called a *transition mutation*. A base-pair substitution exchanging a purine for a pyrimidine or a pyrimidine for a purine is called a *transversion mutation*. Other types of point mutations include **addition mutations** (inserting a new nucleotide into the sequence) and **deletion mutations** (deleting a nucleotide from the sequence). Additions and deletions can have profound effects on the function of the affected gene.

Functional Changes to Genes

If a mutation has no effect on an organism's fitness, that mutation is said to be neutral. A neutral mutation could change the amino acid sequence of a protein without changing its function or could result in no change to an amino acid sequence (e.g. changing the codon AAA to AAG through a base substitution would still result in the amino acid lysine.) The type of neutral mutation in which the amino acid sequence is unchanged is called a **silent mutation**.

Some nucleotide mutations can cause significant changes to the function of a gene. A **missense mutation** occurs when a base substitution changes a codon (creating a **missense codon**) which results in the translation of a different amino acid. Missense mutations can be neutral and result in completely functional proteins. Missense mutations can also significantly change a polypeptide's function. Sickle cell anemia, for example, is a disease caused by a single amino acid difference in hemoglobin.

Mutations are rare. Mutations in somatic cells are not passed to offspring; mutations in germ cells are.

The Cell
BIOLOGY 2

FIGURE 2.18 Base-pair Substitutions

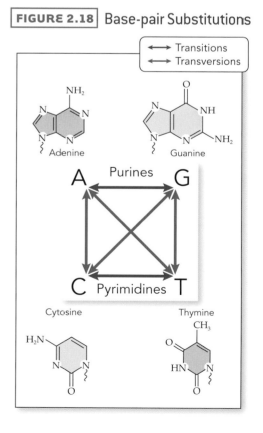

Note that these categories of mutations are overlapping. There are multiple possible categories for any one change. A base substitution could be silent, but could also be neutral and not silent. A base substitution can be a missense mutation if it changes a codon to code for a different amino acid, and this missense mutation may or may not be neutral. A base substitution can also cause a nonsense mutation if it creates a stop codon. As you review the definitions of mutation categories, spend some time thinking through how a mutation may fit into more than one category at a time.

A nonsense mutation occurs when a change to the nucleotide sequence creates a stop codon where none previously existed. For example, a nonsense mutation could be caused by a base substitution changing the codon UCA, which codes for the amino acid serine, into the stop codon UAA. Nonsense mutations tend to have serious consequences for the cell because they terminate translation and usually create a truncated, non-functional protein.

The addition and deletion of nucleotides can result in a frameshift mutation. A frameshift mutation occurs when the deletions or additions occur in multiples other than three. Because the genetic code is read in groups of three nucleotides, an addition or deletion of one or two nucleotides will change the *reading frame* of the code. An altered reading frame means that the entire sequence after the mutation will be shifted so that the three base sequences are grouped incorrectly. If a single T nucleotide were inserted into the series: AAA|GGG|CCC|AAA, so that it reads AAT|AGG|GCC|CAA|A, each 3-nucleotide sequence downstream from the mutation would be altered so each amino acid coded for could change. On the other hand, if three T nucleotides were inserted randomly, the downstream sequence would not be shifted, and only one or a few 3-nucleotide sequences would be changed: AAT|TAG|GTG|CCC|AAA. This is a non-frameshift mutation. Non-frameshift mutations may still result in a partially or even completely active protein, while frameshift mutations most often result in completely non-functional proteins. Frameshifts may also result in nonsense mutations if the new reading frame includes a premature stop codon.

FIGURE 2.19 Mutations at the Level of the Gene

Changes in DNA caused by mutations are included in the RNA sequence through the process of transcription. These changes can have a variety of effects on the translated amino acid sequence and resulting protein function.

- DNA exon
- RNA template
- Amino acid sequence

No mutation
This example illustrates the normal process of transcription and translation when no mutation has occurred. The amino acid sequence produced is intact and functional.

Base substitution - silent
A base-pair substitution has occurred, changing A to G on the DNA exon, thus changing U to C on the mRNA. Because the codons UGU and UGC both code for cysteine, the amino acid sequence remains unchanged and the protein is fully functional. This is an example of a silent mutation.

Addition/deletion - continuing protein
The addition (or deletion) of a nucleotide causes a frameshift. From that point forward, codons are translated on a different reading frame, resulting in different amino acids. If an early stop codon is not introduced, a whole protein is translated. This type of mutation usually results in non-functional proteins.

Base substitution - missense
A base-pair substitution has occurred, changing A to C on the DNA exon, thus changing U to G on the mRNA. A codon that used to code for cysteine (UGU) now codes for tryptophan (UGG). This an example of missense mutation. Missense mutations may alter protein functionality, depending on the location and properties of the substituted amino acid.

Deletion/addition - truncated protein (nonsense)
The deletion (or addition) of a nucleotide causes a frameshift. From that point forward, codons are translated on a different reading frame, resulting in different amino acids. If an early stop codon is introduced, the protein is truncated. This type of mutation usually results in non-functional proteins.

Base substitution - nonsense
A base-pair substitution has occurred, changing A to T on the DNA exon, thus changing U to A on the mRNA. A codon that used to code for cysteine (UGU) is now a stop codon (UGA). This is an example of a nonsense mutation. Transcription of the polypeptide chain ends prematurely, and the resulting protein is usually non-functional.

Mutations at the Level of the Chromosome

Changes at the chromosomal level often have serious consequences for the organism. Structural changes may occur to a chromosome in the form of deletions, duplications, translocations, and inversions. Chromosomal **deletions** occur when a portion of the chromosome breaks off, or when a portion of the chromosome is lost during homologous recombination and/or crossing over events. These topics will be discussed in greater detail later in this lecture. **Duplications** occur when a DNA fragment breaks free of one chromosome and incorporates into a homologous chromosome. **Gene duplication** (also called **gene amplification**) can increase the amount of a gene's product. Deletion or duplication can occur with entire chromosomes (*aneuploidy*) or even entire sets of chromosomes (*polyploidy*).

When a segment of DNA from one chromosome is exchanged for a segment of DNA on another chromosome, the resulting mutation is called a reciprocal **translocation**. In inversion, the orientation of a section of DNA is reversed on a chromosome. Translocation and inversion can be caused by transposition. Transposition takes place in both prokaryotic and eukaryotic cells. The DNA segments called **transposable elements** or **transposons** can excise themselves from a chromosome and reinsert themselves at another location. Transposons can contain one gene, several genes, or just a control element. A transposon within a chromosome will be flanked by identical nucleotide sequences. A portion of the flanking sequence is part of the transposon. When moving, the transposon may excise itself from the chromosome and move, copy itself and move, or copy itself and stay, moving the copy. Transposition is one mechanism by which a somatic cell of a multicellular organism can alter its genetic makeup without meiosis.

FIGURE 2.20 Transposons

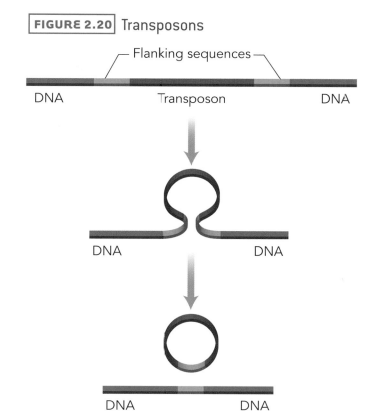

FIGURE 2.21 Mutations at the Level of the Chromosome

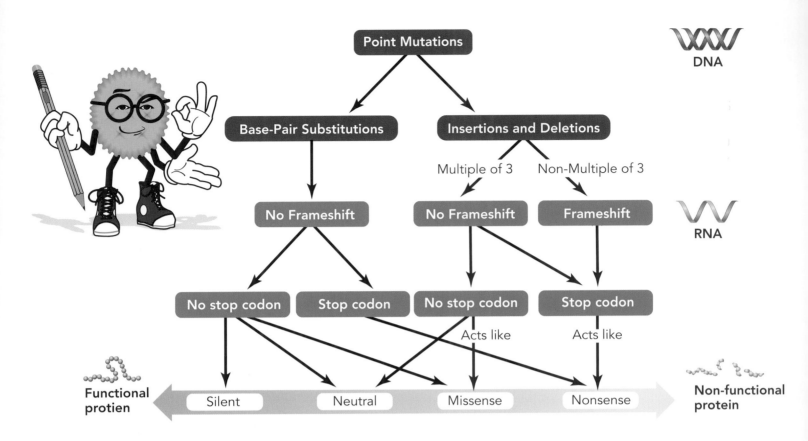

Point Mutations

Base-Pair Substitutions → No Frameshift

Insertions and Deletions
- Multiple of 3 → No Frameshift
- Non-Multiple of 3 → Frameshift

No Frameshift → No stop codon / Stop codon

No Frameshift → No stop codon (Acts like)

Frameshift → Stop codon (Acts like)

Functional protien ← Silent | Neutral | Missense | Nonsense → Non-functional protein

DNA

RNA

A single breast cancer cell has an uneven surface with blebs (blue) and cytoplasmic projections (red, at left). Clumps of cancerous (malignant) cells form tumors, which possess the ability to invade and destroy surrounding tissues and travel to distant parts of the body to seed secondary tumors. Malignant cells proliferate and grow in a chaotic manner, with defective cell division retained within each new generation of cells. Variations from the original cell type also occur in the size and structure of the cancer cell.

DNA Repair

DNA damage is caused by a number of factors, including oxidation by free radicals, errors in DNA replication, and exposure to environmental carcinogens such as cigarette smoke or ultraviolet light. The cell has several systems in place to repair mutated or damaged DNA in order to ensure that genes remain accurately coded in the genome. The role of DNA polymerase in correcting mismatched pairs of nucleotides in DNA replication has already been discussed. Damaged portions of DNA may also be altered through direct repair, in which damaged nucleotides are chemically changed back to their original structures. Ultraviolet light, for instance, covalently links two neighboring thymine bases together, causing a kink in the DNA strand. Special enzymes cleave these cross-links, restoring DNA to its helical structure. Oxidized bases can be corrected through excision repair, in which damaged nucleotides are removed and replaced. Despite the cell's repair mechanisms, damage to DNA can take place and can have serious consequences for cellular function and organismal health.

Cancer

As discussed in the Cell Lecture in *Biology 2: Systems*, cancer is the unrestrained and uncontrolled growth of cells that results when the regulation of the cell cycle has gone awry. However, cancer also has a genetic component that is related to mutation. Certain genes that stimulate normal growth in human cells are called *proto-oncogenes*. Proto-oncogenes can be converted to **oncogenes**, genes that cause cancer, by mutagens such as UV radiation or chemicals, or simply by random mutations. Mutagens that can cause cancer are called **carcinogens**. The genome also contains **tumor suppressor genes** that help regulate normal cell growth. Some examples of tumor suppressor genes are the retinoblastoma (Rb) and p53 proteins, which act at checkpoints during the cell cycle. When the normal functions of tumor suppressor genes are inactivated by mutation, cells growth may proceed uncontrolled.

2.9 | The Genome and Inheritance: Meiosis

Even before the discovery of the existence of a genome and its role in directing the daily production of cellular products, scientists were aware of the concept of heritability. Certain traits seem to run in families, and children tend to look like their parents. Early experiments using bacterial genomes confirmed that DNA is the genetic material responsible for heritability rather than proteins or other cellular components that were contenders at the time. This section and the one that follows will explore the fundamental role of DNA in passing on traits from one generation to the next, first by examining meiosis, the process by which genetic material is apportioned to the next generation, and then through a review of the principles of inheritance and Mendelian genetics.

The Purpose and Products of Meiosis

Meiosis can be thought of as a special case of mitosis that takes place solely in the reproductive organs. Sexual reproduction takes place when genetic information from two individuals merge to produce offspring. For sexual reproduction to occur, reduction division of the genetic information is needed in order to create haploid reproductive cells, or **gametes**, from diploid parent cells. In humans, only the spermatogonium and the oogonium undergo meiosis. All other cells are somatic cells and undergo mitosis only. Meiosis is an important part of sexual reproduction and occurs only in eukaryotes. This section details the process of meiosis in animals, which is how it is most likely to be seen on the MCAT®.

While meiosis, like mitosis, is a form of cell division, the goals and end products of meiosis are different. The purpose of mitosis is to make exact copies of somatic cells in the body, whereas the purpose of meiosis is to create gametes that are suitable to be paired sexually with another gamete to contribute genetic information to the next generation. During mitosis, a cell undergoes one round of nuclear division to produce two diploid daughter cells, each bearing identical genetic information. In contrast, during meiosis, germ cells undergo two rounds of nuclear division to produce four haploid daughter cells, the gametes, each with a unique genetic makeup. The primary difference in the mechanisms of mitosis and meiosis can be found in metaphase of meiosis I in how the chromosomes align. The regulation of meiosis takes place in much the same way as that of mitosis.

The Mechanism of Meiosis

Cells that will undergo meiosis first go through replication of their chromosomes in the S phase of interphase so that at the beginning of meiosis, the chromosomes are duplicated and diploid. Meiosis consists of two rounds of division called meiosis I and meiosis II. Each round of meiosis consists of successive stages of prophase, metaphase, anaphase, and telophase.

The purpose of **meiosis I** is to separate homologous chromosomes to produce two haploid cells, each with one copy of the 23 chromosomes. All cells other than germ cells are diploid, which means they have two copies of each chromosome for a total of 46 chromosomes. Meiosis I is therefore known as a reduction division. Meiosis I proceeds similarly to mitosis, with differences described below. **Prophase I** is perhaps the most important stage of meiosis to understand. In prophase I, homologous chromosomes line up alongside each other, matching their genes exactly. At this time, they may exchange sequences of DNA nucleotides in a process called **crossing over**. The **genetic recombination** that occurs in eukaryotes during crossing over is of critical importance for providing variation in the genetic makeup of the gametes, and consequently, the offspring. Each of the duplicated chromosome in prophase I appears as an 'X' containing two sister chromatids. The side by side homologues exhibit a total of four chromatids, and are called

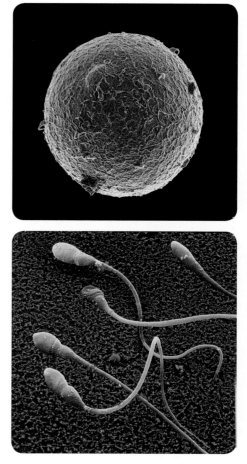

Electron micrographs of sperm and an egg. These two haploid cell types, formed by meiosis, join with each other to form a diploid zygote.

Consider Key 3: If you see mitosis, think of cellular replication, often to replace damaged or dying cells in the body. If you see meiosis, think of reproduction and the processes involved in passing genes to future generations.

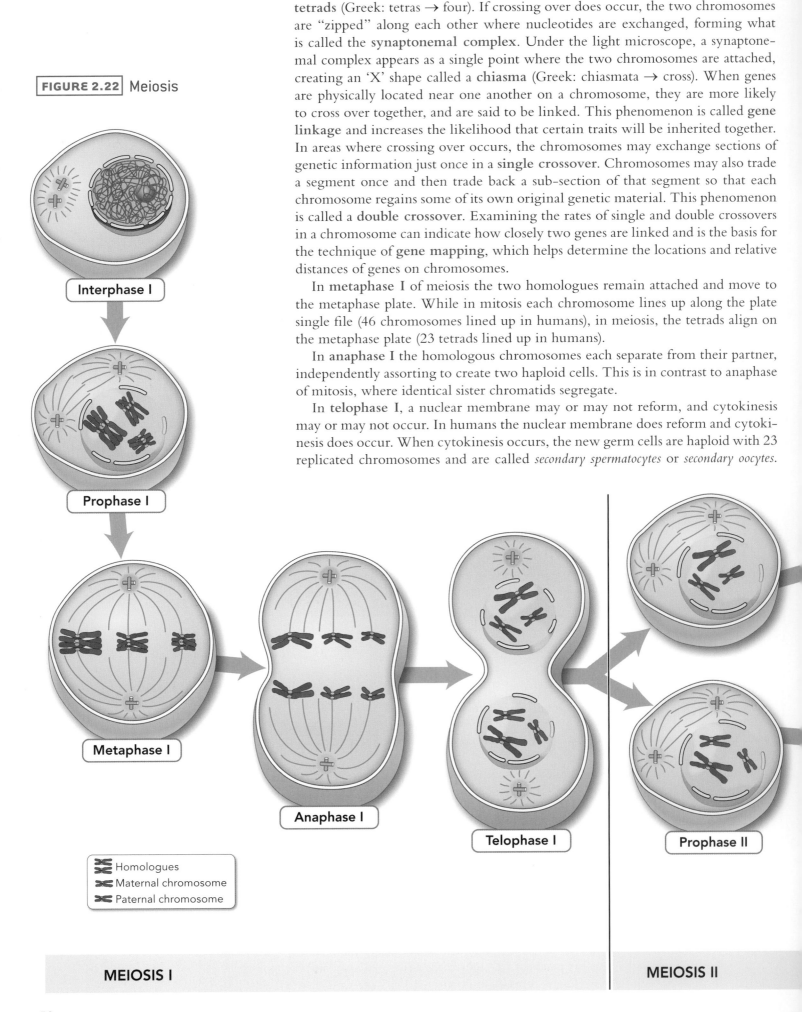

tetrads (Greek: tetras → four). If crossing over does occur, the two chromosomes are "zipped" along each other where nucleotides are exchanged, forming what is called the **synaptonemal complex**. Under the light microscope, a synaptonemal complex appears as a single point where the two chromosomes are attached, creating an 'X' shape called a **chiasma** (Greek: chiasmata → cross). When genes are physically located near one another on a chromosome, they are more likely to cross over together, and are said to be linked. This phenomenon is called **gene linkage** and increases the likelihood that certain traits will be inherited together. In areas where crossing over occurs, the chromosomes may exchange sections of genetic information just once in a **single crossover**. Chromosomes may also trade a segment once and then trade back a sub-section of that segment so that each chromosome regains some of its own original genetic material. This phenomenon is called a **double crossover**. Examining the rates of single and double crossovers in a chromosome can indicate how closely two genes are linked and is the basis for the technique of **gene mapping**, which helps determine the locations and relative distances of genes on chromosomes.

In **metaphase I** of meiosis the two homologues remain attached and move to the metaphase plate. While in mitosis each chromosome lines up along the plate single file (46 chromosomes lined up in humans), in meiosis, the tetrads align on the metaphase plate (23 tetrads lined up in humans).

In **anaphase I** the homologous chromosomes each separate from their partner, independently assorting to create two haploid cells. This is in contrast to anaphase of mitosis, where identical sister chromatids segregate.

In **telophase I**, a nuclear membrane may or may not reform, and cytokinesis may or may not occur. In humans the nuclear membrane does reform and cytokinesis does occur. When cytokinesis occurs, the new germ cells are haploid with 23 replicated chromosomes and are called *secondary spermatocytes* or *secondary oocytes*.

In the case of the female, one of the oocytes, called the first **polar body**, is much smaller and degenerates. This occurs in order to conserve cytoplasm, which is only contributed to the zygote by the ovum.

Meiosis II proceeds through **prophase II**, **metaphase II**, **anaphase II**, and **telophase II**, appearing much like mitosis under the light microscope. The final products are haploid gametes, each with 23 chromosomes. In the case of the spermatocyte, four sperm cells are formed. In the case of the oocyte, a single ovum is formed after the degeneration of the polar bodies. (In the female, telophase II produces one gamete and a second polar body.)

If during anaphase I or II the centromere of any chromosome does not split, this is called **nondisjunction**. As a result of primary nondisjunction (nondisjunction in anaphase I), one of the cells will have two extra chromatids (a complete extra chromosome) and the other will be missing a chromosome. The extra chromosome will typically line up along the metaphase plate and behave normally in meiosis II. Nondisjunction in anaphase II will result in one cell having one extra chromatid and one cell lacking one chromatid. Nondisjunction can also occur in mitosis, but the ramifications are less severe because the genetic information in the new cells is not passed on to every cell in the body. One possible outcome of

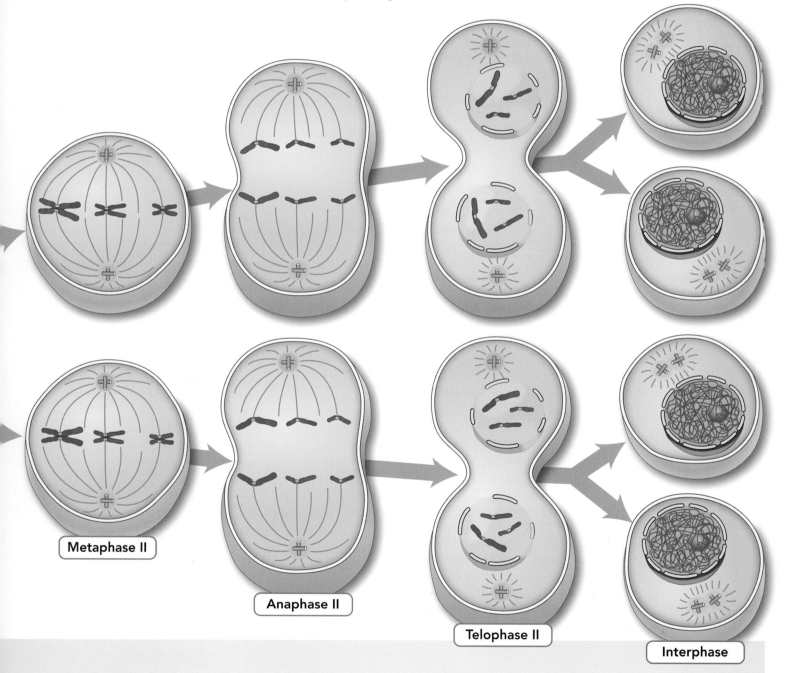

Metaphase II

Anaphase II

Telophase II

Interphase

A spermatogonium or oogonium undergoes DNA replication during the S phase of the cell cycle to become a primary spermatocyte or a primary oocyte. Primary spermatocytes and primary oocytes are still diploid, but contain replicated chromosomes with sister chromatids. The figure indicates the presence of sister chromatids with the subscript "s" for diploid primary spermatocytes and oocytes ($2n_s$) and for haploid secondary spermatocytes and oocytes (n_s), which have undergone a reduction division.

nondisjunction is having three copies of a single chromosome (a condition known as trisomy), which can have significant effects. Down syndrome, for instance, is caused by nondisjunction of chromosome 21.

Meiosis as Gamete Production

The purpose of meiosis is to make haploid gametes that can be used in sexual reproduction. The production of gametes, or **gametogenesis**, occurs in several stages. Gametogenesis occurs via similar paths in males and females, with some key differences. The process in males is more straightforward. Once a male reaches sexual maturity, gametogenesis is ongoing, replenishing the body's supply of gametes as needed. In males, the diploid progenitor cells responsible for giving rise to gametes through the process of meiosis are called spermatogonia. A **spermato-**

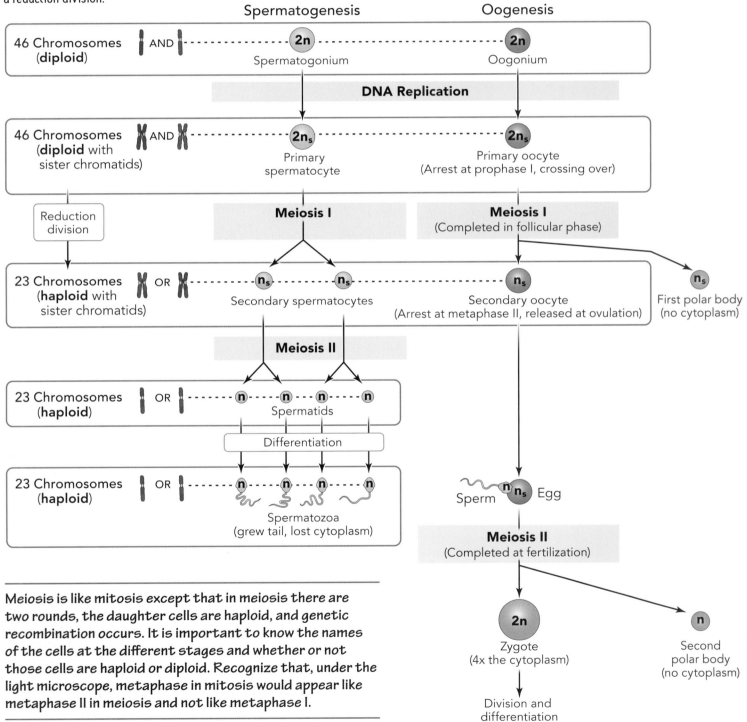

Meiosis is like mitosis except that in meiosis there are two rounds, the daughter cells are haploid, and genetic recombination occurs. It is important to know the names of the cells at the different stages and whether or not those cells are haploid or diploid. Recognize that, under the light microscope, metaphase in mitosis would appear like metaphase II in meiosis and not like metaphase I.

TABLE 2.3 > Stages of Development in Male and Female Gametes

Stages in Males	Stages in Females	Chromosomes	Stage is Reached
Spermatogonium	Oogonium	Diploid	Progenitor cell present at birth
Primary spermatocyte	Primary oocyte	Diploid	After mitosis
Secondary spermatocyte	Secondary oocyte	Haploid	After meiosis I
Spermatid	Ootid*	Haploid	After meiosis II
Sperm (or spermatozoa)	Ovum*	Haploid	After maturation process

Technically joined with a sperm by this stage to form a zygote, which is diploid

gonium undergoes mitosis to produce two diploid copies known as *primary spermatocytes*. Each primary spermatocyte undergoes the reduction division of meiosis I to become two haploid secondary spermatocytes. After the division of meiosis II, each secondary spermatocyte becomes two *spermatids*. A spermatid undergoes a process of maturation in which it loses its cytoplasm and gains a tail to become a mature male gamete known as **sperm**.

There are many parallels between the process of gamete production in males and females. In females, the diploid progenitor cell for gametogenesis is known as the **oogonium**. The oogonium undergoes mitosis to produce two *primary oocytes*. Unlike in males, this step in females primarily takes place before a female is born and the process does not proceed further until the female has reached puberty. Primary oocytes remain arrested in prophase I of meiosis until they receive the hormone signal to participate in the menstrual cycle (see the Endocrine System Lecture in *Biology 2: Systems* for more information on menstruation and ovulation). In preparation for ovulation, a primary oocyte completes meiosis I, producing a secondary oocyte. At this step, again, males and females differ. While meiosis I in males produces two secondary spermatocytes from each primary spermatocyte, the contents of a primary oocyte are not divided evenly among its daughter cells. One daughter cell receives all of the cytoplasm and becomes a secondary oocyte. The other daughter cell, which receives no cytoplasm, is the first polar body and is discarded. The resulting secondary oocyte, now haploid, begins the process of meiosis II but is arrested at the stage of metaphase II. In this arrested state, the secondary oocyte is released from the ovary and travels down the Fallopian tube. The secondary oocyte completes meiosis II only when penetrated by a sperm during the act of fertilization. The penetration of the sperm immediately initiates the completion of meiosis II, dividing the secondary oocyte into a second polar body, which is also discarded, and an ootid, which matures into an **ovum**. The joining of the genetic material of the sperm and the ovum produces a **zygote**.

Note that the process of gametogenesis in males produces four functional gametes (sperm) from each primary spermatocyte. In contrast, each primary oocyte in females results in only one functional ovum (the rest are polar bodies). The reason behind this has to do with conserving cytoplasm. Once an ovum is fertilized, the resulting zygote will need to undergo many rounds of division before it is able to implant on the uterine wall and establish a blood supply. The increased amount of cytoplasm present in an ovum provides the nutrients necessary to sustain a zygote as it becomes a blastula and travels from the Fallopian tube to the uterus. See the Endocrine System Lecture for more on development.

TABLE 2.4 > Summary of Chromosomes and Sister Chromatids

Process	Start	Finish
Replication	Diploid (46 chromosomes)	Diploid with sisters (46 chromosomes, 92 chromatids)
Mitosis	Diploid with sisters (46 chromosomes, 92 chromatids)	Diploid (46 chromosomes)
Meiosis I	Diploid with sisters (46 chromosomes, 92 chromatids)	Haploid with sisters (23 chromosomes, 46 chromatids)
Meiosis II	Haploid with sisters (23 chromosomes, 46 chromatids)	Haploid (23 chromosomes)

If you're having trouble keeping track of chromosome number in replication, mitosis, and meiosis, use this table to review what happens with the number of chromosomes and sister chromatids in each of these processes.

Note that meiosis only describes the process by which nuclear genetic information is passed from one generation to the next. For the MCAT®, know that genetic information can also be passed from organism to organism in other ways. Extranuclear inheritance, which is also called cytoplasmic inheritance (e.g. in the mitochondria and chloroplasts), takes place via its own mechanisms. Genetic leakage, the flow of genetic information from one species to another, can also take place under certain conditions.

2.10 | The Genome and Inheritance: Mendelian and Population Genetics

Many ideas about the role of genetics in heritability were shaped by the early work of Gregor Mendel. Gregor Mendel was a 19th century monk who performed hybridization experiments using pea plants. The difference between Mendel and those who had come before him was that Mendel quantified his results, carefully counting and recording his findings. Mendel examined a variety of traits that naturally occur in pea plants and examined the heritability of these traits through controlled breeding of the plants. He found that when he crossed purple flowered plants with white flowered plants, the **first filial**, or **F₁ generation**, included only purple flowers. He called the purple trait **dominant**, and the white trait **recessive**. Mendel examined seven traits in all, and each trait proved to have dominant and recessive alternatives. When Mendel self-pollinated the F₁ generation plants, the F₂ generation contained some plants that expressed the dominant trait and some that expressed the recessive trait in a ratio of **3:1** (which is now referred to as the **Mendelian ratio**) (Figure 2.24). When the F₂ generation was self-pollinated, 33% of the dominants produced only dominants, and the rest of the dominants pro-

FIGURE 2.24 Mendelian Ratio: 3 to 1

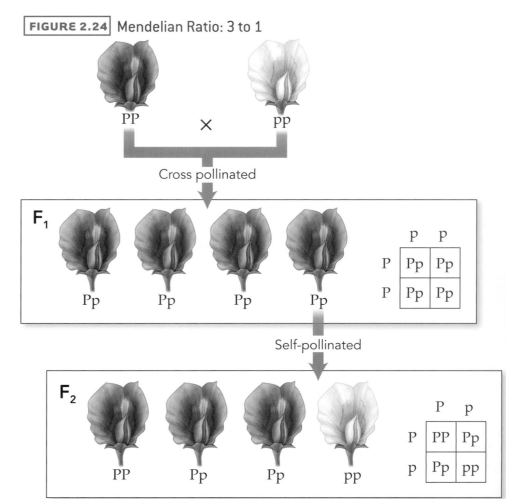

To test his model, Mendel performed a test cross, which is a cross between an unknown genotype and a known, recessive genotype. In his test cross, Mendel crossed the F₁ generation of his flowers (purple) with a homozygous recessive parent plant (white). Because there were white offspring resulting from this cross of a purple F₁ plant and a white parent plant, Mendel was able to prove that the F₁ generation was heterozygous.

duced the Mendelian ratio. The white flowered plants produced only white flowered plants. Mendel used this data to conclude that, even if plants expressed the dominant trait (purple), they might still retain latent information on the recessive trait (white) because they were able to produce white flowered plants in successive generations.

The key to understanding Mendel's experiments is to examine the alleles involved. For any one trait, a diploid individual will have two chromosomes containing separate genes that each code for that trait. These two chromosomes are homologous by definition. Their corresponding genes are located at the same locus, or position, on their respective chromosomes. Each gene contributes one allele, which codes for a specific outcome in that trait. There may be single or multiple allele types possible at each locus. One chromosome may carry the allele coding for purple flowers (represented by P), while the other chromosome may carry the allele for white flowers (represented by p). The "normal" or most common allele type for a certain trait within a population is deemed the wild type allele. With regard to alleles for a certain trait, an individual's genetic makeup is called a genotype while the expression of the trait (i.e. the way the organism actually looks) is called the phenotype. In the example given above, the possible genotypes are PP, Pp, and pp, while the possible phenotypes are purple and white. The genotype ratio is 1:2:1, while the phenotype ratio is 3:1. The phenotype is expressed through the action of enzymes and other structural proteins, which are encoded by genes. In complete dominance, as is the case with Mendel's purple and white flowers, the dominant allele masks expression of the recessive allele. This concept is demonstrated by the outcome that flowers with the genotype Pp appear purple. An individual with a genotype having two dominant (PP) or two recessive (pp) alleles is said to be homozygous for that trait. An individual with a genotype having one dominant and one recessive allele (Pp) is said to be heterozygous for the trait, and is called a hybrid.

Mendel's First Law of Heredity, the Law of Segregation, states that alleles segregate independently of each other when forming gametes during meiosis. Any gamete is equally likely to possess any allele. Also, the phenotypic expression of the alleles is not a blend of the two, but an expression of the dominant allele (the principle of complete dominance).

Penetrance is the term used to refer to the probability of a gene or allele being expressed if it is present. In complete dominance, the penetrance of the dominant allele is 100%. A similar concept is that of expressivity, which is a measure of how much the genotype is expressed as a phenotype. Unlike penetrance, which is based on a binary condition (expressed vs. not expressed), expressivity describes the degree of expression of a certain trait. When a heterozygous individual exhibits a phenotype that is intermediate between its homozygous counterparts, the alleles are said to demonstrate incomplete dominance. An example of incomplete dominance is a pink rose, in which the flower color of a heterozygote is some shade between red and white. By convention, alleles showing incomplete dominance are represented with the same capital letter, and distinguished with a prime or superscript. For instance, a cross between red flowered sweet peas and white flowered sweet peas may produce pink flowers. The genotype for the pink flowered individual would be expressed as either CC' or C^rC^w. If the heterozygote exhibits both phenotypes, the alleles are co-dominant. Human blood type alleles are co-dominant because a heterozygote exhibits A and B antigens on the blood cell membranes.

The Cell
≡ BIOLOGY 2

Immune System
≡ BIOLOGY 2

To better understand penetrance and expressivity, imagine a population of 100 people, all with a gene coding for brown hair. If 90 people have brown hair, the penetrance is 90%. Within those 90 people, the shade of brown hair can differ, with some people having dark brown hair and some with light brown hair. This is expressivity.

FIGURE 2.25 Dihybrid Cross

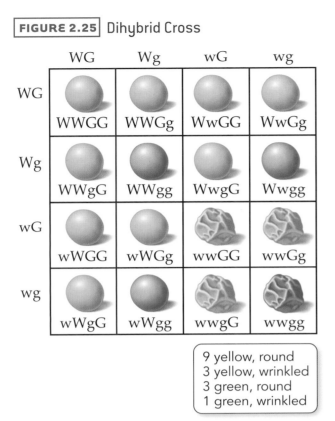

	WG	Wg	wG	wg
WG	WWGG	WWGg	WwGG	WwGg
Wg	WWgG	WWgg	WwgG	Wwgg
wG	wWGG	wWGg	wwGG	wwGg
wg	wWgG	wWgg	wwgG	wwgg

9 yellow, round
3 yellow, wrinkled
3 green, round
1 green, wrinkled

FIGURE 2.26 Sex-linked Traits

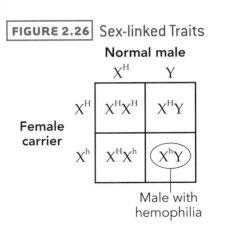

Normal male

Female carrier

Male with hemophilia

Figure 2.25 shows a helpful tool called a **Punnett square**, used for predicting genotypic ratios of offspring from parent genotypes. The genotypes of all possible gametes of one parent are displayed to the left of the column, and all possible gametes of the second parent are displayed above the first row. The alleles are then combined in the corresponding boxes to show the possible genotypes of the offspring. According to the law of segregation, each gametic genotype is equally likely. Therefore, each offspring genotype is also equally likely.

Mendel's Second Law of Heredity, the **Law of Independent Assortment**, states that genes located on separate chromosomes assort independently of each other. In other words, genes that code for distinct traits (such as pea shape and pea color), when located on separate chromosomes, do not affect each other during gamete formation. (Notice that the Law of Independent Assortment discusses genes that code for distinct traits, in contrast to the Law of Segregation, which instead discusses multiple alleles of a single gene.) If two genes are located on the same chromosome, the likelihood that they will remain together during gamete formation is indirectly proportional to the distance separating them. The closer they are on the chromosome, the more likely it is that they will not be separated by genetic recombination and instead will remain together. In Figure 2.25, we use a Punnett square to predict the phenotypic ratio of a **dihybrid cross**. 'W' is the allele for a round pea shape, which is dominant, and 'w' is the allele for wrinkled pea shape, which is recessive. 'G' is the allele for yellow color, which is dominant, and 'g' is the allele for green color, which is recessive. We make the assumption that the genes for pea shape and pea color are on separate chromosomes, and will assort independently of each other. Notice that the **phenotypic ratio of a dihybrid cross is 9:3:3:1**.

The expression of some traits is dependent on the sex of the individual. This is because the chromosomes of males and females differ. In humans, the 23rd pair of chromosomes establishes the sex of the individual, and each partner in the pair is called a **sex chromosome**. Sex chromosomes are designated as either X or Y. Human females usually carry two X chromosomes, while males usually have one X and one Y chromosome. In comparison to the X chromosome, the Y chromosome is greatly abbreviated and contains only a few genes. Genes located on the sex chromosomes are said to be **sex-linked**. The Y chromosome generally does not carry the allele for the sex-linked trait; the allele that is carried by the X chromosome in the male is expressed whether it is dominant or recessive. Because the female has two X chromosomes, her genotype is found through the normal rules of dominance. In most somatic cells, however, one of the X chromosomes will condense, and most of its genes will become inactive. The tiny dark object formed is called a **Barr body**. Barr bodies are formed at random, so the active allele is split approximately evenly among the cells. In most cases, the recessive phenotype is still only displayed in homozygous recessive individuals. The female may carry a recessive trait on her 23rd pair of chromosomes without expressing it. If she does, she is said to be a **carrier** for the trait. Such a recessive trait has a strong chance of being expressed in her male offspring regardless of the genotype of her mate.

Hemophilia is one example of a sex-linked disease. The Punnett square shown in Figure 2.26 shows a cross between a female carrier for hemophilia and a healthy male. Since there are two possible phenotypes for the males, and one is the recessive phenotype, the male offspring from such a pairing have a 1 in 2 chance of having the disease.

In reality, most traits are not inherited in the "one gene, one trait" manner of Mendelian genetics. Most phenotypes are the result of a significant number of genes, whose protein products combine to create a trait. Height, for instance, is determined by over 50 unique genes. Remember that environment can also play a role in determining how and when genes and traits are expressed.

The Hardy-Weinberg Principle

The Hardy-Weinberg Principle is a tool used to predict the probability of off-spring genotypes in an entire population. For example, it may predict the probability that an individual is a carrier for or will be affected by a certain disease when individual genotypes are unknown.

As discussed in the Cell Lecture in *Biology 2: Systems*, the **gene pool** is the total collection of all alleles in a population, and any change in the gene pool constitutes evolution. Hardy-Weinberg provides a snapshot of a population under the assumption that there is no net change happening in allelic frequencies over time. That theoretical state of suspended evolution is called **Hardy-Weinberg equilibrium**. Recall the conditions that a population must meet to be considered in Hardy-Weinberg equilibrium. They can be thought of as the inverse of the conditions under which evolution will occur.

> The Cell
> ☰ BIOLOGY 2

1. No selection for the fittest organism,

2. Random mating,

3. Large population,

4. Immigration or emigration must not change the gene pool, and

5. Mutational equilibrium.

No real population ever ceases to evolve, so no real population possesses these characteristics completely. However, if a population approximates Hardy-Weinberg equilibrium, the following equation can be employed to predict the frequencies of genotypes and phenotypes from allelic frequencies within a population:

$$p^2 + 2pq + q^2 = 1$$

This equation predicts the genotype frequencies of a gene with only two alleles in a population in Hardy-Weinberg equilibrium. If p represents the frequency of dominant alleles and q represents the frequency of recessive alleles in the population, the first term in the equation (p^2) indicates the fraction of homozygous dominant genotypes in a population (like AA), the second term ($2pq$) indicates the fraction of heterozygotes (Aa), and the third term (q^2) indicates the fraction of homozygous recessive genotypes in the entire population (aa). The difference between the results here and those of Mendel for AA, Aa, and aa, are as follows: rather than having a 1 in 2 chance of inheriting an allele (A or a) from one of the two parents, as in Mendel's calculation, here the probability corresponds to the proportion of that allele (A or a) in the entire population.

To work through an example of using this equation, assume that 'A' is the dominant allele and 'a' is the recessive allele, and that they are the only alleles for a specific gene. Now imagine that 80% of the alleles are 'A'. This means that 80% of the gametes will be 'A' and 20% will be 'a'. The probability that two 'A's come together is simply $0.8^2 = 0.64$. The probability that two 'a's come together is $0.2^2 = 0.04$. Any remaining zygotes will be heterozygous, leaving 32% heterozygotes, ($2 \times 0.8 \times 0.2 = 0.32$). The fraction of heterozygotes can also be calculated by adding the probabilities of the two gametic combinations that result in heterozygotes – Aa and aA. Using the formula, we represent the frequency of 'A' as p and the frequency of 'a' as q. Because there are only two alleles, **p + q = 1**.

Answer from page 44:

20 possible amino acids and 100 positions gives 20^{100} possible sequences.

These questions are NOT related to a passage.

Question 41

Suppose in a 10,000-person population, the incidence of β-thalassemia, an autosomal recessive blood disorder, is 81 persons. Assuming Hardy-Weinberg equilibrium, what is the population incidence of carriers for the β-thalassemia gene?

- **A.** 50 in 10000
- **B.** 100 in 10000
- **C.** 1000 in 10000
- **D.** 1500 in 10000

Question 42

Translation, transcription, and replication take place in which of the following life cycle phases?

- **A.** G_1
- **B.** S
- **C.** G_2
- **D.** M

Question 43

A scientist monitors the nucleotide sequence of the third chromosome as a cell undergoes normal meiosis. What is the earliest point in meiosis at which the scientist can deduce with certainty the nucleotide sequence of the third chromosome of each gamete?

- **A.** Prophase I
- **B.** Metaphase I
- **C.** Prophase II
- **D.** Telophase II

Question 44

Radiation therapy is used to treat some forms of cancer by damaging DNA, thus killing the rapidly reproducing cancerous cells. Why might radiation treatment have a greater effect on cancer cells than on normal cells?

- **A.** Normal cells have more time between S phases to repair damaged DNA.
- **B.** Damaged DNA is more reactive to radiation.
- **C.** Cancer cells have lost the ability to repair damaged DNA.
- **D.** The effect of radiation is the same, but there are more cancer cells than normal cells.

Question 45

When a human female is born, the development of her oocytes is arrested in:

- **A.** prophase of mitosis.
- **B.** prophase I of meiosis.
- **C.** prophase II of meiosis.
- **D.** interphase.

Question 46

In the pedigree below, the darkened figures indicate an individual with hemophilia, a sex linked recessive disease. The genotype of the female marked A is:

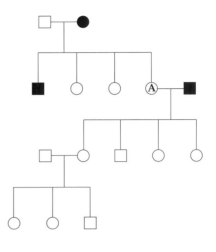

- **A.** $X^H X^h$.
- **B.** $X^H X^H$.
- **C.** $X^h X^h$.
- **D.** $X^h Y$.

Question 47

Sickle cell anemia is an autosomal recessive disease. A male with the disease and a female that is not diseased, but carries the trait, produce two girls. What is the probability that neither girl carries a recessive allele?

- **A.** 0%
- **B.** 25%
- **C.** 50%
- **D.** 66%

Question 48

If, in a very large population, a certain gene possesses only two alleles and 36% of the population is homozygous dominant, what percentage of the population are heterozygotes?

- **A.** 16%
- **B.** 24%
- **C.** 36%
- **D.** 48%

STOP

Hardy-Weinberg equilibrium

$$p + q = 1$$

$$p^2 + 2pq + q^2 = 1$$

TERMS YOU NEED TO KNOW

5' cap
A site
Activators
Addition mutation
Advantageous mutation
Allele
Alternative splicing
Anaphase
Anaphase I
Anaphase II
Anticodon
Aster
Barr body
Base substitution mutation
Bidirectional replication
Carcinogens
Carrier
Centrioles
Centromeres
Centrosomes
Chiasma
Chromatids
Chromatin
Chromosomal mutation
Chromosomes
Co-dominant
Codon
Complete dominance
Crossing over
Cytokinesis
Degenerative
Deleterious mutation
Deletion mutation
Deletions
Dihybrid cross
Dihybrid cross phenotypic ratio: 9:3:3:1

Diploid
DNA binding proteins
DNA helicase
DNA ligase
DNA methylation
DNA polymerase
Double crossover
DNA replication
Dominant
Duplications
E site
Elongation (in replication and translation)
Euchromatin
Exons
Expressivity
F_1 Generation
First filial
Frameshift mutation
Gametes
Gametogenesis
Gene
Gene duplication (gene amplification)
Gene linkage
Gene mapping
Gene mutation
Gene pool
Genetic code
Genetic recombination
Gene repression
Genome
Genotype
Haploid
Hardy-Weinberg equilibrium
Heterochromatin
Heterozygous

Histones
Homologues
Homozygous
Hybrid
Incomplete dominance
Initiation (in replication and translation)
Initiation codon
Initiation complex
Initiation factors
Introns
Inversion
Jacob-Monod model
Kinetochore
Lac operon
Lagging strand
Large subunit
Law of Independent Assortment
Law of Segregation
Locus
Meiosis
Meiosis I
Meiosis II
Mendelian ratio: 3:1
Metaphase
Metaphase I
Metaphase II
Missense codon
Missense mutation
Mitosis
mRNA
Mutagens
Mutation
Non-coding RNA (ncRNA)
Nondisjunction
Nonsense mutation
Nucleolus

Nucleosome

Okazaki fragments

Oncogenes

Oogonium

Operon

Origin of replication

Ovum

P site

Penetrance

Phenotype

Point mutation

Polar body

Poly A tail

Polyploidy

Positive control

Post-translational modifications

Primary transcript

Primase

Promoter

Prophase

Prophase I

Prophase II

Punnett square

Random errors

Recessive

Release factors

Repetitive DNA

Repressors

Ribosome

Ribozyme

RNA polymerase

RNA primer

rRNA

Semiconservative

Semidiscontinuous

Sex chromosome

Sex-linked

Signal peptide

Signal-recognition particle (SRP)

Silent mutation

Single copy DNA

Single crossover

Single or multiple

Small subunit

snRNA

snRNPs

Sperm

Spermatogonium

Spindle apparatus

Spindle microtubules

Splicing

Spliceosome

Stop codon (termination codon, nonsense codon)

Synaptonemal complex

Supercoils

Telomeres

Telophase

Telophase I

Telophase II

Termination (in replication and translation)

Test cross

Tetrads

The Central Dogma

Traits

Transcription

Transcription factors

Translation

Translocation

Transposable elements (transposons)

Triplet code

tRNA

Tumor suppressor genes

Wild type

Wobble pairing

Zygote

DON'T FORGET YOUR KEYS

1. DNA is potential; RNA is regulation; protein is action.

2. Location matters – nucleus or cytoplasm?

3. See mitosis, think replication; see meiosis, think reproduction.

Metabolism

3.1 | Introduction

Organisms consume nutrients to satisfy their need for energy. Because food is not always readily available or constantly consumed, organisms must regulate the storage and use of energy so that they do not run out. When a cell uses a molecule for energy, it generally tries to turn it into acetyl-CoA or other Krebs cycle intermediates, which are then used to create ATP, the cell's primary energy molecule. When a cell stores a molecule, it polymerizes multiple monomers of the same kind, condensing their size and making them more convenient to store. Examples of this process include glycogenesis and fatty acid storage.

While some tissues can produce energy from a variety of molecules, others rely almost exclusively on glucose to function. Because of this demand, the blood glucose level regulates both intracellular and systemic pathways. This control comes from the hormones insulin and glucagon, which promote the storage and use of blood glucose, respectively. After a recent meal, insulin directs tissues to use and store glucose that was absorbed in the intestines. When the body is in a fasting state, glucagon directs the liver to release glucose it had previously stored for use by other organs. The liver does not have enough glucose to supply the entire body, so other sources of energy such as fatty acids help to spare glucose for the brain and red blood cells, which depend on glucose.

ATP and NADH: Energy Currency for Cells

The food humans consume contains energy from a number of sources, including carbohydrates, lipids, and proteins. To make this energy available to the cell, energy derived from these food sources is stored in compounds such as NADH and ATP. NADH stores energy in the high-energy electrons of a hydride ion, and ATP stores it in high-energy phosphate bonds. NADH is primarily produced during glycolysis and the citric acid cycle and is converted to ATP via the electron

> ### THE 3 KEYS
>
> 1. Metabolic pathways move toward either the storage or production of energy.
>
> 2. Blood glucose levels drive systemic and intracellular pathways.
>
> 3. NADH and ATP are the cell's energy molecules.

transport chain. The citric acid cycle and the electron transport chain make up a common final pathway of metabolism – the breakdown of many molecules leads here, where they are ultimately converted into ATP, carbon dioxide and water. ATP powers most reactions that require a driving force in the cells, including muscle contraction and the activity of the Na^+/K^+ pump.

The MCAT® emphasizes reciprocal regulation, positive and negative feedback, and hormonal control over metabolism. Make sure you understand the regulated steps of each pathway and how the major products of one pathway become the substrates of the next. The MCAT® also likes to ask questions about how the inhibition of enzyme function in one pathway could affect another pathway that acts on a common substrate. Here's one example: how would a mutation in pyruvate dehydrogenase change the activity of the pentose phosphate pathway? Such a mutation would prevent pyruvate from being converted into acetyl-CoA, which would back up glycolysis. Instead of glucose-6-phosphate feeding into glycolysis, it would be shunted into the PPP, which would lead to increase in flux through that pathway. Don't spend time memorizing all of the enzyme names in each pathway. Instead, focus on how the pathways are interconnected and regulated. If you are presented with an enzyme name in an MCAT® passage, use the name to help you identify the reaction type. For more information on types of enzyme reactions, see Section 1.10 in Chapter 1.

3.2 | Use Versus Storage

The first part of this lecture focuses on the directionality of metabolic pathways toward either the use or storage of a molecule. Metabolic pathways proceed in one direction to store extra energy molecules after a meal if they are not immediately needed. Through the reversal of the same pathways, the stored energy molecules can be released many hours after a meal, when the intestines are empty of food.

The most important energy molecules on the MCAT® are carbohydrates and lipids. Proteins can also provide energy for the body, but this is mostly outside the scope of the MCAT®. Carbohydrates are stored primarily in the muscle and liver as glycogen. This storage process is called glycogenesis. Carbohydrates can be taken out of storage and broken down for energy. Processes that use carbohydrates include the breakdown of glycogen, or glycogenolysis, and the breakdown of glucose, or glycolysis.

Lipids, in the form of fatty acids, undergo roughly the same processes. They are primarily stored in adipocytes, or fat cells, in the form of triglycerides. They are also taken out of storage and broken down for energy. The chemical breakdown of a fatty acid is called beta-oxidation.

Understand Key 1: Metabolic pathways either generate energy from sources like carbohydrates, amino acids, and fats, or they store energy for later use in molecules like glycogen and fatty acids.

FIGURE 3.1 | Use Versus Storage

Molecules have two metabolic fates: storage and use. Molecules can be brought out of storage and used to synthesize new molecules.

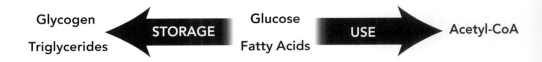

Glucose Metabolism

Use of Glucose

After a meal, the body uses newly absorbed glucose to satisfy its energy needs. The first step in this process is glycolysis, the breakdown of glucose into pyruvate. Glycolysis is a "use" pathway; it involves the acquisition and use of glucose within a single cell. At the end of glycolysis, pyruvate can be turned into acetyl-CoA, which enters the citric acid cycle and the electron transport chain. A number of pathways feed into the citric acid cycle and electron transport chain. These final two processes will be examined later in the lecture.

Glycolysis is a series of reactions that converts a 6-carbon glucose molecule into two 3-carbon molecules of **pyruvate**. All living cells and organisms are capable of breaking down glucose to pyruvate; glycolysis is the most common chemical pathway for this process. Glycolysis is a particularly important metabolic pathway because it can occur with or without the presence of oxygen (**aerobic** or **anaerobic** conditions). Glycolysis occurs in the **cytosol** (fluid portion) of living cells.

The ten steps of glycolysis can be split into two equal halves. In the first half, two phosphate groups from two different ATP molecules are added to glucose. These phosphate groups are bulky and charged, so they trap glucose inside the cell. They also prime the glucose, allowing the 6-carbon glucose to be split into two 3-carbon molecules (glycerol 3-phosphate and dihydroxyacetone phosphate). The first step of the first half of glycolysis occurs upon the entry of glucose into any human cell. Because this half requires the use of ATP, it is called the *energy input phase*. It is also called the *six-carbon phase* because it precedes the split of glucose.

> Glycolysis has traditionally been tested in some detail on the MCAT®.

> Don't memorize all of the names of the enzymes in glycolysis. Use the suffix of the enzyme to figure out what chemistry it does. For more review on enzyme types, see Chapter 1.10 of *Biology 1: Molecules*.

FIGURE 3.2 Gibbs Free Energy for the Steps of Glycolysis

Notice that the steps in the energy input phase seem to have an overall greater negative change in Gibbs free energy than the energy output phase. These reactions with a very negative ΔG will be spontaneous and likely irreversible, which is important for gluconeogenesis.

ATP input gives me the energy I need to get over the glycolysis wall!

FIGURE 3.3 Glycolysis

Glucose

Glucose 6-phosphate

Phosphate

Fructose 6-phosphate

Fructose 1,6-bisphosphate

Dihydroxyacetone phosphate

Glyceraldehyde 3-phosphate

1,3-Bisphosphoglycerate

3-Phosphoglycerate

2-Phosphoglycerate

Phosphoenolpyruvate

Pyruvate

×2

Don't worry about memorizing the enzymes involved in glycolysis; it is very unlikely that the MCAT® would test them explicitly. Just recognize that glucose is converted to two 3-carbon pyruvate molecules and that a net product of 2 ATP results from substrate-level phosphorylation, as well as 2 NADH.

Of course, all these reactions are governed by enzymes. A typical MCAT® question will ask what happens when a certain enzyme is inhibited by a poison. The poison will create a buildup of reactants and a dramatic reduction of products of the reaction that the enzyme governs. A related question would test an inborn error of metabolism, in which an enzyme in a person was missing or nonfunctional because of a mutation. The effect would be just like that of an inhibitory poison. A third question might ask you to predict the effect of a hormone on an enzyme-catalyzed reaction. In the case of glycolysis, insulin will speed up the reaction, and glucagon will slow it down.

In the second half of glycolysis, the two newly created 3-carbon molecules are each converted to pyruvate. Through this process, two ATP are produced per 3-carbon molecule (four ATP total). In addition, one NADH is generated from NAD^+ per 3-carbon molecule (two NADH total). Because energy molecules are created in the second half of glycolysis, it is called the *energy output phase*. It is also called the *three-carbon phase* because it occurs after the split of glucose. The net product of glycolysis for each glucose molecule is two ATP and two NADH. The actual molecular steps of glycolysis can be seen in Figure 3.3.

The production of ATP in glycolysis is somewhat unusual. Most ATP in the cell is produced by the electron transport chain, where the chemiosmotic gradient produced by pumping H^+ across the inner mitochondrial membrane drives the formation of ATP via ATP synthase. In glycolysis, the production of ATP occurs by the transfer of a phosphate from another reactive molecule to an ADP in a process called **substrate-level phosphorylation**. In substrate-level phosphorylation, the phosphate group being donated to ADP is initially attached to another molecule and is transferred to ADP by a kinase enzyme. In ATP synthase, the phosphate molecule is not bound to a larger molecule but is instead freely soluble.

The substrates of glycolysis include more than just glucose. Other monosaccharides such as fructose and galactose feed into glycolysis as well. Much of the fructose and galactose ingested by humans is converted into glucose by the liver, but a fructose or galactose molecule can also enter glycolysis as an intermediate of the six-carbon phase.

Fermentation, also known as anaerobic respiration, describes metabolism in the absence of oxygen. This process includes glycolysis as well as the reduction of pyruvate to ethanol or lactic acid and the oxidation of NADH back to NAD^+. Yeast and some microorganisms produce ethanol in fermentation, while human muscle cells and other microorganisms produce lactic acid. During fermentation, NAD^+ is restored from NADH for use in glycolysis, and the lactic acid or ethanol, along with carbon dioxide, is expelled from the cell as a waste product. In the **Cori Cycle**, lactic acid expelled from cells is transported through the blood to the liver, where it is oxidized back to pyruvate. This pyruvate is converted to glucose and can be sent back to other tissues to help produce ATP. Fermentation is not an optimal process, producing only 2 ATP per glucose molecule. By contrast, the Krebs cycle can produce as many as 36 ATP from one molecule of glucose, as discussed later in this lecture. Without the regeneration of NAD^+ from NADH, ATP could not be generated at all.

There is also an alternative pathway to glycolysis – the **pentose phosphate pathway (PPP)**. This pathway first diverges from glycolysis after glucose is phosphorylated and eventually rejoins at glyceraldehyde-3-phosphate (abbreviated as PGAL or G3P). Rejoining glycolysis allows the original glucose molecule to both create anabolic compounds and generate ATP via glycolysis and oxidative phosphorylation.

The main purpose of the PPP is to create NADPH and some five-carbon sugars, including ribose, that are used as the building blocks for DNA and RNA. The first half of the pathway, referred to as the oxidative branch, generates NADPH. NADPH is used in various synthetic, or anabolic, functions of the body, such as making cholesterol, and it also acts as an antioxidant. Without NADPH, cells could not build many structural components of the plasma membrane or store energy in the form of fatty acids. The second half of the PPP, referred to as the non-oxidative branch, creates important five-carbon sugars for the cell, like ribose for nucleotides.

The PPP is constitutively active in all cells to ensure that the oxidative state of the cell remains in balance. If the intracellular environment becomes too oxidizing or reducing, DNA, RNA, and protein damage occurs, which will usually induce apoptosis. While it occurs to some extent in all tissues, flux through the PPP is greatest in tissues involved in lipid synthesis, such as in the liver and adi-

MCAT® THINK

We normally think about glycolysis as running forward, from glucose to pyruvate. Would glycolysis ever run backward? Under what conditions would this happen?

See answer on page 93.

Don't memorize all the steps of the PPP. Just know that it has both oxidative and non-oxidative branches and the purpose is to make NADPH and five-carbon sugars.

pocytes. In contrast to glycolysis, the pentose phosphate pathway is not regulated by an external hormone, but rather by levels of NADPH. High levels of NADPH inhibit the first step in the oxidative half of the PPP. Because the cell needs some NADPH to maintain its neutral oxidative state, the negative feedback does not completely shut off the pathway but instead slows the progression of molecules through it.

Storage and Release of Glucose

Glucose has the potential to be used by all cells via glycolysis. Some types of cells, such as muscle and liver cells, can also store glucose as glycogen for later use. Muscle cells store glucose for their own use. Liver cells store glucose so that they can later release it for use by other cells. The storage of glycogen is called **glycogenesis**, while the breakdown of glycogen is called **glycogenolysis**. Liver cells also have the unique ability to synthesize glucose from non-carbohydrate products, such as proteins and lactic acid, in a process called **gluconeogenesis**. Glucose produced by gluconeogenesis is also released for use by other cells.

Glycogen is a polymer of glucose molecules linked by α–1,4' glycosidic bonds. The primary substrate for glycogenesis is glucose 6-phosphate, the product of the first step of glycolysis. Glycogen synthesis uses one UTP, which is a triphosphate nucleotide that is energetically equivalent to ATP. Glycogenolysis does not require ATP. Instead, an inorganic phosphate is enzymatically added to each α–1,4' bound glucose. Glycogen has occasional α–1,6' glycosidic bonds that create side chains. The metabolism of these side branches is more complicated, but is unlikely to be tested on the MCAT®.

Synthesis of Glucose

In the fasting state, soon after glycogen breakdown begins, the liver begins the process of gluconeogenesis, synthesizing new glucose molecules out of materials that are not necessarily carbohydrates. Gluconeogenesis is important because it takes products that would otherwise be unable to contribute to ATP generation, such as lactic acid, and turns them into glucose. Gluconeogenesis, in conjunction with glycogenolysis, helps to maintain the blood glucose level many hours after a meal has been eaten.

Gluconeogenesis is almost identical to glycolysis run in reverse, with a few enzymes that are unique in order to overcome unfavorable reactions. Recall that enzymes catalyze both the forward and the reverse reactions. A few of the reactions of gluconeogenesis with particularly large ΔG values have enzymes that are distinct from those of glycolysis. Gluconeogenesis produces free glucose that can be used by other organs.

To be a substrate for gluconeogenesis, the molecule must have a 3-carbon backbone. Fatty acids are mostly broken down, or catabolized, two carbons at a time into acetyl-CoA, so they cannot act as substrates for gluconeogenesis. Glycerol, the three-carbon backbone of a triglyceride, does have a three-carbon unit and can be used for gluconeogenesis. Lactic acid can also be used as starting material. Some, but not all, amino acids can be used for gluconeogenesis as well.

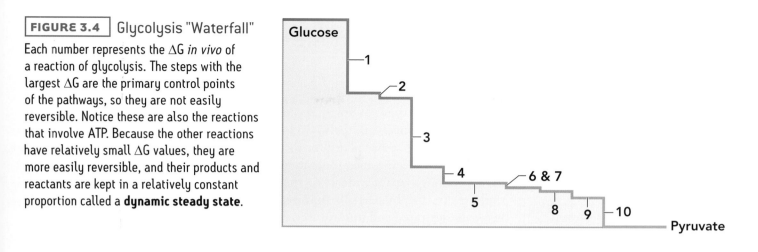

FIGURE 3.4 | Glycolysis "Waterfall"

Each number represents the ΔG *in vivo* of a reaction of glycolysis. The steps with the largest ΔG are the primary control points of the pathways, so they are not easily reversible. Notice these are also the reactions that involve ATP. Because the other reactions have relatively small ΔG values, they are more easily reversible, and their products and reactants are kept in a relatively constant proportion called a **dynamic steady state**.

Glycolysis and gluconeogenesis, like glycogenesis and glycogenolysis, are competing processes that are regulated by competing hormones. Prominent hormones for these reactions include insulin and glucagon. Like all hormones, their effects are widespread and diverse. In general, insulin promotes glycolysis and glycogenesis (decreasing blood glucose), while glucagon promotes gluconeogenesis and glycogenolysis (increasing blood glucose). Overall, insulin tends to be anabolic because, although it breaks down glucose in glycolysis, it uses these molecules to synthesize glycogen, fatty acids, nucleic acids, and steroids. Glucagon, by contrast, is catabolic because it breaks down these molecules and uses them to power ATP synthesis.

All of these pathways – glycolysis, gluconeogenesis, glycogenesis, and glycogenolysis – intersect at a molecule called *glucose-6-phosphate*. Glucose–6–phosphate may be converted to *glucose-1-phosphate* and then to glycogen for storage if glucose is plentiful. If glucose 6-phosphate follows the glycolytic pathway, it is converted to *fructose-6-phosphate* in the second step of glycolysis.

FIGURE 3.5 | Central Role of Glucose-6-Phosphate

3.4 | Fatty Acid Metabolism

Use of Fatty Acids

There are many types of lipids, as discussed in Lecture 1 of this manual. As far as metabolism is concerned, the MCAT® primarily tests fatty acids and triglycerides. These molecules store energy for the body. Because they contain long chains of alkanes, they are the most potent reducing agents in the body. Carbohydrates have alcohol groups that decrease the reducing potential of the carbons to which they are attached by partially oxidizing them. A similar comparison can be made between **saturated** and **unsaturated fats**. Because unsaturated fats have two fewer electrons for every double bond present, their reducing potential is decreased. Unsaturated fats store less energy, measured as calories, in the body. This is part of the basis of recommendations to include more unsaturated fats in the diet than saturated fats. For a review of oxidizing and reducing agents, see the Solutions and Electrochemistry Lecture in the *Chemistry* manual.

Electrochemistry
CHEMISTRY

Fatty acids can be used in two different ways in the body. First, they can be used directly by the organ into which they diffuse. They are broken down into acetyl-CoA in a process called **beta-oxidation**. Second, in the liver, they can be converted into a new molecule, called a ketone body, which can be shared with other organs for energy. This process is called **ketogenesis**, and it occurs during a prolonged fast when the body is no longer able to synthesize sufficient glucose via gluconeogenesis. Typically, ketogenesis begins some time after beta-oxidation.

In the fasting state, beta-oxidation begins at about the same time that gluconeogenesis begins. Fatty acids are freed from adipocytes, where they are held as triglycerides. The enzyme lipase releases the fatty acids and allows them to travel in the bloodstream via lipoproteins to the liver and any other organs that can use them. The fatty acids diffuse through the cell membrane and enter into the mitochondria, where they begin to undergo beta-oxidation. The process is called beta-oxidation because fatty acids are oxidized two carbons at a time.

| Acetone | Acetoacetic acid | Beta-hydroxybutyrate |

The acetone produced in ketone body formation is the same acetone you might use as a solvent in organic chemistry labs or when removing fingernail polish. It smells fruity, and you can smell this on the breath of a person who is producing ketone bodies. Beta-hydroxybutyrate is not actually a ketone, but rather a carboxylic acid. For the purposes of biology and biochemistry, it is still called a ketone body.

Beta-oxidation occurs in two steps. Fatty acids are first converted into *acyl-CoA*, at the expense of 1 ATP, along the outer membrane of the mitochondrion. The acyl-CoA is then brought into the mitochondrial matrix, where it is cleaved two carbons at a time to make acetyl-CoA. This reaction also produces $FADH_2$ and NADH for every two carbons taken from the original fatty acid. Acetyl-CoA then enters into the citric acid cycle. The glycerol backbone of the triglyceride is converted into an intermediate of glycolysis.

Don't worry about memorizing all of the enzyme names in beta-oxidation. Remember that beta-oxidation occurs in four steps: oxidation, hydration, oxidation, and thiolysis (OHOT) to give a two carbon acetyl-CoA. The four opposite reactions define fatty acid synthesis: condensation, reduction, dehydration, and reduction (CRDR).

Beta-oxidation works well for even-chain fatty acids, producing around 108 ATP per 16-carbon fatty acid, but odd-chain fatty acids end with a three-carbon fatty acid. This three-carbon molecule, as well as glycerol, can act as a substrate for gluconeogenesis when transported out of the mitochondria into the cytosol. Because the single three-carbon fatty acid makes up just a small fraction of any triglyceride molecule, lipids are not usually considered substrates for gluconeogenesis.

In addition to directly providing energy to cells via beta-oxidation, fatty acids can provide energy indirectly through **ketone bodies** produced by ketogenesis. There are three primary ketone bodies produced in humans: acetone, acetoacetic acid, and beta-hydroxybutyrate. Each of these is a small molecule with a carbonyl group. The carbonyl allows them to dissolve in the blood stream via hydrogen bonding, while also not adding charge, which would make crossing the cell membrane difficult. The biological purpose of ketone bodies is to spare glucose for the brain and red blood cells by providing an alternative source of energy for the other organs. If needed, the brain can also use ketone bodies to supply a portion of its energy.

Ketogenesis takes place in the mitochondria of liver cells. The process is similar to gluconeogenesis, in that a substrate (fatty acid) enters the liver and is processed into a new molecule (ketone body) that can be sent to other organs. Ketone bodies, however, are *not* substrates for gluconeogenesis. During periods of prolonged fasting or starvation, the liver oxidizes fatty acids for its own energy needs, using other carbon sources like glycerol and amino acids to create glucose. Because the liver oxidizes an excess of fatty acids, some of the acetyl-CoA produced from beta-oxidation is converted into ketone bodies that are transported through the blood for use in other tissues. These tissues include muscle and brain cells, where ketone bodies are converted back into acetyl-CoA and fed into the citric acid cycle to aid in the synthesis of ATP.

> Link gluconeogenesis, glycogenolysis, and beta-oxidation together in your mind as the processes that happen a few hours after you eat. In cases of extreme starvation, think of ketogenesis as well.

Storage and Release of Fatty Acids

Lipids are insoluble in the bloodstream, so they are transported in association with proteins. The entire complex of lipid and protein is known as a **lipoprotein**. Lipoproteins are produced primarily in the liver, intestines, and adipocytes, and are expelled from these cells via exocytosis. The intestines produce a special type of lipoprotein called a chylomicron, which contains a higher ratio of lipid to protein. Chylomicrons are the primary transport molecules that carry lipids from the intestines to the liver. The liver, in turn, repackages chylomicrons as *very low density lipoproteins (VLDL)* and *high density lipoproteins (HDL)*. VLDL transport lipids such as triglycerides, phospholipids, and cholesterol from the liver to other parts of the body, such as muscle and adipocytes. HDL, in contrast, picks up stray fatty acids and triglycerides from the periphery and brings them to the liver.

> Biological Molecules
> ≡ BIOLOGY 1

> **Make sure you know the types of lipoproteins and what they transport.**

The liver also has the ability to generate fatty acids out of materials that are not lipids. After a meal full of carbohydrates, the excess of sugar produces too much acetyl-CoA for the liver to use. In the presence of insulin, the excess acetyl-CoA is converted into fatty acids in the cytosol. This process is in contrast to ketogenesis, which also begins with excess acetyl-CoA in the liver, but is associated with low insulin levels and takes place in the mitochondria.

Lipids are stored inside adipocytes as triglycerides. Triglycerides organize fatty acids in a condensed, organized way, just as glycogen organizes glucose molecules. Immediately after a meal, lipids are transported by VLDL to adipocytes and stored for future use. In a fasting state (around the time of gluconeogenesis), triglycerides are broken down in the cell by lipase. **Lipase** is an enzyme that hydrolyzes triglycerides and releases free fatty acids into the bloodstream. This lipase is very similar to the lipase that breaks down triglycerides in the intestines. The fatty acids released are then taken around the body to various tissues that use them for beta-oxidation. In times of extreme starvation, the body will also turn fatty acids into ketone bodies in the liver.

Intestinal lipase tries to get triglycerides into cells. Hormone sensitive lipase tries to get triglycerides out of cells.

FIGURE 3.6 | Central Role of Acetyl-CoA

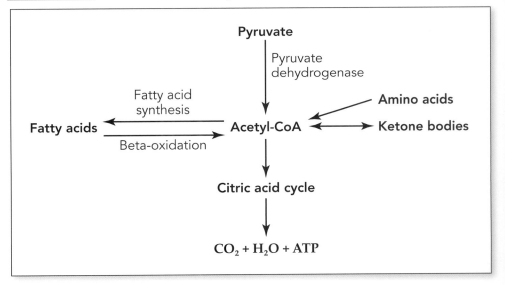

Link glycolysis, glycogenesis, and triglyceride storage together in your mind as defining the fed state. Glucose is used by all tissues for immediate energy needs, and any extra glucose and other high energy molecules are put into storage.

3.5 | Protein Metabolism

Protein and amino acid metabolism includes protein formation and protein breakdown. Protein formation, or protein **anabolism**, occurs primarily during the fed state and should be associated with glycolysis, glycogenesis, and lipid storage. Protein breakdown, or protein **catabolism**, occurs primarily during the fasting state and should be associated with gluconeogenesis, glycogenolysis, beta-oxidation, and ketone body synthesis.

While protein formation occurs primarily in the fed state, recall that translation depends on mRNA and the ribosome, and that regulatory control has many levels beginning at the level of the DNA. (The structures of proteins and amino acids are discussed in the Biological Molecules and Enzymes Lecture, and translation is discussed in the Genetics Lecture.) Proteins are made from amino acids, and the bulk of a cell's amino acids are incorporated into proteins, which are constantly being synthesized and degraded. Aside from this pool of amino acids, there is no true storage form of amino acids analogous to glycogen or triglycerides.

Protein breakdown begins with the hydrolysis of amino acid chains in the small intestines. Recall that amino acids are connected by amide bonds, which can be hydrolyzed into an amine plus a carboxylic acid. Enzymes such as **trypsin**, **chymotrypsin**, and **carboxypeptidase** cleave proteins into small mono-, di-, and tri-amino acids. The final small amino acid chains are cleaved by enzymes of the brush border. They are then absorbed and released into circulation by intestinal epithelial cells. Amino acid breakdown begins with the removal of the nitrogen group, producing ammonia and a carbon chain. The ammonia is fed into the *urea cycle* to become urea, which is excreted in the urine. The carbon chain can then serve as a substrate for various stages of the citric acid cycle.

Amino acids can be used to synthesize a number of biological substances besides proteins. Some of them can be substrates for gluconeogenesis, while others are substrates for ketogenesis. They are also used to form neurotransmitters and hormones, as well as heme, the oxygen-carrying portion of hemoglobin. Amino acids can even be used to create other amino acids. Eleven of the twenty amino acids can be synthesized from other amino acids. The other nine are referred to as essential amino acids, which must be obtained from the diet. For a review of the amino acids, including their various side chains and functional groups, see Section 1.6 of Chapter 1.

For the MCAT®, understanding the nature of each metabolic pathway and how the pathways fit together will be rewarded over the memorization of individual molecules and steps. Read this lecture for the "main idea" of each metabolic pathway and how it contributes to the energetic needs of the body.

These questions are NOT related to a passage.

Question 49

Which of the following is true of saturated and unsaturated fats containing an equal number of carbons?

○ **A.** Saturated fat stores less energy than unsaturated fat since saturated fat is more oxidized.
○ **B.** Saturated fat stores more energy than unsaturated fat since saturated fat is more oxidized.
○ **C.** Unsaturated fat stores less energy than saturated fat since unsaturated fat is more oxidized.
○ **D.** Unsaturated fat stores more energy than saturated fat since unsaturated fat is more reduced.

Question 50

Which of the following would be expected to cross a cell membrane without the aid of an accessory protein?

○ **A.** Glucose
○ **B.** Glycine
○ **C.** Ketone bodies
○ **D.** Triglycerides

Question 51

A runner is brought to the emergency room after vomiting on the side of the road during a high intensity run. When his laboratory tests reveal lactic acidosis, the physicians determine that the most likely reason for the patient's low blood pH is:

○ **A.** insufficient oxygen intake leading to gluconeogenesis.
○ **B.** insufficient glucose intake leading to fermentation.
○ **C.** insufficient oxygen intake leading to fermentation.
○ **D.** insufficient glucose intake leading to gluconeogenesis.

Question 52

Which of the following produces the most ATP per unit mass?

○ **A.** Saturated fats
○ **B.** Unsaturated fats
○ **C.** Glucose
○ **D.** Protein

Question 53

Which of the following processes occurs under both aerobic and anaerobic conditions?

○ **A.** Electron transport chain
○ **B.** Krebs cycle
○ **C.** Glycolysis
○ **D.** Oxidative phosphorylation

Question 54

Glycolysis takes place in the cytoplasm of an animal cell. Which of the following is NOT a product or reactant in glycolysis?

○ **A.** Glucose
○ **B.** Pyruvate
○ **C.** ATP
○ **D.** O_2

Question 55

Heart and liver cells can produce more ATP for each molecule of glucose than other cells in the body. This is most likely due to:

○ **A.** a more efficient ATP synthase on the outer mitochondrial membrane.
○ **B.** an additional turn of the Krebs cycle for each glucose molecule.
○ **C.** a more efficient mechanism for moving NADH produced in glycolysis into the mitochondrial matrix.
○ **D.** production of additional NADH by the citric acid cycle.

Question 56

Which of the following is an example of substrate-level phosphorylation?

○ **A.** The phosphorylation of glucose by glucokinase
○ **B.** The reduction of NAD^+ by triosephosphate dehydrogenase
○ **C.** The removal of a phosphate group from glucose 6-phosphate by glucose 6-phosphatase
○ **D.** The addition of an inorganic phosphate to ADP by pyruvate kinase

Regulation of Metabolism

This section will describe the guiding principles of metabolic regulation. On the level of the organism, the primary source of energy is glucose. While nothing in biology is ever absolute, there are two rules that are almost always true in metabolism. The first is that blood glucose only can come from the intestines or the liver. The second is that red blood cells *always* require glucose and the brain can use either glucose or ketones during periods of prolonged fasting.

Glucose Supply

Immediately after a meal, the intestines are a source of abundant glucose. The amount of glucose presents a metabolic challenge – if the blood glucose level gets too high, some will spill out in the urine. The kidney can only reabsorb glucose at a certain rate (see the Digestive and Excretory Systems Lecture in *Biology 2: Systems* for kidney physiology). In this state of glucose abundance, the body actively works to store glucose via glycogenesis. Extra glucose is also converted to fatty acids and stored as triglycerides in adipocytes. When there is a supply of glucose coming from the intestines, metabolic pathways tend to use glucose and store excess glucose as glycogen and triglycerides.

A few hours after a meal, the liver becomes the primary supplier of blood glucose. The liver can make glucose in two different ways: it can break down its glycogen stores via glycogenolysis, and it can manufacture new glucose from non-carbohydrate molecules via gluconeogenesis. The glucose supply from the liver is nowhere near as abundant as that which comes from the intestines during and immediately after a meal. When glucose is being provided by the liver, metabolic pathways release glucose and fatty acids for use.

Glucose Demand

The brain and the red blood cells present a fixed glucose demand. Both require a steady supply of glucose to function. Glucose is one of the few molecules that can penetrate the protective barrier between the blood and the brain, known as the blood-brain barrier. Red blood cells require glucose because they do not have mitochondria; their metabolism is limited to fermentation in the cytosol.

When glucose is abundant and coming mostly from the intestines, all organs will use blood glucose. When the glucose supply comes from the liver, it is limited. Most organs will begin to use fatty acids from adipocytes for their energy needs. The muscles are a special case in that they have their own internal glycogen supply that allows them to rapidly respond to changes in ATP requirements. Muscles keep glucose produced from their glycogen stores for internal use rather than releasing it because they do not have the necessary phosphatase to release glucose from the cell. They can use fatty acids as an energy source as well. All organs, except red blood cells, can also use ketone bodies for energy.

Hormones Communicate Glucose Levels

Blood glucose is primarily regulated by the competing hormones insulin and glucagon, although epinephrine and cortisol are also involved. When insulin levels are high, glucagon levels are typically low. Insulin is released from the pancreas in response to increased blood glucose levels and promotes glycolysis in all tissues, glycogenesis in the liver and muscle, fatty acid synthesis in the liver, and fatty acid storage in adipocytes. Glucagon is released from the pancreas in response to decreased blood glucose levels and promotes glycogenolysis in the liver and muscle, gluconeogenesis in the liver, fatty acid release in adipocytes, and beta-oxidation in almost all tissues. In late starvation, the absence of insulin promotes ketogenesis. Epinephrine is released in response to stress and, like glucagon, promotes glycogenolysis, the removal of glucose from storage. Cortisol is also released

Regulation is an important concept for the MCAT®. Make sure you understand how positive and negative feedback regulate the movement of molecules through each pathway and how this affects homeostasis.

Physiologically normal individuals do not excrete glucose in their urine. However, people with diabetes, who have insufficient or ineffective insulin, do excrete glucose. One of the tests for diabetes is to check for glucose in the urine.

Apply Key 2: Blood glucose levels drive key systemic and intracellular pathways. Low blood glucose leads to glucagon release from the pancreas, which in turn promotes glycogen breakdown in tissues, lipolysis in fat cells, and gluconeogenesis in the liver.

Endocrine System
BIOLOGY 2

in response to stress, but promotes gluconeogenesis instead. Both epinephrine and cortisol act to raise blood glucose levels but go about this change in different ways. Epinephrine acts quickly, while cortisol produces a more sustained effect.

Chemical signals in the bloodstream control metabolic pathways by regulating the enzymes of metabolism. All biochemical signal molecules must have receptors in order to have an effect. Insulin, epinephrine, and glucagon are hydrophilic hormones, so they have receptors on the outside of the cell membrane. Cortisol, a glucocorticoid, is a hydrophobic hormone and has receptors in the nucleus. Hormones control metabolic enzymes in the same ways that all enzymes are controlled:

1. phosphorylation,

2. regulation of the synthesis of enzymes,

3. use of control enzymes, and

4. local metabolic effects.

Insulin and glucagon tend to exert their effects via reversible phosphorylation, though they can use any of the first three mechanisms above. Glycogen synthase, the enzyme that makes glycogen, is inactivated by phosphorylation. This process is mediated by insulin acting through a membrane protein. As another example, cortisol and glucagon regulate glucose 6-phosphatase, the last enzyme of gluconeogenesis, by increasing its synthesis. Control enzymes are perhaps the most complicated. An example is phosphofructokinase-2. The exact function of this enzyme is beyond the scope of the MCAT®, but it is activated by insulin and catalyzes the creation of a molecule that is a potent activator of glycolysis.

Local metabolic effects occur in accordance with **Le Châtelier's principle**. Increasing substrate concentration causes an increase in the amount of product that is formed. This effect is not controlled by a hormone, but rather by local molecule concentrations. Ketogenesis provides an example of local metabolic effects When there is too much acetyl-CoA for the citric acid cycle in the liver to use, the liver begins to generate ketone bodies. Insulin must also be absent for this to happen. The lack of insulin is simply permissive; excess acetyl-CoA is the driving force behind ketogenesis.

Thermodynamics
CHEMISTRY

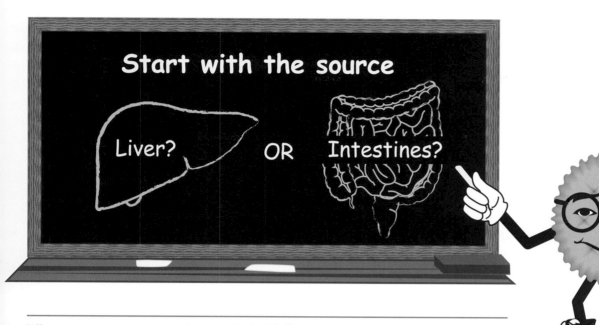

Start with the source

Liver?   OR   Intestines?

Whenever you see a question on the MCAT® that asks about metabolic pathways, always start by considering the source. Is the source of energy the intestines or the liver? If the question refers to someone who has just eaten a meal, or says that only one or two hours have passed since eating, the source is the intestines. In this case, you are in luck! All organs carry out glycolysis, the citric acid cycle, and the electron transport chain. Carbohydrates and lipids are stored as glycogen and triglycerides, respectively.

If more than two or three hours have passed since a meal, the source is the liver. Metabolism is more complex when this is the case. First, think about how the liver creates glucose for other organs – the liver must be carrying out glycogenolysis and gluconeogenesis. Second, think about fixed demand. Ask yourself what parts of the body REALLY need the glucose – the red blood cells and the brain are carrying out glycolysis. Remember that red blood cells cannot use the citric acid cycle and the electron transport chain because they do not have mitochondria. Third, think about variable demand. Ask yourself how all of the other organs in the body get their energy – they obtain it from fatty acids, not glucose. All other organs use beta-oxidation! There are only two exceptions to this rule that you must know. One is that muscles have their own supply of glycogen. The second is that many hours after eating a meal (approximately eight to twelve hours), the liver also makes ketone bodies, which can be used by all parts of the body except red blood cells.

Think about source, fixed demand, and variable demand when you answer any metabolism question on the MCAT®. The MCAT® will often give you one piece of information and require you to fill in another. Try two examples:

1) If the liver is undergoing gluconeogenesis, what is happening in an adipocyte?
   In this scenario, the liver is behaving as a source of glucose. The fixed demand (the red blood cells and the brain) have priority for this supply. All other tissues use beta-oxidation. Therefore, adipocytes must be carrying out fatty acid breakdown. They can also use some fatty acids for beta-oxidation themselves.

2) If the liver is undergoing glycolysis, what is happening in the muscle?
   In this scenario, the source must be the intestines. Therefore, all organs are undergoing glycolysis, including muscle. Since muscles also form their own glycogen stores, they are carrying out glycogenesis as well.

Question 57

If gluconeogenesis is occurring in the liver, which metabolic pathway will be happening in a red blood cell?

- ○ **A.** Gluconeogenesis
- ○ **B.** Glycogenolysis
- ○ **C.** The citric acid cycle
- ○ **D.** The pentose phosphate pathway

Question 58

Glucose 6-phosphatase is the enzyme that catalyzes the last step of gluconeogenesis, the formation of glucose from glucose 6-phosphate. If a child were born without a functional version of this enzyme, which of the following problems would be expected?

- ○ **A.** Decreased glycolysis in the liver during the fed state
- ○ **B.** Decreased glycogenesis in the liver during the fed state
- ○ **C.** Decreased exit of glucose from muscle cells during the fasting state
- ○ **D.** Decreased blood glucose levels during the fasting state

Question 59

When hormone-sensitive lipase is active during the fasting state, which of the following processes will not be active in a muscle cell?

- ○ **A.** Glycolysis
- ○ **B.** Gluconeogenesis
- ○ **C.** The citric acid cycle
- ○ **D.** The electron transport chain

Question 60

Which of the following cells does NOT produce carbon dioxide?

- ○ **A.** Red blood cells
- ○ **B.** Muscle
- ○ **C.** Liver
- ○ **D.** Adipocytes

Question 61

During the fasting state, and assuming that bloodstream oxygen levels are normal, which of the following does NOT serve as a substrate of gluconeogenesis in the liver?

- ○ **A.** Lactate
- ○ **B.** Glycerol
- ○ **C.** Odd chain fatty acids
- ○ **D.** Even chain fatty acids

Question 62

Which of the following organs CANNOT use fatty acids as an energy source?

- ○ **A.** The liver
- ○ **B.** Muscle
- ○ **C.** The brain
- ○ **D.** The kidney

Question 63

Which of the following does NOT represent a correct pathway for the control of metabolism at the biochemical level?

- ○ **A.** Insulin phosphorylates an enzyme to inactivate it.
- ○ **B.** Glucagon phosphorylates an enzyme to inactivate it.
- ○ **C.** An abundance of ATP in the cell slows glycolysis.
- ○ **D.** Epinephrine triggers the destruction of enzymes in the cell.

Question 64

One hour after a meal, which hormone would be expected to be elevated?

- ○ **A.** Insulin
- ○ **B.** Glucagon
- ○ **C.** Epinephrine
- ○ **D.** Cortisol

3.7 | Energy: ATP and NADH

On the cellular level, the primary source of energy is the nucleotide **adenosine triphosphate (ATP)**, which contains three phosphate groups. Phosphate groups are very hydrophilic, and donation of these groups can change the conformation of proteins. The addition of a phosphate group to Na^+/K^+ ATPase allows the enzyme to change configuration and pump Na^+ and K^+ against their concentration gradients. **NADH** is also an important source of cellular energy. It stores energy in the high energy electrons of its hydride and is used to drive ATP formation in the electron transport chain.

The phosphate groups of ATP contain phosphoanhydride bonds, or phosphoric acids that are linked at an oxygen atom. Their chemical reactivity is similar to that of the anhydrides discussed in the Oxygen Containing Reactions Lecture in the *Chemistry* manual. Hydrolysis of phosphoanhydride bonds, which is spontaneous and exothermic, can provide the energy required for less energetically favorable reactions. For an exothermic reaction, ΔH, or the change in enthalpy, is negative. For a spontaneous reaction, ΔG, or the change in Gibbs free energy, is also negative.

Cells must constantly maintain functional levels of ATP to power metabolic reactions. ATP is synthesized by the addition of one phosphate group to adenosine *di*phosphate (ADP).

> Note that a hydride ion is an H^- ion. It consists of a proton and two electrons. A hydride ion is not the same as a hydrogen proton, which has no electrons.

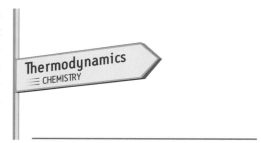

Thermodynamics
CHEMISTRY

> Understand Key 3: ATP and NADH are the cell's energy molecules. They are formed during catabolic processes, such as glycolysis, the citric acid cycle, the electron transport chain, and fatty acid oxidation and help power cellular functions.

FIGURE 3.7 | ATP and ADP

ATP synthase operates by brute force. It forces the ADP and phosphate group to join by smashing them together.

Since the hydrolysis of ATP has a negative ΔG, the synthesis of ATP has a positive ΔG of equal magnitude. The energy for this synthesis is extracted from the diet. All ATP is synthesized by the addition of a phosphate group to adenosine diphosphate; this addition is called phosphorylation. **Oxidative phosphorylation** occurs when oxidation reactions provide the energy for phosphorylation. It requires the presence of oxygen as a final electron acceptor. In the mitochondria, a series of oxidation reactions results in the creation of a proton gradient that powers a turbine-like enzyme, ATP synthase, which catalyzes the synthesis of ATP. In substrate-level phosphorylation, oxidation and phosphorylation are not coupled. ADP is simply one of several substrates in an enzyme-catalyzed reaction that results in transfer of a phosphate group to ADP. There are enzymes in both glycolysis and the citric acid cycle that catalyze substrate-level phosphorylation.

The energy to run oxidative phosphorylation comes from NADH, which is the reduced form of nicotinamide adenine dinucleotide (NAD^+). NAD^+ consists of two nucleotides joined together by phosphate groups. Recall that a nucleotide consists of a base, a five carbon sugar, and at least one phosphate group. One of the base groups of one of the nucleotides in NAD^+ can exist in either an oxidized or reduced state. In the reduced state, NAD^+ has accepted a hydride ion (H^-) to become NADH. In other words, it has gained electrons. NADH carries electrons to the electron transport chain, acting as a **soluble electron carrier**. The hydride ion serves as the source of electrons passed down the electron transport chain to oxygen, powering the movement of three H^+ into the intermembrane space of the mitochondrion. By diffusing down their concentration gradient, these hydrogen ions power ATP synthase.

FIGURE 3.8 | NAD$^+$ and NADH

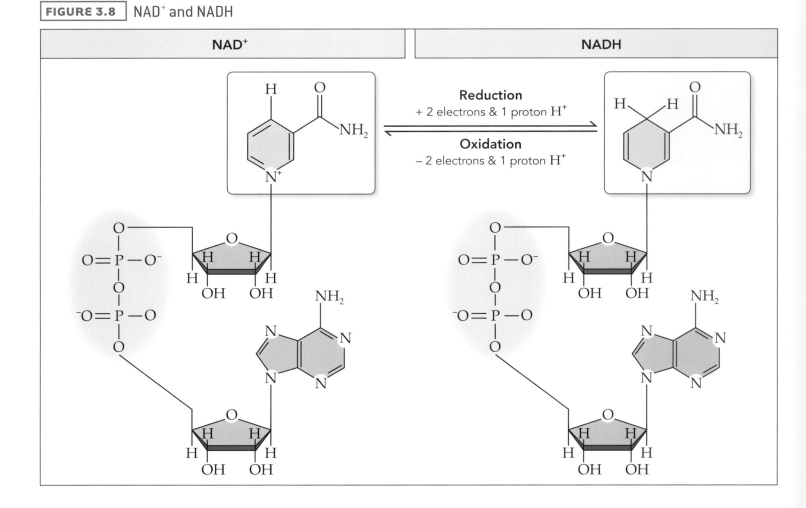

NADH and the Citric Acid Cycle

While NADH can be produced by a few different cellular processes (including glycolysis, as mentioned previously), most NADH in the cell comes from the citric acid cycle. This allows the high levels of NADH produced in the citric acid cycle to more easily contribute to ATP synthesis, which also occurs in the mitochondria. Pathways that feed into the citric acid cycle include glycolysis (after pyruvate is converted into acetyl-CoA), beta-oxidation, and ketone body use. The citric acid cycle takes place in the **mitochondrial matrix**. The outer membrane of a mitochondrion is permeable to small molecules, such as pyruvate and NADH. These molecules pass into the intermembrane space via facilitated diffusion through a large membrane protein. The inner **mitochondrial membrane**, however, is almost impermeable to small molecules in order to maintain the chemiosmotic gradient produced by pumping H^+ across the membrane. Although pyruvate, fatty acids, and ketone bodies move into the matrix via facilitated diffusion, the hydrolysis of ATP is usually required to transport each NADH.

Acetyl-CoA is a coenzyme that transfers two carbons (from pyruvate) to the 4-carbon oxaloacetic acid to begin the **citric acid cycle** (also called the **Krebs cycle** or the **tricarboxylic acid cycle, TCA**). During the cycle, two carbons are lost as CO_2, and oxaloacetic acid is regenerated. The citric acid cycle is called a "cycle" because the end product, oxaloacetic acid, is combined with acetyl-CoA to restart the series of reactions. Each turn of the citric acid cycle produces 1 ATP, 3 NADH, and 1 $FADH_2$. $FADH_2$ acts similarly to NADH to help move H^+ across the inner mitochondrial membrane, as will be described in more detail below.

Notice that the output given above is per turn of the citric acid cycle. Since each glucose molecule is split in half, one glucose molecule powers two turns of the citric acid cycle. This means that 6 NADH are made per glucose in the citric acid cycle, compared to the 2 NADH made per glucose in glycolysis. A similar ratio exists for beta-oxidation, which produces 1 NADH per two carbons versus 3 NADH in the citric acid cycle. The one GTP produced during the citric acid cycle serves as the phosphate donor to ADP to produce ATP. This process occurs by substrate-level phosphorylation, just like in glycolysis.

During aerobic respiration, most ATP is produced inside the mitochondrion.

Carbons are "lost as CO_2" in the citric acid cycle because carboxylic acid is undergoing a decarboxylation reaction. This reaction is discussed in the Oxygen Containing Reactions Lecture in the Chemistry manual.

FIGURE 3.9 | Citric Acid Cycle

At the beginning of the citric acid cycle in the mitochondrial matrix, a two-carbon acetyl-CoA is added to a four-carbon oxaloacetate, producing a six-carbon molecule. Each turn of the cycle produces 3 NADH, 1 $FADH_2$, 1 GTP that is converted to ATP via substrate-level phosphorylation, and 2 CO_2.

Don't memorize all of the names of the enzymes in the citric acid cycle. Use the suffix of each enzyme to help you figure out the chemistry. For a review of enzyme types, see Lecture 1.10 in Biology 1: Molecules.

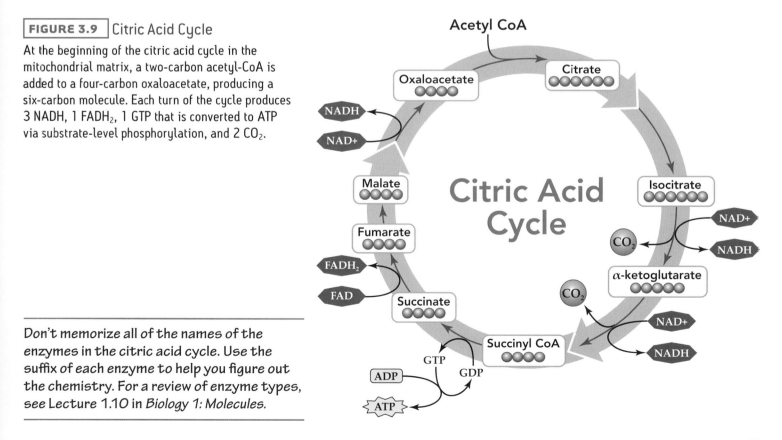

Regulation of the citric acid cycle is tied to the amount of NAD$^+$ available. NAD$^+$ is generated by the oxidation of NADH by the electron transport chain. If the electron transport chain is inhibited, as when there is a lack of oxygen, NADH cannot be oxidized to NAD$^+$. In this case, the citric acid cycle is inhibited and the cell shifts its energy production toward anaerobic pathways. This is an example of the local metabolic effects discussed earlier in this lecture. Because of this close connection to the electron transport chain, the citric acid cycle is considered to be aerobic. NADH provides another source of regulation: the citric acid cycle produces NADH, so if an excess of NADH builds up, the reactions slow down.

Note that acetyl-CoA is not the only substrate that can enter the citric acid cycle. Some molecules can be modified to various citric acid cycle intermediates that can then enter the cycle. Amino acids come with carbon backbones of varying lengths. After amino acids are deaminated in the liver, the deaminated product may be chemically converted to pyruvic acid or acetyl-CoA, or it may enter the citric acid cycle at various stages depending upon the length of the carbon backbone. Glutamic acid, for example, has a five carbon backbone and can be converted into the citric acid cycle intermediate α–ketoglutarate.

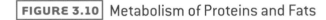

FIGURE 3.10 Metabolism of Proteins and Fats

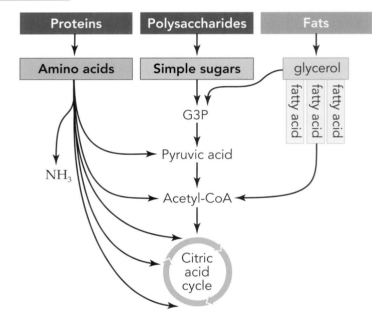

ATP and the Electron Transport Chain

The electron transport chain (ETC) (Figure 3.11) is a series of proteins that carries electrons from NADH to O_2. These proteins include **ubiquinone** and **cytochromes**, which are intermediate electron carriers in the electron transport chain. They pick up electrons from NADH and transfer them to O_2, which is reduced to H_2O. Remember that when any molecule gains electrons, it is reduced. When that molecule gives them away, it is oxidized.

In the ETC, complex I receives two electrons from NADH and transfers them to the lipid-soluble carrier, ubiquinone. The process of electron transfer within complex I pumps 4 H$^+$ across the membrane. Complex II receives electrons from FADH$_2$ and transfers them to a quinone carrier, Q, to make QH$_2$. Unlike complex I, no protons are pumped across the membrane. Next, complex III receives the electrons from QH$_2$ and transfers them to cytochrome c, resulting in the movement of 4 H$^+$ across the membrane. Finally, complex IV removes the electrons from cytochrome c and transfers them to oxygen. Complex IV also moves 2 H$^+$ across the membrane to contribute to the proton gradient.

Remember that the citric acid cycle occurs twice for each glucose; once for each pyruvate generated by glycolysis.

To be used for energy, amino acids must first be deaminated, after which they can enter the citric acid cycle as pyruvate or as one of the citric acid cycle intermediates. Nucleotides must also be deaminated before entering the cycle as an intermediate. Fats are converted to acetyl-CoA, which can then enter the citric acid cycle.

The electron transport chain can be thought of as an assembly line. Electrons are picked up at one end and handed down the line to oxygen.

Another electron carrier, cytochrome c, has a second function – when it leaks out of the mitochondria in the event of cellular damage, it triggers apoptosis (cell death).

The electron transport chain is fundamentally a reduction-oxidation reaction. NADH loses electrons (is oxidized) to become NAD$^+$. Oxygen gains electrons (is reduced) to form water. This is crucial to understand for the MCAT$^®$.

> Don't worry about memorizing the specific names of the proteins in the ETC. Just make sure to know which ones contribute to establishing the proton gradient and how drugs blocking their action or a mutation that decreases the efficacy of pumping might impact ATP production.

As electrons are passed along, protons are pumped into the intermembrane space, establishing a proton gradient called the **proton-motive force**. As the protons diffuse back into the mitochondrial matrix along their electrochemical gradient, they travel through **ATP synthase**, generating ATP. The horizontal flow of protons causes ATP synthase to turn. As it turns, it combines a phosphate group with an ADP to generate ATP. This mechanism of fueling ATP production is called **chemiosmotic coupling**, an example of oxidative phosphorylation in the body. A net product of 2 to 3 ATP is manufactured for each NADH, depending on whether an ATP was spent to transport NADH into the mitochondrial matrix. $FADH_2$ works in a similar fashion to NADH, except that $FADH_2$ reduces a protein further along in the ETC series, so only about 2 ATP are produced for each $FADH_2$.

Oxygen is a key regulator of the electron transport chain. When it is present, the electron transport chain runs as described above. When it is absent, there is no acceptor to which the final electron carrier of the chain can pass its electrons, leaving the electron carrier in a reduced state. Eventually, the entire chain backs up and NADH has nowhere to pass its electrons, so the citric acid cycle slows, as discussed previously. The excess NADH also shifts the cell into anaerobic fermentation, so NADH is converted to NAD^+ by the conversion of pyruvate to lactate.

FIGURE 3.11 | Electron Transport Chain

Notice that the intermembrane space has a lower pH than the matrix, due to the buildup of protons.

You don't have to memorize the names of the molecules or the enzymes of the citric acid cycle except for the ones that are red and bold; however, you should recognize them as being part of the citric acid cycle if they are presented in a diagram. Pay special attention to acetyl-CoA and ATP synthase. Also know the difference between oxidative phosphorylation and substrate-level phosphorylation.

Finally, you should definitely know the net products and reactants for respiration:

Glucose + $O_2 \rightarrow CO_2 + H_2O$

(This reaction is not balanced.)

This is a combustion reaction. Notice that the oxygen you breathe in does not become CO_2, although it is exchanged for CO_2. Instead it becomes H_2O. Be sure you remember that the final electron acceptor is oxygen. This is why oxygen is necessary for aerobic respiration.

You should know that aerobic respiration, including glycolysis, produces about 36 net ATP. You should also know that 1 NADH produces 2 to 3 ATP and that 1 $FADH_2$ produces about 2 ATP. Know how many NADH, $FADH_2$, and ATP molecules are produced in each turn of the citric acid cycle, and that one glucose produces two turns.

TABLE 3.1 > Molecular Accounting

	Glycolysis	Pre-Krebs	Krebs	Total	ATP/mol	ATP total
ATP	2	0	2	4	1	4
NADH	2	2	6	10	3	30 - 2 = 28*
$FADH_2$	0	0	2	2	2	4
						NET 36

* The cost of transporting each glycolysis-produced NADH from the cytosol into the mitochondrion is one ATP.

The CDC recommends controlled calorie intake, increased physical activity, and improved eating behaviors. It looks like this shopper is making good food choices.

3.8 | Metabolic Disorders

Disruption of the regulatory mechanisms involved in metabolism can lead to a variety of metabolic disorders. **Obesity** is a metabolic disorder that has quickly become one of the important medical problems of the twenty-first century. Body mass index, or BMI, expresses weight compared to height and has traditionally been used to define obesity, although it is an imperfect measure. Obesity is defined as a BMI above 30. As of 2010, the CDC estimates that over one-third of adults in the United States are obese. Obesity has been associated with increased risk of heart disease, stroke, diabetes, and some types of cancer.

Diabetes is a key example of a metabolic disorder, characterized by a lack of or a resistance to insulin. Type I diabetes is an autoimmune disease where the immune system attacks the β-cells of the pancreas. As a result, insulin levels are almost nonexistent in the blood of type I diabetic patients. Regular blood glucose monitoring and administration of insulin helps control type I diabetes. Type II diabetes results from a combination of genetic and lifestyle factors. Type II diabetes is characterized by increasing resistance to the action of insulin at the target cell. Cells become unable to regulate glucose intake and blood glucose levels can become dangerously high, sometimes resulting in coma and death. A healthy lifestyle is key to preventing type II diabetes.

Over the past century, high-calorie foods have become more prevalent, and lifestyles have become increasingly sedentary. However, the source of obesity is more complicated than just eating more calories than are burned off during activity. Obesity is also influenced by genetics and the complex interaction of hormones and metabolites in the body.

One of the best studied hormones affecting appetite is leptin, which interacts with the hypothalamus to signal satiety, or a feeling of fullness. Obesity has been associated with deficiency or lack of response to leptin, but obesity should not be thought of as a leptin deficiency any more than it should be thought of as the result of greater calorie intake than expenditure. There are hundreds of hormones and molecules that regulate the drive to eat and the way the body processes food.

Weight loss is complex and involves multiple interrelated factors. Diets can be modified to include healthier and lower calorie food, and lifestyles can be modified to include more physical activity. Sociological and psychological forces often pull a person back into old habits. In the clinic, the approach to weight loss is multifaceted, but usually centers on diet and exercise. Pharmaceutical companies have begun to create drugs that can modify metabolic pathways, but determining which pathways can be safely targeted with the result of meaningful weight remains difficult. In the future, medications may play a larger role in treatment, but it is unlikely that they will ever be the entire solution.

TABLE 3.2 > Metabolism Summary

Pathway	Cellular Location	Substrates	Products	Regulated Steps
Glycolysis	Cytosol	Glucose	Pyruvate, ATP, NADH	1) Glucose → glucose-6-phosphate 2) Fructose-6-phosphate → fructose-1,6-bisphosphate 3) PEP → pyruvate
Citric acid cycle	Mitochondrial matrix	Acetyl-CoA	ATP (GTP), CO_2, NADH, $FADH_2$	1) Oxaloacetate + acetyl-CoA → citrate 2) Isocitrate → α-ketoglutarate 3) α-Ketoglutarate → succinyl-CoA
Electron transport chain	Inner mitochondrial matrix	NADH, $FADH_2$	ATP, H_2O	
Gluconeogenesis	Cytosol	Pyruvate	Glucose	1) Pyruvate → oxaloacetate → PEP 2) Fructose-1,6-bisphosphate → fructose-6-phosphate 3) Glucose-6-phosphate → glucose
β-Oxidation	Mitochondrial matrix	Fatty Acids	Acetyl-CoA, NADH, $FADH_2$	Acyl-CoA ester transport across the mitochondrial membrane
Fatty acid synthesis	Cytosol	Acetyl-CoA, NADPH	Fatty acids	Attachment of acetyl-CoA to fatty acid synthase
Glycogenesis	Cytosol	Glucose	Glycogen	De-phosphorylation of glycogen synthase
Glycogenolysis	Cytosol	Glycogen	Glucose	Phosphorylation of glycogen phosphorylase
Pentose phosphate pathway	Cytosol	Glucose	NADPH, 5 Carbon sugars	Oxidation of glucose-6-phosphate

Question 65 is based on the following information:

The first reaction of glycolysis converts glucose into glucose 6-phosphate at the expenditure of one ATP. The full reaction is shown, with thermochemical data below it.

Glucose + ATP → Glucose 6-phosphate + ADP

Glucose + Phosphate → Glucose 6-phosphate
$\Delta G = 20.9$ kJ/mol

ATP → ADP + P_i
$\Delta G = -48.1$ kJ/mol

Question 65

What is the ΔG of the conversion of one mole of glucose into glucose 6-phosphate?

- **A.** -27.2 kJ
- **B.** +27.2 kJ
- **C.** -69.0 kJ
- **D.** +69.0 kJ

Questions 66 – 72 are NOT based on a descriptive passage.

Question 66

Oxidative phosphorylation is reliant on the transfer of electrons in the electron transfer chain. Which of the following molecules is an electron acceptor?

- **A.** NAD^+
- **B.** NADH
- **C.** $FADH_2$
- **D.** NADPH

Question 67

Which of the following best describes the reaction of NAD^+ to NADH?

- **A.** NAD^+ accepts a proton and is reduced to NADH.
- **B.** NAD^+ donates a proton and is reduced to NADH.
- **C.** NAD^+ accepts hydride and is reduced to NADH.
- **D.** NAD^+ accepts hydride and is oxidized to NADH.

Question 68

The reaction that generates ATP from ADP and an inorganic phosphate would be expected to have which of the following values of ΔG?

- **A.** $\Delta G > 0$
- **B.** $\Delta G = 0$
- **C.** $\Delta G < 0$
- **D.** ΔG cannot be predicted without more information about the reaction.

Question 69

After electrons are passed from one protein complex to another, the final electron acceptor of the electron transport chain is:

- **A.** ATP.
- **B.** H_2O.
- **C.** NADH.
- **D.** O_2.

Question 70

In a human renal cortical cell, the Krebs cycle occurs in the:

- **A.** cytosol.
- **B.** mitochondrial matrix.
- **C.** inner mitochondrial membrane.
- **D.** mitochondrial intermembrane space.

Question 71

As electrons move within the electron transport chain, each intermediate carrier molecule is:

- **A.** oxidized by the preceding molecule and reduced by the following molecule.
- **B.** reduced by the preceding molecule and oxidized by the following molecule.
- **C.** reduced by both the preceding and following molecules.
- **D.** oxidized by both the preceding and following molecules.

Question 72

Which of the following molecules serves as a membrane-soluble carrier of electrons in the electron transport chain?

- **A.** Ubiquinone
- **B.** Succinyl-CoA dehydrogenase
- **C.** Pyruvate dehydrogenase complex
- **D.** ATP synthase

Acetyl-CoA
Adenosine triphosphate (ATP)
Aerobic
Anabolism
Anaerobic
Apoptosis
ATP synthase
Beta-oxidation
Carboxypeptidase
Catabolism
Chemiosmotic coupling
Chymotrypsin
Citric acid cycle (Krebs cycle)
Cori cycle
Cortisol
Cytochrome

Cytosol
Dynamic steady state
Electron transport chain (ETC)
Epinephrine
Fermentation
Glucagon
Gluconeogenesis
Glycogenesis
Glycogenolysis
Glycolysis
Inborn error of metabolism
Insulin
Ketogenesis
Ketone bodies
Le Châtelier's principle
Lipase

Lipoproteins
Mitochondrial matrix
Mitochondrial membrane
Obesity
Oxidative phosphorylation
NADH
Pentose phosphate pathway (PPP)
Products of citric acid cycle: 1 ATP, 3 NADH, 1 $FADH_2$
Proton-motive force
Pyruvate
Saturated fats
Soluble electron carrier
Substrate-level phosphorylation
Trypsin
Ubiquinone
Unsaturated fats

MCAT® THINK ANSWER

Pg. 73: When blood glucose is low, the body works to restore glucose to the blood. The blood serves all of the tissues in the body as a glucose bank account with a minimum balance requirement. When blood glucose levels drop, as when a person is exercising or fasting, the hormone glucagon is released and triggers both gluconeogenesis and glycogenolysis. The reverse of glycolysis is gluconeogenesis - rebuilding glucose from pyruvate. Glycogen is broken down into glucose molecules in the process of glycogenolysis. Both processes recreate glucose and send it back to the blood. Gluconeogenesis occurs in the liver and a very small extent in the cortex of the kidney. Newly synthesized glucose enters the bloodstream to bring blood glucose back to homeostasis, making glucose available to other tissues that may need it.

DON'T FORGET YOUR KEYS

1. Metabolic pathways move toward either the storage or production of energy.

2. Blood glucose levels drive systemic and intracellular pathways.

3. NADH and ATP are the cell's energy molecules.

Laboratory Techniques

4.1 Introduction

Understanding laboratory techniques is vital to success on the MCAT® and as a physician. Physicians must be able to interpret studies that utilize such techniques in order to practice evidence-based medicine, and lab techniques are increasingly important in clinical practice as well. It is critical that physicians have the ability to explain these techniques to patients and determine when they should be used.

Succeeding on the MCAT® requires an understanding of the use and scientific principles of certain laboratory techniques, which can be divided into three categories:

1. Separations divide mixtures into their components based on intermolecular forces and can be used for purification, identification, or collection.

2. Spectroscopy and spectrometry provide structural information that can be used to identify compounds.

3. Genetic techniques have many clinical and research applications, including the isolation/identification of genes and the manipulation of DNA on the molecular level.

Familiarize yourself with lab techniques for two reasons. First, they may appear in questions testing basic scientific principles. Second, you will have a better understanding of the experiments and conclusions presented in passages when you understand the techniques used. Techniques such as protein and nucleic acid electrophoresis, PCR, cloning, and DNA sequencing are particularly important to understand for the MCAT®.

4.2 Separating Compounds

Separations are a variety of lab techniques that use intermolecular forces to separate a mixture into its component parts. Certain separation techniques are better suited for certain mixtures based on the particular properties of the compounds in the mixture, and some techniques can provide quantitative information on a mixture's components. Compounds can be separated according to solubility, melting point, boiling point, or any other physical property that causes two substances in a mixture to behave differently from one another. Unique terminology is assigned to each type of separation: extraction, distillation, crystallization, and chromatography.

Extraction

Extraction is a separation technique based on solubility. The principle underscoring this technique is that "like dissolves like." Extraction involves two immiscible (not mixable) phases, most commonly an aqueous layer and a less dense organic mixture. As shown in Figure 4.1, these two layers have different polarities, so they are immiscible. The steps below are used to perform an extraction on a mixture of compounds. Note that the compounds must typically be of significantly different polarity in order to be fully separated.

1. Add a weak acid and shake. The acid protonates strong bases in the organic layer, making them polar and thus causing them to move to the aqueous layer. The aqueous layer is separated and then washed with a base to neutralize the added acid, leaving only the strong organic base(s).

> The sequence of an extraction is key to the separation of components. A weak acid or base will bind only strong complements, whereas a strong acid or base will react with all (weak and strong) complements. To separate multiple components, the first extraction uses a weak acid or base to extract only the strong complements. Then a strong acid or base is used to extract the remaining weak components. If the reverse order was used, a strong acid or base in the first separation would react with all - strong and weak - complements such that they would be extracted all at once from the organic to the aqueous layer, rather than being sequentially separated from one another.

FIGURE 4.1 | Extraction

2. Add a strong acid and shake. The acid protonates weak bases in the organic layer, making them polar. The polar bases dissolve in the aqueous layer and are drained off. The separation is then washed with a base to neutralize the added acid, leaving only the organic weak base(s).

3. Add a weak base. The base deprotonates only the strongest organic acids, making them polar enough to dissolve in the aqueous layer. The polar acids are then drained off. The separation is washed with an acid to neutralize the added base, leaving only the strong organic acid(s).

4. Add a strong base. The strong base reacts with any weak acids that remain in the organic layer. The deprotonated acids dissolve in the aqueous layer and are drained off. Finally, this separation is washed with an acid to remove the added base, leaving only the weak organic acid(s).

One commonly used extraction technique is called a phenol-chloroform extraction, which can be used to separate nucleic acids from cellular proteins. DNA and RNA can be isolated from cells using phenol-chloroform extraction to be used for genomic sequencing, various blotting techniques, and gene expression studies.

Distillation

Distillation is a technique used to separate compounds that have significantly different boiling points. A solution of two volatile liquids with boiling point differences of at least 20°C can be separated by slow boiling. The compound with the lower boiling point (and therefore the higher vapor pressure at a given temperature) will boil off first and can be captured and condensed in a cool tube. Distillation can be used to purify fresh water from salt water, or to increase the purity of an alcohol-water mixture, among many other uses.

If a solution of two volatile liquids exhibits a positive deviation to Raoult's law, the solution will boil at a lower temperature than either pure compound. The result will be a solution with an exact ratio of the two liquids. Such a solution cannot be separated by distillation.

Fractional distillation is a more precise method of distillation that can be used to separate liquids whose boiling points are fairly close together. In fractional distillation, the vapor is run through glass beads, allowing the compound with the higher boiling point to repeatedly condense and fall back into the solution.

Crystallization

Crystallization is based on the principle that pure substances form crystals more easily than impure substances (i.e. pure substances have higher freezing/melting points). Crystallization is used to purify solid compounds. The classic example is an iceberg. An iceberg is formed from the ocean but contains only pure water, not salt water, since pure water forms crystals more easily than salt water. Crystallization is a very inefficient method of separation; in other words, it is very difficult to arrive at a pure substance through crystallization. For most salts, crystallization is an exothermic process.

During the process of freezing, most of the salty impurities are frozen out of the iceberg. This is an example of crystallization.

FIGURE 4.2 Fractional Distillation

Thermometer

Water out

Glass beads packed in fractionating column

Water in

Vert

Product

Mixture

Heat

Chromatography

Chromatography is used to purify a compound from a mixture and/or to determine the ratio of compounds in a mixture. It involves the separation of a mixture by passing it over or through a matrix that adsorbs (binds) different compounds more or less strongly according to their properties, ultimately altering the rate at which they lose contact with the matrix. The mixture is usually dissolved into a solution to serve as the mobile phase, while the matrix is often a solid surface. By adsorbing compounds from the mixture, the matrix surface establishes the stationary phase. The compounds in the mixture that have a greater affinity for the surface move more slowly. Typically the stationary phase is polar, causing more polar compounds to elute more slowly. Chromatography separates the mixture into separate and distinct layers, one pertaining to each component of the mixture.

In **column chromatography** (Figure 4.3), a solution containing the mixture is dripped down a column containing the solid phase (usually glass beads made of the polar molecule SiO_2). The more polar compounds in the mixture travel more slowly down the column, creating separate layers for each compound. Each compound can be collected as it elutes with the solvent and drips out of the bottom of the column. In general, gravity drives the movement of the mixture in column chromatography. One variant of column chromatography is **high pressure liquid chromatography (HPLC)**, in which the column and solution use an apparatus that puts the system under high pressure.

FIGURE 4.3 | Column Chromatography

Solvent continuously applied to columns

Mixture to be separated

Chromatography column with glass beads

Compounds are eluted and collected

Compound 1   Compound 2   Compound 3

In **paper chromatography** (Figure 4.4), a small portion of the sample to be separated is spotted onto paper. One end of the paper is then placed into a nonpolar solvent. The solvent moves up the paper via capillary action and dissolves the sample as it passes over it. As the solvent continues to move up the paper, the more polar components of the sample move more slowly because they are attracted to the polar paper. The less polar components dissolve more easily to move up the paper with the solvent. The result is a series of dots representing the different components of the sample, with the most polar near the bottom and the least polar near the top. An R_f *factor* can be calculated for each component by dividing the distance traveled by the component by the distance traveled by the solvent. Non-polar components have an R_f factor close to one; polar components have a lower R_f factor. The R_f factor can be used to identify each component.

Thin-layer chromatography is similar to paper chromatography except that a coated glass or plastic plate is used instead of paper, and the results are visualized via an iodine vapor chamber.

FIGURE 4.4 | Paper Chromatography

- Solvent line
- Component 1
- Component 2
- Mixture

d_s d_1

$$R_f \text{ for component 1} = \frac{d_1}{d_s}$$

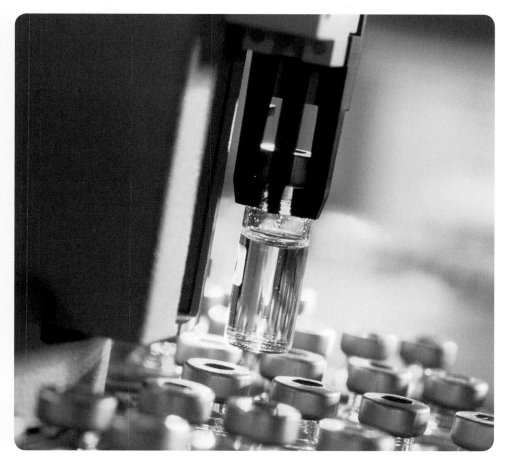

Gas chromatography is carried out to separate complex mixtures of compounds into individual components, allowing the composition to be analyzed and particular fractions to be isolated.

In **gas-liquid chromatography**, the stationary phase is liquid. The mixture is dissolved into a heated carrier gas (usually helium or nitrogen) and passed over a liquid phase bound to a column. Compounds in the mixture equilibrate with the liquid phase at different rates and pass through an exit port as individual components. Gas-liquid chromatography outputs a graph that shows peaks that elute at different times. The area under each peak corresponds to the amount of each molecule eluted.

Other types of chromatography are particularly well-suited for the separation of peptides and proteins. In **size-exclusion chromatography**, molecules are separated by their size and sometimes molecular weight, often through gel filtration. While it may seem counterintuitive, large molecules elute first in size-exclusion chromatography. This is because they do not penetrate well into the stationary phase, so they travel quickly down the length of the column. Small molecules, by contrast, are able to diffuse through the network of the stationary phase, lengthening the time they spend in the column and eluting later. In **ion-exchange chromatography**, molecules are separated based on their net surface charge. This form of chromatography utilizes cationic or anionic "exchangers" that slow down the movement of charged molecules. **Affinity chromatography** uses highly specific interactions to slow down select molecules, rather than simply separating out all molecules that have a particular property. Affinity chromatography can make use of receptor-ligand, enzyme-substrate, and antigen-antibody interactions, among others.

FIGURE 4.5 | Gel Electrophoresis

1 DNA (or RNA) fragments are loaded into wells at the top of the gel and an electrical field is applied.

Samples

Gel

2 DNA (or RNA) fragments of different lengths migrate different distances through the agarose gel, forming distinct bands.

Higher mass fragments

Lower mass fragments

The recipe for finding a piece of DNA via gel electrophoresis and a Southern blot is:

1. Chop up some DNA,

2. Use an electric field (gel electrophoresis) to spread out pieces according to size,

3. (Southern) blot it onto a membrane,

4. Add a radioactive probe made from DNA or RNA,

5. Visualize.

Separation and Purification of Nucleic Acids and Peptides

This lecture has focused so far on separations of molecules that are fundamentally different from one another, including separations of polar compounds from non-polar compounds, volatile compounds from much less volatile ones, and so on. There are also techniques that can be used to separate very similar compounds from one another, including different peptides or proteins, mixtures of nucleic acids of varying sizes, or mixtures of enantiomers.

Mixtures of nucleic acids (DNA and RNA fragments) or mixtures of proteins/polypeptides can be separated based on size and charge by **gel electrophoresis**. In gel electrophoresis, the molecular mixture is placed in a gel, and an electric field is applied.

Because nucleic acids are negatively charged, they migrate through the gel in response to the electric field. Larger particles move more slowly, since the agarose gel used for separation of nucleic acids forms a porous matrix and smaller pieces can more easily wind through the pores. After applying the electric field for an appropriate amount of time, nucleic acid fragments of different lengths will have migrated different distances, forming distinct "bands" that can be visualized, usually after blotting, which is discussed below.

Proteins are too large to be separated by pores, so a different type of gel is used. Proteins in a mixture are normally denatured in the presence of a detergent before they are placed in the gel. The detergent coats each protein with negative charge proportional to its length. When an electric field is applied, proteins migrate at a rate proportional to their charge and length. Like nucleic acids, proteins of a distinct size will be visualized as a "band" in the gel. Proteins can also be separated via gel electrophoresis based on their **isoelectric points (pI)**, discussed in the Acids and Bases Lecture of the *Chemistry* manual. In isoelectric focusing, a gel with a stable pH gradient is used. When an electric field is applied, the proteins in a pH region below their isoelectric point will be positively charged and move towards the cathode (the negatively charged electrode). As it migrates into regions of the gel with increasing pH, the overall positive charge on the protein will decrease, making the protein progressively more neutral. Once all the protein reaches the position in the gel where the gel pH equals the pI of the protein, the protein has no net charge and stops moving. Proteins appear as sharp bands when the gel is exposed.

In order to identify the size or quantity of DNA, RNA, or polypeptide present in a band, gel electrophoresis is often performed with a "ladder" alongside. A ladder is a mixture of DNA, RNA, or polypeptide fragments of known sizes or quantities. The migration distances of the experimental mixture's bands can be compared against those of the ladder's bands to determine approximate size. Computerized visualization software can be used to compare the intensity of a band to the intensity of a known standard in order to approximate quantity. Bands from the gel can also be isolated and purified for further study or manipulation.

Once gel electrophoresis has been used to separate molecules according to their physical properties, particular nucleic acids or proteins can be visualized using "blotting." Blotting is a technique by which molecules are transferred from the gel onto a membrane, maintaining the same spatial relationship of bands based on size. This transfer to a membrane allows for easier manipulation or visualization of the molecules.

Southern blotting is a technique used to identify target fragments of a known DNA sequence in a large population of DNA. A Southern blot begins with DNA that has already been cleaved and then resolved (separated) by gel electrophoresis. The gel is first placed in a basic solution in order to denature the DNA fragments, meaning that the double-stranded structure separates into single strands. A membrane, such as a sheet of *nitrocellulose*, is placed on top of or below the gel, and the resolved, single-stranded DNA fragments are transferred to the membrane. A labeled probe with a nucleotide sequence complementary to the target fragment

Southern blotting: A researcher transfers an electrophoresis gel containing DNA into a tray of salt solution prior to blotting the DNA onto nitrocellulose paper. The purple dye shows how far electrophoresis has progressed. Southern blotting is a technique used to reveal specific fragments of DNA (deoxyribonucleic acid) in a complex mixture. The total DNA is cut into fragments and separated by gel electrophoresis according to size. The DNA is then blotted onto a sheet of nitrocellulose, and a radioactive DNA is probe added to the nitrocellulose. The resulting banding pattern can be used to map the structure of particular genes.

A Southern blot identifies specific sequences of DNA by nucleic acid hybridization, and a Northern blot uses the same technique to identify specific sequences of RNA.

is added to the membrane. The probe hybridizes with and marks the target fragment. The membrane is then visualized to reveal the location of the probe and the target fragment. A radiolabelled probe was traditionally used, which required membrane exposure to radiographic film. There are now other detection methodologies available, such as fluorescence.

A *Northern blot* is just like a Southern blot, but it identifies RNA fragments, not DNA fragments.

A **Western blot** is used to detect a particular protein in a mixture of proteins. Although some of the specific steps are different, the basic process of transferring the resolved protein mixture from a gel to a separate membrane after electrophoresis is the same as in Southern and Northern blotting.

While there are numerous ways to visualize a protein following a Western blot, antibodies are commonly used. In this technique, an antibody (the *primary antibody*) specific to the protein in question is placed on the membrane. This primary antibody will only bind to the protein of interest. A *secondary antibody-enzyme* conjugate is then added. The secondary antibody recognizes and binds to the primary antibody and marks it with an enzyme for subsequent visualization. The reaction catalyzed by the enzyme attached to the secondary antibody produces a colored, fluorescent, or radioactive reaction product that can be visualized.

The **separation of enantiomers** from a **racemic mixture**, called chiral resolution, is a particular challenge because enantiomers have almost exactly the same physical and chemical properties. Generally speaking, there are two ways to resolve enantiomers. The first uses differences in crystallization of the enantiomers; in this case, direct visualization of the crystals can be used to separate enantiomers. Second, there are a number of stereospecific enzymes that can be added to a racemic mixture and will react with only one enantiomer in the mixture, creating a compound that can be separated using the types of techniques described previously. Once the altered enantiomer has been removed, the reaction can be reversed to produce the pure enantiomer. Enantiomers in a racemic mixture can also be converted into diastereomers, which have different physical and chemical properties that can be used for separation.

Remember Key 1: Don't let separation techniques scare you. Just remember that you can use the physical and chemical properties of different molecules to separate them from one another. Start by identifying which property is being used, and then apply what you know about those properties to help you answer the questions.

Question 73

Which of the following is NOT true concerning gel electrophoresis?

- ○ **A.** Nucleic acids can be separated by size based on migration through pores.
- ○ **B.** Nucleic acids migrate through gel in the presence of an electric field due to their negative charge.
- ○ **C.** Proteins can be separated by size based on migration through pores.
- ○ **D.** Proteins can be separated based on isoelectric point.

Question 74

Laboratory tests that measure the levels of elemental calcium and magnesium in a patient's blood can be confounded by the presence of carbonic acid, H_2CO_3. Which of the following molecules would most likely be mixed with a blood sample, then the resulting mixture separated, to improve the accuracy of calcium measurements?

- ○ **A.** NaOH
- ○ **B.** H_3PO_4
- ○ **C.** CH_3CH_2OH
- ○ **D.** NH_3

Question 75

In order to isolate insulin from a protein mixture taken from pancreatic beta cells of a mouse, scientists designed a column coated with antibodies against insulin. Isolation via this method can best be described as:

- ○ **A.** high pressure liquid chromatography.
- ○ **B.** ion exchange chromatography.
- ○ **C.** size exclusion chromatography.
- ○ **D.** affinity chromatography.

Question 76

In thin layer chromatography, polar compounds will:

- ○ **A.** rise more slowly through the silica gel than nonpolar compounds.
- ○ **B.** rise more quickly through the silica gel than nonpolar compounds.
- ○ **C.** move to the left through the silica gel.
- ○ **D.** move to the right through the silica gel.

Question 77

Which of the following statements is (are) true concerning separations?

- I. Any two compounds with sufficiently different boiling points can be separated completely by distillation.
- II. Crystallization is an efficient method of compound purification for most compounds.
- III. Distillation is most effective when it is carried out slowly.

- ○ **A.** I only
- ○ **B.** III only
- ○ **C.** I and III only
- ○ **D.** II and III only

Question 78

Which of the following blotting techniques is (are) used for nucleic acids?

- I. Southern
- II. Northern
- III. Western

- ○ **A.** I only
- ○ **B.** I and II only
- ○ **C.** II only
- ○ **D.** I, II, and III

Question 79

Which of the following is NOT a valid method for separation of a racemic mixture?

- ○ **A.** Visualization of crystals
- ○ **B.** Extraction via aqueous and polar phases
- ○ **C.** Utilization of stereospecific enzymes followed by separation
- ○ **D.** Conversion to diastereomers followed by separation

Question 80

In gel electrophoresis, DNA fragments are separated according to size. Which of the following is true of this process?

- ○ **A.** Positively charged DNA fragments move toward the cathode.
- ○ **B.** Positively charged DNA fragments move toward the anode.
- ○ **C.** Negatively charged DNA fragments move toward the cathode.
- ○ **D.** Negatively charged DNA fragments move toward the anode.

STOP

Spectroscopy

Spectroscopy is the study of the interaction between matter and electromagnetic radiation (light). Distinct regions of the electromagnetic spectrum interact differently with matter, providing information about the structures of molecules.

TABLE 4.1 > Spectroscopy Summary

Type of Spectroscopy	Region of Electromagnetic Spectrum	Structural Information Provided
Nuclear Magnetic Resonance (NMR)	Radio waves	Arrangement of carbon and hydrogen atoms
Infrared (IR)	Infrared light	Presence of functional groups
Ultraviolet-Visible (UV-Vis)	Ultraviolet light and visible light	Presence of conjugated π systems

Nuclear Magnetic Resonance (NMR) spectroscopy is the study of the interaction between atomic nuclei and radio waves. Nuclei with odd atomic or mass numbers possess a mechanical property called *nuclear spin*. Hydrogen-1, for example, has an odd atomic and mass number. Carbon-13 has an even atomic number but an odd mass number. A spinning proton, like any other rotating sphere of charge, generates a magnetic field, in this case around the nucleus.

When subject to an external magnetic field, the magnetic field of the nucleus aligns either with or against the external field. Nuclei whose fields align with the external field are said to occupy lower energy α spin states. Those whose fields are aligned against the external field are said to occupy higher energy β spin states. The stronger the magnetic field, the greater the difference in energy, ΔE, between the low energy and high energy states.

As discussed in Lecture 1 of the *Chemistry* manual, the energy of a photon is equal to Planck's constant times the frequency of the associated electromagnetic wave: $\Delta E = h\nu$. Photons whose energies are equal to the ΔE between the two spin states can cause nuclei to flip orientations. Atoms whose spins are aligned with the external field flip and align against it when they absorb a photon with energy equal to ΔE. Nuclei that have flipped to the β spin state are said to be in resonance with the external magnetic field. When protons return to their original spin states, they release electrical impulses that are detected by an NMR spectrometer.

Understand Key 2: The spectroscopy techniques "read" the functional groups on compounds to provide information about chemical structure, reactivity, polarity, among many other physics properties. Spectroscopy techniques are used to identify the specific features of molecules.

Electricity
≡ PHYSICS

The stronger the magnetic field, the greater the difference in energy between the α and β spin states.

FIGURE 4.6 | α and β Spin States

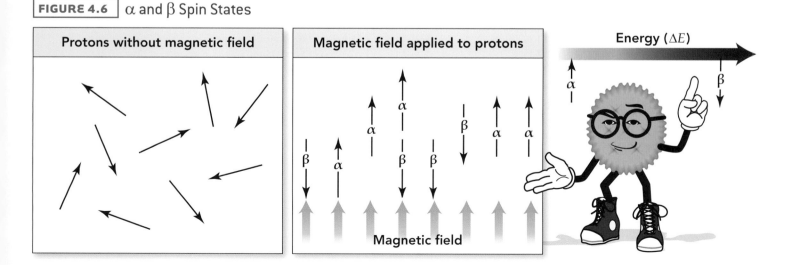

FIGURE 4.7 | NMR and Magnetic Field Strength

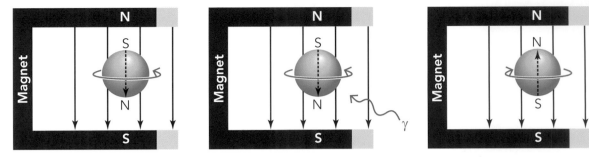

Low energy state   High energy state

Don't be intimidated by unfamiliar phrases like magnetic resonance and nuclear spin. Protons and electrons will behave just like any other type of moving charge.

FIGURE 4.8 | NMR Spectrum

The molecule has two chemically distinct hydrogen populations, which give rise to two peaks. H_a has one hydrogen on each of the neighboring carbons, for a total of two neighboring hydrogens. Using the n+1 rule, three peaks are generated. H_b has only one hydrogen on a neighboring carbon. Using the n+1 rule, two peaks are generated.

In NMR, the frequency of the electromagnetic radiation is held constant while the magnetic field strength is varied. Hydrogen atoms within distinct compounds or functional groups experience different surrounding electron densities and are uniquely affected by the magnetic fields of nearby protons. Electrons shield protons from the external magnetic field, so the external field must be strengthened for a shielded proton to achieve resonance. Due to this effect, protons within a compound absorb electromagnetic energy of the same frequency at different magnetic field strengths.

An NMR spectrum is a graph of the magnetic field strengths absorbed by the hydrogen, carbon, or other odd atomic number atoms of a specific compound at a single frequency. The field strength is measured in parts per million, ppm, and, despite the decreasing numbers indicated in the spectrum, increases from left to right. The leftward direction is called downfield and the rightward is called *upfield*. All the way to the right is a peak at 0 ppm. This peak represents the hydrogen atoms of *tetramethylsilane*, a reference compound that is used to calibrate the instrument.

Very little specific information about NMR is required for the MCAT®. Remember that unless otherwise indicated, NMR is concerned with hydrogen atoms. An MCAT® problem could provide an NMR spectrum and ask which peaks belong to which hydrogen atoms on a given compound, or which of four compounds would create the given spectrum. Answering this type of question requires an understanding of the following principles:

- Each peak represents chemically equivalent hydrogens,

- Splitting of peaks is caused by "neighboring hydrogens."

Each peak indicates one or a group of chemically equivalent hydrogens, meaning hydrogens whose positions on the compound are indistinguishable by NMR. Hydrogens that are chemically equivalent have the same chemical shift. Chemical shift is the difference between the resonance frequency of the chemically shifted hydrogens and the resonance frequency of hydrogens on a reference compound such as tetramethylsilane.

The area under a peak is proportional to the number of hydrogens represented by that peak. The more chemically equivalent hydrogens, the greater the area. The tallest peak does not necessarily correspond to the greatest area. The *integral trace* is a line drawn above the peaks that rises each time it goes over a peak. The rise of the integral trace is proportional to the number of chemically equivalent hydrogens in the peak beneath it. A newer instrument, called a digital trace, records numbers that correspond to the rise in the line. The exact number of hydrogens cannot be determined from the integral or digital trace. However, comparing the values assigned to different peaks provides the ratio of hydrogens between peaks.

The position of a peak on the NMR spectrum is dictated by electron shielding, so the positions of different groups of hydrogens can be predicted based on the presence of electron-withdrawing and electron-donating groups. Electron-withdrawing groups tend to lower shielding and thus decrease the magnetic field strength at which resonance takes place. Hydrogens adjacent to electron-withdrawing groups tend to have peaks downfield (to the left). Electron-donating groups tend to increase shielding and increase the field strength required for resonance.

Splitting (also called **spin–spin splitting**) of a peak into several smaller peaks is caused by neighboring hydrogens that are not chemically equivalent. A neighboring hydrogen is one that is bound to an atom adjacent to the atom to which the other hydrogen is connected. The number of peaks due to splitting for a group of chemically equivalent hydrogens is given by the simple formula n + 1, where *n* is the number of **neighboring hydrogens** that are not chemically equivalent. The number of neighboring hydrogens for a given peak can be determined by subtracting 1 from the number of smaller peaks into which the peak is split.

To interpret proton NMR spectroscopy, follow these steps:

- Identify chemically equivalent hydrogens.

- Identify and count neighboring hydrogens that are not chemically equivalent. Use n + 1 to determine the number of peaks created by splitting for the chemically equivalent hydrogens.

- If necessary, identify electron withdrawing/donating groups near the chemically equivalent hydrogens. Withdrawing groups will move the signal to the left; donating groups will move the signal to the right.

Aldehyde protons have a very distinctive shift at 9.5 ppm. Watch for it.

In a rare situation, carbon NMR may also appear on the MCAT®. Remember, the nucleus must have an odd atomic or mass number to register on NMR, so carbon-13 is the only carbon isotope that would register. Treat carbon NMR the same way as proton NMR, but ignore splitting.

For the MCAT®, it is helpful to know a few chemical shifts:
- aldehyde protons appear around 9.5 ppm
- carboxylic acid protons appear between 10-12 ppm
- benzene protons appear around 8 ppm
- alcohol protons appear between 1-5 ppm
- methyl protons appear at shifts less than 1 ppm.

NMR can be more complicated than is described here, but the MCAT® would provide any additional information necessary to solve complex problems. Figure 4.9 presents an additional NMR spectrum that can be used to test understanding. Before reading further, try to predict which hydrogens belong to which group of peaks (see answer on p. 124).

(see answer on p. 124)

FIGURE 4.9 | NMR Spectrum with Integral Trace

IR spectroscopy uses molecular dipoles to find information about functional groups. A dipole exists when the centers of positive and negative charge do not coincide. When exposed to an electric field, these oppositely charged centers move in opposite directions, either toward or away from each other. In infrared radiation, the direction of the electric field oscillates, causing the positive and negative centers within polar bonds to move toward each other and then away from each other. When exposed to radiation in the **infrared region** of the electromagnetic spectrum, the polar bonds within a compound stretch and contract, causing **intramolecular vibrations and rotations**.

Different bonds vibrate at different frequencies. When the resonance frequency of the oscillating bond is matched by the frequency of infrared radiation, the IR energy is absorbed. In **IR spectroscopy**, an infrared spectrometer slowly changes the frequency of infrared light shining on a compound and records the frequencies of absorption in number of cycles per centimeter, cm^{-1}. If a bond has no dipole moment, infrared radiation does not cause it to vibrate and no energy is absorbed.

FIGURE 4.10 | Vibration of a Dipole

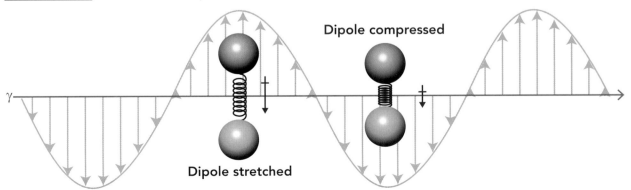

The most predictable section of the IR spectrum is in the 1600 to 3500 cm^{-1} region. Figure 4.11 depicts the shapes and frequencies of absorption associated with common functional groups, which should be known for the MCAT®.

Limited predictions about the vibration of a bond can be made based on the masses of the atoms involved and the stiffness of the bond between them. Atoms with greater mass resonate at lower frequencies. Stiffer bonds, such as double and triple bonds, resonate at higher frequencies. Bond strength and bond stiffness follow the same trend: $sp > sp^2 > sp^3$.

An IR spectrum can help identify which functional groups are included in a compound, but it does not reveal the shape or length of the carbon skeleton. Two compounds are very unlikely to have exactly the same IR spectrum, so a compound's spectrum can act as its "fingerprint." Many of the complex vibrations

> The MCAT® may require knowledge of the IR spectra of certain functional groups. The most likely spectra that would be tested by MCAT® are C=O, a sharp dip around 1700 cm^{-1}, and O-H, a broad dip around 3200-3600 cm^{-1}. A few other common groups include C≡C, a sharp dip around 2200 cm^{-1}, and C-O a sharp dip around 1100 cm^{-1}. The broad dips for O-H and N-H are due to the effects of hydrogen bonding.

FIGURE 4.11 | IR Absorption of Common Functional Groups

MCAT® THINK

So far, we've talked about how
the bonds in molecules absorb
infrared radiation of a characteristic frequency. However, bonds
also emit radiation. The higher
the temperature, the greater the
amount of radiation emitted by
bonds. Because cancerous tissue
tends to be warmer than surrounding tissue, medical imaging
professionals have suggested that
infrared radiation detectors could
be used to identify breast cancer.
This still controversial method
of detection is known as thermal
imaging, or thermography.

that distinguish one compound from a similar compound are found in the 600 to
1400 cm⁻¹ region, called the fingerprint region. Figure 4.12 shows three sample
spectra that include the fingerprint region. Know where the fingerprint region is
and why it is called the fingerprint region, but use the higher frequency range to
identify functional groups.

FIGURE 4.12 Sample IR Spectra

The **ultraviolet** region of the electromagnetic spectrum has much shorter
wavelengths than infrared light, between 200 and 400 nm, and at a much higher
energy level. **Ultraviolet (UV) spectroscopy** detects **conjugated systems** (double
bonds separated by one single bond) by comparing the intensities of two beams
of light from the same monochromatic light source. One beam is shone through
a sample cell and the other is shone through a reference cell. The sample cell
contains the sample compound to be analyzed dissolved in a solvent, while the
reference cell contains only the solvent. The difference in energy absorbed by the
sample and the reference is recorded as a UV spectrum of the sample compound.

The UV spectrum provides limited information about the length and structure of the conjugated portion of the molecule. When a photon collides with an electron in a molecule in the sample, the photon may be absorbed, bumping an electron up to a vacant molecular orbital. These are typically π-electron movements from bonding to nonbonding orbitals (π → π*). Electrons in σ-bonds usually require more energy to reach the next highest orbital, so they are typically unaffected by wavelengths greater than 200 nm. Conjugated systems with π-bonds, on the other hand, have vacant orbitals at energy levels close to their highest occupied molecular orbital (HOMO) energy levels. Such a vacant orbitals is called LUMO (lowest unoccupied molecular orbital). UV photons can momentarily displace electrons to the LUMO.

If a conjugated system is present in the sample, the measured intensity of the radiation after passing through the sample will be lower than that of the reference, due to absorption. The absorbance of the sample can be calculated as the logarithm of sample intensity divided by reference intensity. Absorbance also equals the product of concentration of the sample (c), the length of the path of light through the cell (l), and the molar absorptivity (ε):

$$A = \varepsilon c l$$

Molar absorptivity is a measure of how strongly the sample absorbs light at a particular wavelength. It can be thought of mathematically, as $\varepsilon = A/cl$.

The longer the chain of conjugated double bonds, the greater the wavelength of absorption. The rule of thumb is that each additional conjugated double bond increases the wavelength by about 30 to 40 nm. An additional alkyl group attached to any atom involved in the conjugated system increases the spectrum wavelength by about 5 nm. Isolated double bonds do not affect the absorption wavelength.

UV spectra lack detail. Samples must be extremely pure or the spectrum is obscured. Figure 4.13 shows the UV spectrum of 2-methyl-1,3-butadiene dissolved in methanol. The methyl group increases the absorption wavelength slightly. The methanol solvent makes no contribution to the spectrum. Spectra are typically represented by lists rather than being printed. The spectrum below would be listed as:

$$\lambda_{max} = 222 \text{ nm} \qquad \varepsilon = 20,000$$

Carbonyls, compounds with carbon-oxygen double bonds, also absorb light in the UV region. Acetone has a broad absorption peak at 280 nm. In this instance, unshared pairs of electrons are excited into a nonbonding π-orbital (n→ π*).

The rule of thumb for UV absorption is a 30 to 40 nm increase for each additional conjugated double bond, and a 5 nm increase for each additional alkyl group.

Isolated   Conjugated

FIGURE 4.13 | UV Absorbance of 2-methyl-1,3-butadiene

Keep your spectroscopies straight! NMR deals with the magnetic spin of hydrogen or carbon nuclei; IR spectroscopy deals with the way IR light causes bonds with dipoles to vibrate and rotate; and UV spectroscopy deals with the way UV light affects electrons in conjugated systems.

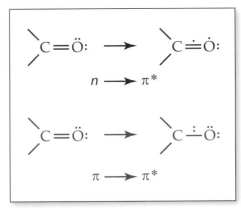

Change in molecular orbital levels upon absorption of a photon.

FIGURE 4.14 Mass Spectrometer

FIGURE 4.14 Mass Spectrometer

A mass spectrometer ionizes and fragments molecules in a sample, and then fires the fragments through a magnetic field. The amount that the fragments deviate is indicative of their mass and charge. This deviation provides detailed information about the sample's composition. A mass spectrometer is shown in the photo above.

If a compound has eight or more double bonds, its absorbance moves into the **visible region** of the electromagnetic spectrum. β-carotene, a precursor of vitamin A, has 11 conjugated double bonds. β-carotene has a maximum absorbance at 497 nm. Electromagnetic radiation of 497 nm has a blue-green color. Because carrots contain β-carotene, they absorb blue-green light, giving them the **complementary color** of red-orange. Structural changes in a compound can push its absorbance into the visible region; this is the mechanism behind the use of indicators in titrations.

Mass Spectrometry

In contrast to spectroscopy, which studies interactions between matter and electromagnetic radiation, spectrometry is the study of interactions between matter and energy sources other than electromagnetic radiation. **Mass spectrometry** is used to determine a compound's molecular weight, and, in the case of high resolution mass spectrometry, its molecular formula.

In a mass spectrometer, the molecules of a sample are bombarded with electrons, causing them to break apart and to ionize. The largest ion is the size of the original molecule but has one less electron. This cation is called the *molecular ion*. If methane were the sample, the molecular ion would be CH_4^+.

After a molecule is broken apart, the ions are accelerated through a magnetic field. The resulting force deflects the ions around a curved path. The radius of curvature of their path depends upon their *mass to charge ratio* (m/z). Most of the ions have a charge of 1+. The magnetic field strength is altered to allow the passage of differently sized ions through the flight tube.

A computer records the numbers of ions that arrive at the detector at different magnetic field strengths as peaks on a chart. The largest peak is called the *base peak*. The peak made by the molecular ions is called the *parent peak*. The parent peak is made by molecules that did not fragment. Look for the parent peak all the way to the right of the spectrum. Only heavy isotopes will be further right. All peaks are assigned *abundances* as percentages of the base peak. In Figure 4.14, the parent peak has an abundance of 10 because it is 10% as high as the base peak.

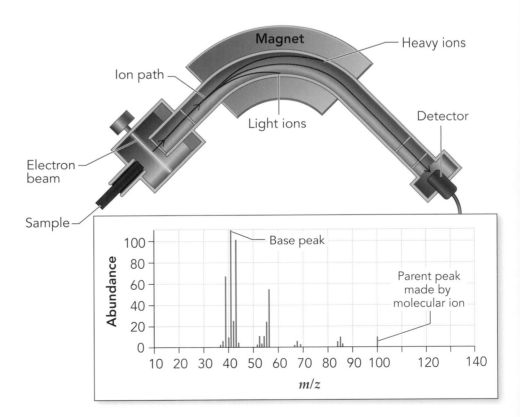

These questions are NOT related to a passage.

Question 81

All of the following are true concerning NMR spectroscopy EXCEPT:

- ○ **A.** protons are distinguished when they absorb magnetic energy at different field strengths.
- ○ **B.** "downfield" is to the left on an NMR spectrum.
- ○ **C.** functional groups are distinguished when they absorb magnetic energy at different field strengths.
- ○ **D.** delocalized electrons generate magnetic fields that can either shield or deshield nearby protons.

Question 82

Which of the following structures is most likely to produce the infrared spectroscopy result depicted below?

- ○ **A.**

- ○ **B.**

- ○ **C.**

- ○ **D.**

Question 83

A carbonyl group will absorb infrared radiation at a frequency of approximately:

- ○ **A.** 700 – 900 Hz.
- ○ **B.** 1630 – 1700 Hz.
- ○ **C.** 2220 – 2260 Hz.
- ○ **D.** 3300 – 3500 Hz.

Question 84

What are the predicted numbers of C^{13} NMR peaks for methylcyclopentane and 1,2-dimethylbenzene, respectively?

Methylcyclopentane   1,2-Dimethylbenzene

- ○ **A.** 2,3
- ○ **B.** 3,4
- ○ **C.** 4,4
- ○ **D.** 5,3

Question 85

Researchers used NMR spectroscopy in an attempt to characterize the molecule depicted in the inset below. Which of the following are represented by the peak at ~3.6 ppm?

- ○ **A.** The "D" hydrogens
- ○ **B.** The "C" oxygen
- ○ **C.** The "B" carbon
- ○ **D.** The "A" hydrogens

Question 86

Which of the following must be FALSE concerning a molecule with a mass spectrometry parent peak of 134?

- ○ **A.** It normally carries no net charge.
- ○ **B.** It has a base peak at 15 m/z.
- ○ **C.** It has a molecular mass of 134 g/mol.
- ○ **D.** Its most abundant isotope has a mass of 160 g/mol.

Question 87

After analyzing both the products and reactants of a reaction, a chemist notices that a peak at roughly 3400 cm^{-1} has disappeared from the product reading. The reaction type was most likely:

- ○ **A.** elimination.
- ○ **B.** addition.
- ○ **C.** hydration of an alkene.
- ○ **D.** reduction of an aldehyde.

Question 88

Which of the following would show absorbance in the UV spectrum (200-400 nm)?

- ○ **A.**

- ○ **B.**

- ○ **C.**

- ○ **D.**

4.4 | Genetic Techniques

As noted in the Genetics Lecture, the scientific understanding of "genes" has evolved greatly over the last several decades. This is in part due to the use of genetic laboratory techniques. It is possible not only to isolate a gene and determine its function and origin, but also to manipulate it. A gene can be copied or altered, or we can cause it to be over- or under-expressed and observe the effects on the organism. Genetic techniques have a myriad of clinical, research, and ethical implications, and understanding them requires a strong grasp of basic biology and biochemistry.

Broadly speaking, there are three types of genetic laboratory techniques:

1. Nucleic acid manipulation. DNA and RNA can be manipulated on a macro or micro level. Techniques can be used to join two strands together, pry two strands apart, chop one piece into smaller pieces, or join smaller pieces into a larger piece.

2. Recombination and cloning. Many copies of the same piece of genetic material can be created and put in new places or otherwise manipulated.

3. Sequencing and function. Techniques can be used to determine the exact nucleotide sequence of a piece of DNA or RNA. A piece of nucleic acid that codes for a protein can also be used to determine the function of that gene or protein.

Nucleic Acid Manipulation

For a variety of reasons that will become clear later in this lecture, it is useful to know how to manipulate nucleic acids. More complicated lab techniques require the ability to convert DNA (or RNA) from 2 strands to 1 (and vice versa), as well as to chop up one big piece into many little pieces (and vice versa).

When heated or immersed in a high concentration salt solution or high pH solution, the hydrogen bonds connecting the two strands of a double-stranded DNA molecule are disrupted and the strands separate. The DNA molecule is said to be **denatured** or *melted*. The temperature required to separate DNA strands is called the *melting temperature* (T_m). Since guanine and cytosine make three hydrogen bonds while thymine and adenine make only two, DNA with more G–C base pairs has a greater T_m. Heating to 95°C (just below the boiling point of water) is generally sufficient to denature any DNA sequence. Denatured DNA is less viscous, denser, and more able to absorb UV light than double-stranded DNA.

Separated strands will spontaneously associate with their original partner or any other complementary nucleotide sequence when not in a denaturing environment. The following double-stranded combinations can be formed: DNA-DNA, DNA-RNA, and RNA-RNA. This is called **nucleic acid hybridization**. Hybridization techniques allow scientists to identify nucleotide sequences by binding a known sequence with an unknown sequence.

Denaturing goes from double strands to single strands. Hybridization goes from single strands to double strands.

Genetics
BIOLOGY 1

Understand Key 3: Genetic techniques are high yield on the MCAT®. Make sure you understand the basics of nucleic acids and proteins by reviewing Lecture 1 of this book for the properties of the biological molecules. It is important to know the steps of PCR and how DNA technology can be used to detect or treat human diseases.

To denature DNA means to separate the two strands of the double helix.

DNA prefers to be double-stranded and will look for a complementary partner.

Recombination and Cloning

Recombination techniques take advantage of a method that bacteria use to defend themselves from viruses: cutting the viral DNA into fragments using restriction enzymes. Bacteria protect their own DNA from these enzymes through **DNA methylation** (adding a −CH₃ group). **Restriction enzymes** (also called restriction endonucleases) *digest* (cut) nucleic acid only at certain nucleotide sequences along the chain (see Figure 4.15). Such a sequence is called a *restriction site* or *recognition sequence*. A restriction site is typically a *palindromic* sequence four to six nucleotides long. (Palindromic means that it reads the same backwards as forwards.) Most restriction endonucleases cleave the DNA strand unevenly, leaving complementary single-stranded ends. These ends can reconnect through hybridization and are termed *sticky ends*. Once paired, the phosphodiester bonds of the fragments can be joined by DNA ligase.

There are hundreds of known restriction endonucleases, each attacking a different restriction site. Any sample of DNA of significant size is likely to contain a recognition sequence for at least one restriction endonuclease.

In the laboratory, scientists take advantage of the fact that two DNA fragments cleaved by the same endonuclease can be joined together regardless of the origins of the fragments. DNA created by this method is called **recombinant DNA**; it has been artificially recombined. Scientists can digest multiple pieces of DNA with the same restriction enzyme and then "paste" the pieces together to make a desired piece of recombinant DNA. This technology can be used to generate a DNA library for the purpose of DNA cloning.

FIGURE 4.15 Recombinant DNA

There are many reasons that it might be necessary to clone or amplify a piece of DNA. Generally speaking, one copy of a piece of DNA is too small to be useful in a laboratory. In order to sequence, recombine, or manipulate the DNA, it is necessary to have many copies, which is achieved by **gene cloning**. Cloning is accomplished either through bacteria and a cDNA library, or through polymerase chain reaction (PCR).

Recombinant DNA can be placed within a bacterial genome using a **vector**, typically a **plasmid** or sometimes an infective virus (Figure 4.17). The bacteria can then be grown in large quantities to form a **clone** of cells containing the vector with the recombinant DNA fragment. The clones can be saved separately to produce a **clone library**.

Not all bacteria will take up the vector, so a library may contain some clones that do not contain vectors. Including a gene in the original vector that lends resistance to a certain antibiotic makes it possible to screen the clone library for bacteria that did not take up the vector. The addition of the antibiotic eliminates clones without resistance, which must not have taken up the vector. Since some vectors will not take up the DNA fragment, some clones that do contain vectors will have vectors that lack the recombinant DNA. To allow screening for these clones, the *lacZ* gene, which enables the bacteria to metabolize the sugar X-gal, can be included in the original vector. An endonuclease with a recognition site that cleaves the *lacZ* gene can then be used to place the DNA fragment into the vector. Since the endonuclease cleaves the *lacZ* gene and the recombinant DNA is inserted in the middle of the *lacZ* gene, the *lacZ* gene will not work when the DNA fragment is placed in the vector. Clones with an active *lacZ* gene turn blue in the presence of X-gal, while clones with the cleaved form of the gene do not turn blue. Clones with the DNA fragment will therefore not turn blue when placed on a medium with X-gal.

Part of the screening process involves finding the desired DNA sequence from a library. **Hybridization** can be used as a technique to find a particular gene in a library. A fluorescently or radioactively labeled complementary sequence of the desired DNA fragment (called a **probe**) is used to search the library. The labeled clones are then identified. In the case of radiolabelling, the labeled clones expose photographic film while the non–radiolabeled clones do not.

Eukaryotic DNA contains introns. Since bacteria have no mechanism for removing introns, it is useful to clone DNA with no introns (Figure 4.16). In order to do this, the mRNA produced by the DNA is reverse transcribed using reverse transcriptase. The DNA product is called **complementary DNA** or **cDNA**. Adding DNA polymerase to cDNA produces a double strand of the desired DNA fragment.

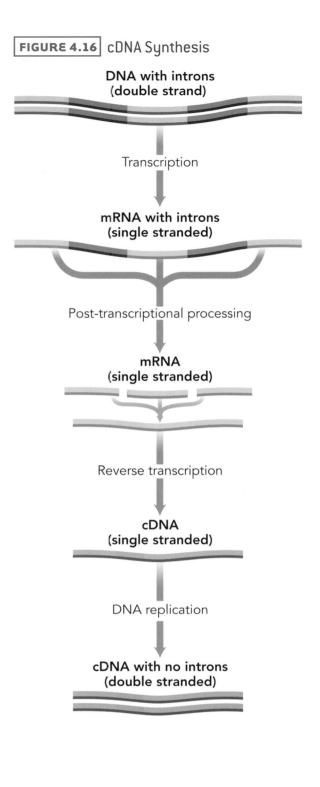

FIGURE 4.16 cDNA Synthesis

DNA with introns (double strand)

Transcription

mRNA with introns (single stranded)

Post-transcriptional processing

mRNA (single stranded)

Reverse transcription

cDNA (single stranded)

DNA replication

cDNA with no introns (double stranded)

To make a DNA library, take a DNA fragment, use a vector to insert it into a bacterium, and reproduce that bacterium like crazy. Now you have clones of bacteria with the DNA fragment.

cDNA is just DNA reverse transcribed from mRNA. The great thing about cDNA is that it lacks the introns that would normally be found in eukaryotic DNA.

FIGURE 4.17 Clone Library

1 **Plasmid (vector) and human DNA are isolated.**

2 **Human DNA fragment is inserted into plasmid.**

   a Human DNA and plasmids are digested with the same restriction enzyme.

   b Human DNA fragments and plasmids are mixed. Some plasmids join with the gene of interest.

   c DNA ligase is added.

3 **Plasmid is placed into bacteria by transformation.**

4 **Cells are cloned.**

   a Bacteria are plated onto medium with ampicillin and x-gal.

   b Only clones containing the recombinant plasmid are able to grow in the presence of ampicillin. Colonies that also contain the DNA fragment are white because their *lacZ* gene is nonfunctional, preventing the breakdown of x-gal.

5 **Identify clone carrying gene of interest.**

   Bacterial clones each carry a copy of the human gene of interest.

The cloning process isn't perfect, so some bacteria in a library won't have the vector and some vectors won't have the DNA fragment. To screen out these undesirable elements, the *lacZ* gene and an antibiotic resistant gene can be included in the preparation of the clone. Also, when preparing the clone, a restriction enzyme should be used that will insert the DNA fragment into the middle of the *lacZ* gene, causing it to be inactivated.

A much faster method of cloning, called **polymerase chain reaction (PCR)**, has been developed using a specialized polymerase enzyme found in a species of bacterium adapted to life in nearly boiling waters. In PCR, the double strand of DNA to be cloned is placed in a mixture with many copies of two DNA primers, one for each strand, a heat resistant polymerase, and a supply of nucleotides. The mixture is heated to 95°C to denature the DNA. When the mixture is cooled to 60°C, the primers hybridize (or **anneal**) to their complementary ends on the DNA strands. Next, the mixture is heated to 72°C to activate the polymerase. The polymerase amplifies the complementary strands, doubling the amount of DNA. The procedure can be repeated many times without adding more polymerase because the polymerase is heat resistant. A heat sensitive polymerase would be denatured by the high temperature required to denature the DNA and would have to be added each cycle. The result is an exponential increase in the amount of DNA. Starting with a single fragment, over one million copies (2^{20}) can be produced by 20 cycles. What used to require days with recombinant DNA techniques can now be done in hours with PCR. Another advantage of PCR is that minute DNA samples can be amplified. In order to use PCR, the base sequence flanking the ends of the DNA fragment must be known so that the complementary primers can be chosen.

Because the amount of target DNA doubles in each cycle, PCR can be used to quantify the amount of DNA in each cycle (and therefore the amount of starting DNA). This is called *quantitative PCR (qPCR)* or *real-time PCR*. Most commonly, qPCR uses a fluorescent dye or probe that binds to DNA and measures its concentration each cycle.

FIGURE 4.18 Polymerase Chain Reaction (PCR)

1 Loading
Target DNA, primers, and heat resistance polymerase are placed into a PCR thermal cycler.

2 Denaturing
Temperature is increased to separate target DNA strands.

3 Annealing
Temperature is decreased and primers hybridize with target DNA.

primers

4 Replication
Heat resistant polymerase replicates target DNA.

polymerase

5 Amplification
Repeating the cycle exponentially amplifies the target DNA.

CYCLE 1	CYCLE 2	CYCLE 3	CYCLE 20
2 copies	2^2 = 4 copies	2^3 = 8 copies	2^{20} = over 1,000,000 copies

Sequencing and Function

Given a piece of DNA or RNA, genetic techniques can be used to determine its sequence, and correspondingly, what protein it will produce. It is also possible to determine the function of that protein.

Although **DNA sequencing** was first performed in the 1970s, it has become much more efficient and orders of magnitude faster. For many years, a *chain-termination method* called the *Sanger method* (Figure 4.19) was the main technique for sequencing. In this method, DNA is repeatedly replicated *in vitro*, with researchers providing all the necessary reagents, including all 4 nucleotides, primers, and enzymes. The researchers also add a small quantity of dideoxynucleotide (ddNTP) into the mix. Because of their structure, ddNTPs are incorporated into the growing DNA strand, but result in termination of replication ("chain-termination") once incorporated. The chain termination method involves setting up four replication tubes, each one containing one type of ddNTP (ddATP, ddTTP, ddCTP, and ddGTP).

In the tube containing both adenine and ddATP, each time the DNA replicated and attempted to incorporate an adenine, there would be a chance that it would instead choose ddATP, resulting in chain termination. If this replication cycle was repeated many times over (as in PCR), there would be some DNA strands that terminated at every adenine. Similarly, there would be strands terminating at every thymine in the ddTTP tube, every guanine in the ddGTP tube, and every cytosine in the ddCTP tube. Gel electrophoresis could then be used to compare the relative lengths of the strands. With this gel, it is relatively straightforward to determine the sequence of the replicated DNA segment.

More recently, rapid "next generation" DNA sequencing methods have been developed using automated systems. One such example utilizes fluorescence, with 4 differently colored molecules attached to each of the four nucleotides. DNA is replicated in vitro with these "colored" nucleotides. The new piece of DNA is thus color-coded, and can be passed through a computerized reader, which translates the sequence of colors into a DNA sequence.

| FIGURE 4.19 | Sanger Method

| FIGURE 4.20 | Automated Sequencing

Nucleotides in DNA are labeled using fluorescence.

Automated DNA sequencing machines utilize capillary electrophoresis and ultra-violet laser to detect fluorescent dyes.

A computer interprets data from the sequencing machines and determines the exact sequence of nucleotides.

Gene expression levels for any given DNA sequence can vary greatly depending on cell type as well as intracellular and extracellular conditions. **Analyzing gene expression** requires measuring the gene's downstream mRNA or protein product. This can be done on a large scale through a *DNA microarray* or *gene chip*. A gene chip compares the levels of mRNA between two cells and/or conditions. One of these microarrays may contain probes (small DNA sequences complimentary to mRNA) for hundreds or thousands of genes.

To run a gene chip, mRNA from two conditions (often the same cell type before and after a stimulus) must be isolated. mRNA from the first situation is labeled in red, while mRNA from the second is labeled in green. Both sets of mRNA are then incubated with the same gene chip. Genes that are down-regulated from situation 1 to 2 appear as red dots in the appropriate area of the gene chip, since more red-labeled mRNA is present to bind to the probes. Likewise, genes that are up-regulated appear green. If a gene's expression level remains unchanged, there will be an equal amount of green and red mRNA, creating a yellow spot on the microarray.

FIGURE 4.21 Gene Chip

Microarrays, or gene chips, show which genes are active in the cells being tested.

In addition to examining gene sequence and expression, researchers are often interested in **determining gene function**. There are a variety of ways that the function of a gene can be determined. One method is to observe gene conservation or evolution among different species. More modern techniques involve direct manipulation of genes. Some of these techniques involve observing the results of a reduction or elimination of gene expression. Others allow observation of the results when a gene is over-expressed, or when the gene is expressed in a cell, tissue, or organism in which it is not normally expressed.

A common method used to examine gene function is to create a genetic *knockout*, in which a target gene is deleted from the genome. Once the gene is knocked out, cells can be analyzed for phenotypic changes, providing information about the function of the gene that was removed. A knockout can refer to a cell line or to an entire organism; the latter is termed a knockout animal. In order to make a knockout animal, it is necessary to knock out the genes from gametes or from embryonic **stem cells** and to grow the animal from a zygote. (Note that if the gene to be knocked out is necessary for embryonic development, it will be impossible to generate a true knockout animal.) As an example, a mouse model of diabetes can be generated by knocking out the gene that codes for the insulin receptor.

Gene expression can also be reduced by the use of *RNA interference*, or *RNAi*. RNAi is a naturally occurring biological process in which small pieces of RNA bind to mRNA molecules, preventing their translation and/or marking them for degradation. Scientists can exploit this process to block expression of specific genes.

It is possible to examine a gene's function by causing it to be overexpressed. One method is to alter the sequence of the gene's surrounding DNA, such as by increasing the strength of the promoter before a gene, thus increasing the expression of that gene. Another method is to express the gene in a new cell line or organism. For instance, the gene that codes for the green fluorescent protein in jellyfish can be placed in the genome of an organism from another species, which then produces the protein and glows green.

Endocrine System
BIOLOGY 2

This photo shows a mosquito larva which has had a green fluorescent protein (GFP) gene, from a jellyfish, inserted into its genome.

MCAT® THINK

Manipulating genes in animals is one of the most common ways to create animal models of human diseases. Here's one example: deletion of certain genes involved in cell cycle checkpoints can result in animals that are more prone to cancer. These animals can be studied to help us better understand the disease pathogenesis and treatment options.

Practical Applications of Genetic Techniques

All of the aforementioned genetic lab techniques have a host of practical applications in medicine and research. They can be used to identify individuals by their genetic code, treat genetic diseases, screen for carriers of genetic disorders, and much more.

Restriction fragment length polymorphism (**RFLP**) analysis identifies individuals, rather than identifying specific genes. The genomes of distinct individuals possess varying restriction sites and distances between restriction sites. In other words, the human population is *polymorphic* for their restriction sites. After fragmenting the DNA sample with endonucleases, a band pattern unique to an individual is revealed on radiographic film via Southern blotting techniques. RFLPs (pronounced "riflips") are the DNA fingerprints used to identify criminals in court cases.

The genome of one human differs from the genome of another at about one nucleotide in every 1000. These differences have been called *single nucleotide polymorphisms* (SNPs). Like RFLPs, SNPs can serve as a fingerprint for an individual's genome.

One of the "holy grails" of medical research is curative treatment of genetic diseases. One method used by researchers is **human gene therapy**. Gene therapy involves genetic manipulation of an affected individual's DNA, in which the defective allele of the gene is replaced by the wild type, or correctly functioning, allele. Theoretically, gene therapy can be accomplished by recombining the DNA in all defective cells, such as with a viral vector, or by altering the genome of a stem cell and letting it replicate in order to correct the deficit. Although there have been some successes with gene therapy, it remains highly experimental and at times has had dangerous side effects.

Genetic laboratory techniques can be also used for screening. Patients can be screened to see if they have certain genetic disorders, and newborns are routinely screened for a panel of genetic conditions. Potential parents can be screened to see if they are carriers of a genetic disorder and if their offspring could therefore be afflicted with the disease. Another type of screening involves antibiotic resistance in bacteria, allowing for treatment with the proper antibiotics. Bacterial resistance screening was traditionally carried out by growing bacteria in a culture and exposing them to antibiotics. Genetic screening techniques are becoming increasingly more common, as they are faster, cheaper, and at times more accurate.

Another significant application of genetic techniques is in **biometry**, the use of statistical methods to understand biological data. Biostatistical analysis can be applied to a wide variety of biological inquiries. One of the major current uses of statistical analysis in biology is the attempt to better understand population genetics. With the wide variety of genetic data now available, it is possible to study population genetics on a large scale. The analysis of this data has had a powerful impact on the field of medicine, allowing researchers to identify genes correlated with certain medical conditions, as well as to better understand global health and epidemiology.

Safety and Ethics of Genetic Techniques

New scientific advances have raised issues around the **safety and ethics of DNA technology**. Some wonder whether it is ethical to alter the DNA of agricultural plants, other animals, and even ourselves. One contentious issue is the use of genetic modifications in agriculture, such as to produce a crop that is resistant to environmental hazards. Others think it might be a "slippery slope" from genetic screening of offspring to "designer babies," where parents could choose the sex and desirable physical or mental attributes of their offspring. Many of the lab techniques involve manipulation of embryonic stem cells, which leads to issues surrounding the purported origins of life. There are also controversial discussions related to gene patenting, biological warfare, and more. Modern advancements in genetic techniques have come with a whole host of complex ethical implications.

It is important to understand how every technique is done, which requires an understanding of the basic science behind it, as well as why it is being done or how it fits into the larger picture of a complex technique. On the MCAT®, many of these techniques, especially ones involving genetics, may be involved in questions about other topics, such as ethics, biostatistics, or safety.

These questions are NOT related to a passage.

Item 89

In PCR amplification, a primer is hybridized to the end of a DNA fragment and acts as the initiation site of replication for a specialized DNA polymerase. The DNA fragment to be amplified is shown below. Assuming that the primer attaches exactly to the end of the fragment, which of the following is most likely the primer? (Note: The N stands for any nucleotide.)

5′-ATGNNNNNNNNNNNNNNNGCT-3′

- **A.** 5′-GCT-3′
- **B.** 5′-TAC-3′
- **C.** 5′-TCG-3′
- **D.** 5′-AGC-3′

Item 90

Which of the following regarding restriction enzymes, such as EcoRI and HindIII, is most likely FALSE?

- **A.** They are made by bacteria as a defense against viruses.
- **B.** EcoRI is synthesized in the cytosol.
- **C.** They recognize sequences that read the same forward and backwards.
- **D.** DNA cut by EcoRI easily joins to DNA cut by HindIII.

Item 91

Which of the following best describes the molecule shown and its effect on replication?

- **A.** There is no 3' hydroxyl group, so a phosphodiester bond will be unable to form and replication will terminate.
- **B.** There is no 3' hydroxyl group, so replication will continue as normal.
- **C.** There is no 5' phosphate group, so replication will continue as normal.
- **D.** There is no 5' phosphate group, so a phosphodiester bond will be unable to form and replication will terminate.

Item 92

Cystic fibrosis is an autosomal recessive trait resulting from the dysfunction of a sodium chloride transporter protein. Which of the following describes the best experimental approach to developing a mouse model of cystic fibrosis?

- **A.** Take the human protein encoding the sodium chloride transporter and express it in mice.
- **B.** Identify the mouse homologue of the sodium chloride transporter and develop a knockout mouse.
- **C.** Identify the mouse homologue of the sodium chloride transporter and feed the mice food laced with RNAi for that protein.
- **D.** Identify the promoter for the mouse homologue of the sodium chloride transporter and change it to a weaker one.

Item 93

Starting with n copies of a gene, x cycles of PCR are performed. How many copies of the gene result from this procedure?

- **A.** n^x
- **B.** n^{2x}
- **C.** $n(2^x)$
- **D.** x^n

Item 94

Pancreatic beta cells were isolated from a mouse after a fast. The same mouse was then fed, followed by another round of beta cell collection. If samples from both groups of cells were run on the same DNA microarray, what color would be seen on the region of the chip containing probes for the insulin gene?

- **A.** Green
- **B.** Yellow
- **C.** Red
- **D.** No color

Item 95

Suppose a forensic scientist is trying to prove that a criminal defendant was at a crime scene. Which of the following would be the LEAST useful piece of evidence?

- **A.** Blood found at the scene showing signs of a rare disorder with which the defendant also suffers
- **B.** Blood found at the scene that is the same blood type as that of the defendant
- **C.** RFLP analysis of DNA found at the crime scene that was identical to DNA taken from the defendant
- **D.** SNP analysis of DNA found at the crime scene that was identical to DNA taken from the defendant

Developmental biologists have developed inducible knockout mice for certain genes. In these animals, an enzyme responsible for excising the gene of interest is only active after treatment with certain pharmaceuticals. This development would be most useful for the study of which of the following genes?

- ○ **A.** The *LacZ* gene
- ○ **B.** A telomerase gene that is active in many cell types during old age
- ○ **C.** A dopamine transporter gene that becomes active during puberty in certain brain regions
- ○ **D.** A *Hox* family gene necessary for proper embryonic neurulation

Affinity chromatography

Analyzing gene expression

Anneal

β-carotene

Biometry

Chemical shift

Chemically equivalent hydrogens

Chromatography

Clone

Clone library

Column chromatography

Complementary color

Complementary DNA (cDNA)

Conjugated systems

Denatured

Determining gene function

Distillation

DNA methylation

DNA sequencing

Extraction

Fingerprint region

Gas-liquid chromatography

Gel electrophoresis

Gene cloning

High pressure liquid chromatography (HPLC)

Human gene therapy

Hybridization

Infrared region

Infrared (IR) spectroscopy

Intramolecular vibrations and rotations

Ion-exchange chromatography

Isoelectric points

Mass spectrometry

Neighboring hydrogens

Nuclear Magnetic Resonance (NMR) spectroscopy

Nucleic acid hybridization

Paper chromatography

Plasmid

Polymerase chain reaction (PCR)

Probe

Racemic mixture

Recombinant DNA

Restriction enzymes

RFLP

Safety and ethics of DNA technology

Separation of enantiomers

Separations

Size-exclusion chromatography

Southern blotting

Splitting (spin-spin splitting)

Stem cells

Thin-layer chromatography

Ultraviolet region

Ultraviolet (UV) spectroscopy

Vector

Visible region

Western blot

FIGURE 4.9 | NMR Spectrum Answers

pg. 106: Each letter, *A*, *B*, and *C*, represents a group of chemically equivalent hydrogens. The groups of peaks from left to right correspond to the *C*, *B*, and *A* hydrogens respectively. Since NO_2 is electron-withdrawing, the *c* hydrogens are further downfield. The *B* hydrogens have 5 neighbors, so their peak has 6 smaller peaks. The digital trace shows that the peak furthest upfield has 1.5 times as many hydrogens as each of the other peaks. The ratio of *A* hydrogens to *B* or *C* hydrogens is 3 to 2, so this peak must represent the *A* hydrogens.

DON'T FORGET YOUR KEYS

1. Separation and purification techniques use properties such as charge, size, and polarity to isolate compounds.

2. "Spec" techniques, such as NMR, IR, UV, and Mass Spec provide information about functional groups and molecular structure.

3. Genetic lab techniques identify or manipulate DNA to study or change healthy and pathological processes.

STOP!

DO NOT LOOK AT THESE EXAMS UNTIL CLASS.

30-MINUTE IN-CLASS EXAM FOR LECTURE 1

Passage I (Questions 1-5)

The three-dimensional shape of a protein is ultimately determined by its amino acid sequence. The folding pattern itself is a sequential, cooperative process where initial folds assist in aligning the protein properly for subsequent folds. Proteins that provide assistance in the folding process by stabilizing partially folded intermediates are called chaperones.

Folding of myosin (the thick filament involved in muscle contraction) in striated muscle is mediated by the chaperone Hsp90. Newly synthesized myosin forms a transient complex with Hsp90 in which the myosin motor domain is partially folded. Myosin transits through this chaperone complex on the pathway to myofibril assembly. This pathway appears to involve an Hsp90 co-chaperone, Unc45b. Unc45b has a region that is conserved among proteins that interact with myosin. Mutations in this domain result in decreased accumulation of striated muscle myosin filaments and disruption of contractile ring formation, both processes that are dependent on myosin function.

Analysis of synthesized myosin subfragments has shown that folding of the myosin motor domain is the rate limiting step and may require folding factors. If Unc45b is indeed a striated myosin specific chaperone, it might be expected to target the myosin motor domain. To test this hypothesis, scientists synthesized full-length myosin (MHC) and two subfragments, one including the myosin motor domain (S1) and one without (S2). They also isolated the native (fully formed and functioning) myosin motor domain subfragment (HMM) from chicken muscle. Unc45b was tagged with an epitope coding sequence to create Unc45b^{Flag}, which was then bound to radioactively tagged anti-Flag antibody. The subfragments and native protein were incubated with either Unc45b^{Flag}/Hsp90 complex or purified Unc45b^{Flag}. Binding of Unc45b^{Flag} or the Unc45b^{Flag}/Hsp90 complex was visualized by autoradiography as a dark band at a characteristic position for each protein or fragment. The results are shown in Figure 1.

Figure 1 Binding of synthesized myosin heavy chain and its subfragments to Unc45b^{Flag} and Unc45b^{Flag}/Hsp90 complex, visualized by tagged Anti-Flag antibody

Question 1

Do the results of this experimental setup allow the conclusion that Unc45b acts as a co-chaperone for the folding of the myosin motor domain?

- ○ **A.** Yes, because they show that the Unc45b^{Flag}/Hsp90 complex binds to the synthesized subfragment myosin motor domain.
- ○ **B.** Yes, because they show that mutations in Unc45b result in decreased accumulation of type II striated muscle myosin filaments.
- ○ **C.** No, because they do not show that the Unc45b^{Flag}/Hsp90 complex enhances the folding of the myosin motor domain.
- ○ **D.** No, because they show that the Unc45b^{Flag}/Hsp90 complex does not bind to the native conformation of the myosin motor domain.

Question 2

Which of the following is the best explanation for why attempts at predicting protein configuration based upon amino acid sequence have been unsuccessful?

- ○ **A.** It is impossible to know the amino acid sequence of a protein without knowing the DNA nucleotide sequence.
- ○ **B.** Chaperones help to determine the three dimensional shape of a protein.
- ○ **C.** The three-dimensional shape of a protein is based upon hydrogen and disulfide bonding between amino acids, and the number of possible combinations of bonding amino acids makes prediction difficult.
- ○ **D.** The amino acid sequence of the same protein may vary slightly from one sample to the next.

Question 3

The scientists first incubated each protein fragment with Anti-Flag antibody only because:

- ○ **A.** they wanted to ensure that the Anti-Flag antibody was visualizable by autoradiography.
- ○ **B.** if the Anti-Flag antibody bound to any of the proteins, it could not be used to assess whether the protein bound to Unc45b^{Flag} or the Unc45b^{Flag}/Hsp90 complex.
- ○ **C.** they wanted to ensure that the Anti-Flag antibody bound to the Unc45b^{Flag}.
- ○ **D.** each protein fragment had a different tertiary structure.

Next ▶

Question 4

Natural selection has resulted in increased chaperone synthesis in the presence of elevated temperatures. How might increased chaperone production in the presence of heat be advantageous to a cell?

- ○ **A.** Heat destabilizes intermolecular bonds, making protein configuration more difficult to achieve. Chaperones counteract this effect by stabilizing the partially folded intermediates.
- ○ **B.** Increased temperatures increase reaction rates, creating an excess of fully formed proteins. Chaperones stabilize the partially folded intermediates and slow this process.
- ○ **C.** Increased chaperone production requires energy. This energy is acquired from the kinetic energy of molecules, so it cools the cell.
- ○ **D.** Elevated temperatures result in increased cellular activity, requiring more proteins. Chaperones increase the rate of polypeptide formation.

Question 5

Which of the following bonds in a protein is likely to be LEAST stable in the presence of heat?

- ○ **A.** A disulfide bond
- ○ **B.** A hydrogen bond
- ○ **C.** A peptide bond
- ○ **D.** The double bond of a carbonyl

Passage II (Questions 6-10)

Galactose is normally metabolized via the Leloir pathway to produce glucose-6-phosphate for glycolysis. The first step of this pathway is the phosphorylation of galactose, catalyzed by galactokinase. A common cause of galactosemia, the inability to digest galactose, is deficiency of the next enzyme in the pathway, galactose-1-phosphate uridyl transferase (GALT). The associated symptoms are believed to result from the buildup of the toxic metabolite galactose-1-phosphate. It has been suggested that the inhibition of galactokinase might be a useful treatment for GALT-deficient patients.

Scientists explored a possible site of inhibition by mutating the residue glutamate-43 in the sugar binding site of human galactokinase and assessing the kinetic consequences. Mutating the glutamate side chain to alanine (creating the mutant E43A) caused no major changes in the kinetic parameters. In contrast, altering this residue to glycine (creating the mutant E43G) caused a substantial drop in the turnover number (the number of substrate molecules converted to product per active site in a solution saturated with substrate, also called k_{cat}) with no corresponding drop in the specificity constant.

Figure 1 Turnover number as a function of galactose concentration for mutant proteins E43A and E43G

The specificity constant is related to K_m as follows:

$$specificity\ constant = \frac{k_{cat}}{K_m}$$

While K_m is a summed measure of the interaction between the substrate and the enzyme across all stages of the catalytic cycle, the specificity constant reports on the initial enzyme-substrate encounter. In the case of E43G, the kinetic changes show that the mutation causes little or no change in the rate of interaction between galactose and the enzyme but that the overall rate of catalysis is reduced.

Question 6

The activity of galactokinase causes a buildup of galactose-1-phosphate when the GALT enzyme is deficient because:

- **A.** galactokinase lowers the energy of activation for the forward reaction in the phosphorylation of galactose and does not affect the energy of activation for the reverse reaction.
- **B.** galactokinase lowers the energy of activation for both the forward and reverse reactions in the phosphorylation of galactose.
- **C.** galactokinase lowers the energy of activation for the forward reaction in the phosphorylation of galactose and raises the energy of activation for the reverse reaction.
- **D.** galactokinase alters the relative amounts of reactant and product at equilibrium, causing the galactose-1-phosphate product to be favored.

Question 7

Which type of inhibition might be expected to lead to a decreased specificity constant?

- **A.** Noncompetitive, because K_m would stay the same and the turnover number would decrease.
- **B.** Noncompetitive, because K_m would increase and the turnover number would decrease.
- **C.** Competitive, because K_m would stay the same and the turnover number would decrease.
- **D.** Competitive, because K_m and the turnover number would both increase.

Question 8

Which of the following is the most likely explanation for the finding that the E43G mutant protein demonstrated a decreased turnover number while the specificity constant was unaffected?

- **A.** The E43G mutant showed no enzymatic function.
- **B.** K_m changed by a factor approximately equal to the factor by which k_{cat} changed.
- **C.** Glycine is a nonpolar amino acid, while glutamate is basic.
- **D.** The E43G mutant protein had an increased K_m compared to the native galactokinase.

Question 9

Suppose that the scientists used an uncompetitive inhibitor to inhibit galactose, rather than mutating a side chain. What would be the expected effect on K_m and V_{max}?

- **A.** K_m would increase or decrease, depending on the specific inhibitor used, and V_{max} would decrease.
- **B.** K_m would increase and V_{max} would stay the same.
- **C.** K_m would stay the same and V_{max} would decrease.
- **D.** K_m and V_{max} would both decrease.

Question 10

Which of the following describes a general feature of proteins that makes them well suited to be enzymes?

- **A.** Proteins have large variability in structure, allowing for substrate specificity.
- **B.** Proteins are defined by their amphipathic nature, which allows them to assemble into membranes that isolate substrates from the watery environment of the cell.
- **C.** Proteins cannot be denatured even in extreme environmental conditions.
- **D.** Proteins have high regularity in structure, allowing for substrate specificity.

Next ▶

Passage III (Questions 11-14)

Hepatitis C virus (HCV) frequently causes chronic infection that can lead to cirrhosis and liver cancer. The density of circulating hepatitis C virus (HCV) particles in the blood of chronically infected patients is quite heterogeneous. The very low density of some particles has been attributed to an association of the virus with triglyceride rich lipoproteins (TRL), namely the low, intermediate and very low density lipoproteins (LDL, IDL and VLDL, respectively) and chylomicrons, as well as apolipoprotein B (apoB) positive lipoproteins. This association likely results in hybrid lipoproteins known as lipoviro-particles (LVP), containing the viral envelope glycoproteins E1 and E2. (Glycoproteins are composed of a protein with a short chain of monosaccharides attached.) The specific infectivity of these particles is higher when the ratio of lipids to proteins is greater. The mechanism of the association of HCV particles with lipoproteins remains elusive, and the role of apolipoproteins in the synthesis and assembly of the viral particles is unknown.

Microsomal triglyceride transfer protein (MTP) is an essential protein in the synthesis and assembly of TRL in the liver and intestine. To evaluate the role of MTP in the synthesis and assembly of lipoviro-particles, the human intestinal cell line Caco-2 was infected with the E1E2 lentiviral vector and then incubated with an MTP inhibitor (Cp 346086). MTP activity was measured one and two days later. The results are shown in Figure 1.

Figure 1 MTP activity in the basal medium, measured in enzyme activity units U per μg, at 24 and 48 h after addition of 1 or 10 nM Cp 346084

The secretions of apoB, E1, and E2 were also measured one and two days later. The quantity of E1 and E2 secreted into the basal medium after 24h or 48h incubation with 1 and 10 nM inhibitor was greatly reduced and correlated with the concentration of secreted apoB (data not shown). The effects on apoB concentration are shown in Figure 2.

Figure 2 Concentrations of secreted apoB in the basal medium at 24h and 48h after addition of 1 or 10 nM Cp 346084

Question 11

Which of the following accurately describes the structure of triglycerides?

○ **A.** Two fatty acids and a polar group attached to a glycerol backbone

○ **B.** Three fatty acids attached to a glycerol backbone

○ **C.** A long-chain alcohol and long-chain fatty acid attached by an ester linkage

○ **D.** A four ringed structure

Question 12

Which additional finding would support the conclusion that apoB lipoproteins contribute to lipoviro-particle formation?

○ **A.** Infected patients lacking apoB lipoproteins had lower levels of circulating VLDL.

○ **B.** A line of apoB negative epithelial cells was found to secrete HCV envelope proteins.

○ **C.** Inhibition of MTP did not lead to reduced secretions of any proteins other than apoB.

○ **D.** A line of liver cells infected with the E1E2 lentiviral vector did not produce significant co-precipitation of apoB and HCV envelope proteins.

Question 13

Which of the following findings is supported by the experimental data?

- ○ **A.** The doses of 1 nM and 10 nM Cp 346086 have the same effect on MTP activity.
- ○ **B.** Secretion of apoB is directly correlated with MTP activity.
- ○ **C.** Secretion of E1 and E2 is inversely correlated with MTP activity.
- ○ **D.** The presence of Cp 346086 did not cause decreased MTP activity.

Question 14

According to the passage, which of the following would most likely be found as a component of glycoproteins like E1 and E2?

- ○ **A.** Starch
- ○ **B.** Glycogen
- ○ **C.** Glucose
- ○ **D.** Cellulose

Passage IV (Questions 15-18)

β-lactam antibiotics have been effectively used in the treatment of bacterial infections due to their relatively high efficacy and minimal side effects. Despite the large number of β-lactams already in use, new compounds must be developed to combat increasing antibacterial resistance.

Two bacterial mechanisms are responsible for antibiotic resistance: structural modification in penicillin binding protein (PBP) targets and production of β-lactamase. PBPs are membrane-associated proteins that catalyze the final step of peptidoglycan biosynthesis in bacteria. Both the transpeptidase and carboxypeptidase activities of PBPs occur at the D-Ala-D-Ala terminus of a disaccharide pentapeptide comprising N-acetylglucosamine and N-acetyl-muramic acid-L-Ala-D-Glu-L-Lys-D-Ala-D-Ala, where D and L refer to chirality of the molecule. Penicillin antibiotics compete with the pentapeptide precursor for binding to the active site of the enzyme.

Molecular docking predicts the preferred orientation of a drug molecule in an enzyme by computing the bound conformation and the binding affinity. Researchers interested in generating novel antibiotics synthesized penicillin analogues, as shown in Figure 1. The modifications to penicillin have different hydrophobic/hydrophilic groups and all possess a −COOH group that can easily be condensed with the −NH2 group of penicillin precursor molecule 6-APA. The binding interactions between the side chain R groups of penicillin binding protein (PDBID 1CEF) and synthesized compounds (4a-h) were predicted via molecular docking and compound 4e found to have the lowest K_m. Next, *E. coli* were treated with compound 4e that was predicted to target MurC, a UDP-N-acetylmuramic acid:L-alanine ligase, an essential enzyme in bacteria for peptidoglycan biosynthesis. Compound 4e showed a K_m of 17 μM and a V_{max} of 44.3 μM/min , compared to a K_m of 12 μM and a V_{max} of 44.2 for the uninhibited enzyme.

Next ▶

R–COCl + →

(4a-h)

4a
Ibuprofen

4d
Ketoprofen

4g
Diclofenic

4b
Dexibuprofen

4e
Naproxen

4h
Mefenamic acid

4c
Flurbiprofen

4f
Indomethacin

Figure 1 Synthesis of penicillin derivatives (4a-h)

Question 15

β-lactamase is responsible for opening the carbonyl on the four-membered ring in penicillin derivative antibiotics. Which of the following amino acids in β-lactamase is LEAST likely to facilitate this reaction?

○ **A.** Isoleucine

○ **B.** Serine

○ **C.** Cysteine

○ **D.** Glutamate

Question 16

Which of the following curves corresponds to the inhibition of PBPs by compound 4e?

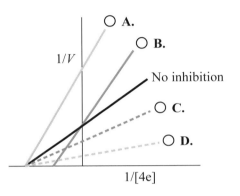

Question 17

Based on information contained in the passage, studies of patients with penicillin-resistant bacterial infections are likely to show:

○ **A.** bacteria that have an increased concentration of peptidoglycan on the cell surface.

○ **B.** bacteria that have a decreased concentration of glycoprotein on the cell surface.

○ **C.** bacteria with decreased expression of β-lactamase.

○ **D.** bacteria with nonsense mutations in transpeptidase.

Question 18

Which of the following enzymes catalyzes the reaction most similar to the synthesis of the penicillin-derivative antibiotics?

○ **A.** Pol β lyase

○ **B.** DNA ligase

○ **C.** Ribozyme

○ **D.** Phosphohexose isomerase

Questions 19 through 23 are NOT based on a descriptive passage.

Question 19

Which type of forces holds together complementary strands of DNA?

○ **A.** Polar covalent bonds

○ **B.** Nonpolar covalent bonds

○ **C.** Hydrogen bonds

○ **D.** Van der Waals forces

Question 20

Lineweaver-Burk plots, where the reciprocal of reaction velocity is plotted as a function of the reciprocal of substrate concentration, are commonly used to demonstrate enzyme kinetics.

Which of the following Lineweaver-Burk plots demonstrates the effects of a competitive inhibitor?

○ **A.**

○ **B.**

○ **C.**

○ **D.**

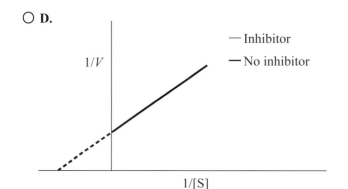

Question 21

All of the following accurately describe differences between RNA and DNA EXCEPT:

○ **A.** In general, DNA is double-stranded and RNA is single-stranded.

○ **B.** In a eukaryotic cell, DNA is found in the nucleus; RNA can be found in both the cytosol and nucleus.

○ **C.** On one of the carbons of the pentose sugar, there is a hydroxyl group in DNA but only a hydrogen in RNA.

○ **D.** RNA contains uracil where DNA contains thymine.

Question 22

Antiphospholipid syndrome is an autoimmune disease caused by synthesis of antibodies that react to proteins that are bound to phospholipids on plasma membranes, often provoking blood clots. These proteins most likely bind to which region of the phospholipid?

○ **A.** Fatty acid chain

○ **B.** Glycerol backbone

○ **C.** Phosphate

○ **D.** Sphingosine

Question 23

The following K_m and V_{max} values were recorded for three inhibitors of GLUT2, a protein known to transport glucose from the liver into the blood. What type of inhibitor is compound C?

Compound	K_m (M)	V_{max} (mol/s)
–	1×10^{-6}	50
A	1×10^{-3}	51
B	1×10^{-9}	30
C	1.2×10^{-6}	25

○ **A.** Competitive inhibitor

○ **B.** Uncompetitive inhibitor

○ **C.** Mixed inhibitor

○ **D.** Noncompetitive inhibitor

STOP. IF YOU FINISH BEFORE TIME IS CALLED, CHECK YOUR WORK. YOU MAY GO BACK TO ANY QUESTION IN THIS TEST BOOKLET.

30-MINUTE IN-CLASS EXAM FOR LECTURE 2

Passage I (Questions 24-27)

The primary abnormality in Down syndrome (DS), trisomy 21, is well known; but how this chromosomal gain produces a complex variety of DS phenotypes, including immune system defects that make DS individuals particularly susceptible to autoimmune disease and recurrent infection, is not well understood. It is postulated that epigenetic effects may contribute to development of the DS immune system phenotype, with altered DNA methylation acting in response to changes in gene dosage.

Experiment 1

Using microarray analysis, scientists profiled DNA methylation in total peripheral blood leukocytes (PBL) and T-lymphocytes from adults with DS and a population of control adults and found gene-specific abnormalities of CpG methylation in DS. Many of the differentially methylated genes have known or predicted roles in lymphocyte development and function. Strong differences ($p<0.0001$) were found between DS and control groups for each of the eight genes tested: *TMEM131, TCF7, CD3Z/CD247, SH3BP2, EIF4E, PLD6, SUMO3*, and *CPT1B*. The differentially methylated genes were found on various autosomes with no specific enrichment on chromosome 21. Results from the *TMEM131* gene are shown in Figure 1.

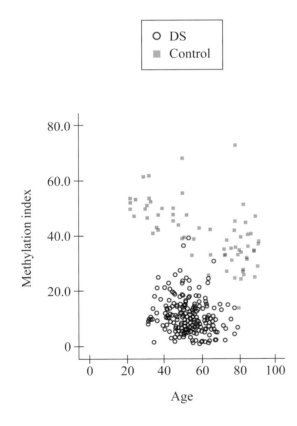

Figure 1 *TMEM131* methylation in DS and control subjects

Experiment 2

Some, but not all, of the differentially methylated genes showed different mean mRNA expression in DS versus control PBL. These five differentially expressed genes (*TMEM131, TCF7, CD3Z, NOD2*, and *NPDC1*) were examined in normal lymphocytes before and after exposure to the demethylating drug 5-aza2'deoxycytidine (5aza-dC) plus mitogens. Results for *TMEM131* expression are shown in Figure 2.

Figure 2 *TMEM131* gene expression in DS subjects and in control subjects after 0, 0.25, and 0.5 µM 5aza-dC

This passage was adapted from "Altered DNA Methylation in Leukocytes with Trisomy 21." Kerkel K, Schupf N, Hatta K, Pang D, Salas M, et al. *PLoS Genetics*. 2010. 6(11) doi:10.1371/journal.pgen.1001212 for use under the terms of the Creative Commons CCBY 3.0 license (http://creativecommons.org/licenses/by/3.0/legalcode).

Question 24

Which of the following conclusions is supported by the findings of Experiment 1?

○ **A.** Immune deficiency in DS individuals is due to hypermethylation at chromosome 21.

○ **B.** Immune deficiency in DS individuals is due to hypomethylation at chromosome 21.

○ **C.** Immune deficiency in DS individuals is due to altered multi-chromosomal methylation.

○ **D.** Immune deficiency in DS individuals is sex-linked.

Question 25

The combined evidence of Experiments 1 and 2 suggests that which of the following might be a possible chain of cause and effect?

○ **A.** DNA methylation→ aneuploidy → differential gene expression

○ **B.** Aneuploidy → DNA methylation → differential gene expression

○ **C.** Aneuploidy → differential gene expression → DNA methylation

○ **D.** DNA methylation → differential gene expression → aneuploidy

Next ▶

Question 26

Which of the following is/are true regarding the *TMEM131* gene?

    I. Increased methylation results in altered expression in DS individuals.

    II. Decreased methylation alters normal PBL to DS levels of gene expression.

    III. In control individuals, gene expression should be expected to decrease with age.

○ **A.** I only

○ **B.** II only

○ **C.** I and III only

○ **D.** II and III only

Question 27

The researchers repeat the Experiment 2 protocol to explore the effect of *5aza-dC* on *CD3Z* gene expression in control PBL. They find that higher doses of *5aza-dC* produce lower levels of *CD3Z* gene expression. These results are best explained by which of the following?

○ **A.** Increased methylation caused by 5aza-dC decreases gene expression.

○ **B.** Methylation sites of the *CD3Z* gene are located in the promoter region.

○ **C.** *CD3Z* is an autosomal gene.

○ **D.** Increased methylation in repressor regions leads to increased expression.

Passage II (Questions 28-32)

For many genes in eukaryotes, the mRNA initially transcribed is not translated in its entirety. Instead, it is processed in a series of steps occurring within the nucleus. The 5′ end of the pre-mRNA is capped with GTP, forming a 5′–5′ triphosphate linkage. Several adenosine residues are added to the 3′ end to form a poly-A tail.

During processing, as much as 90% of the pre-mRNA is removed from the nucleotide sequence as introns and the remaining exons are spliced together into a single mRNA strand (Figure 1).

Figure 1 Post-transcriptional processing of mRNA

A recent study showed that Alus, which are retrotransposed elements, may be important in determining the splicing patterns of pre-mRNA in humans. A large fraction of Alus are found in intronic sequences. The study showed that more Alus flank alternatively spliced exons than constitutively spliced ones; this effect is especially notable for those exons that have changed their mode of splicing from constitutive to alternative during human evolution. In one experiment, two Alu elements that were inserted into an intron in opposite orientations underwent base-pairing and affected the splicing patterns of a downstream exon, shifting it from constitutive to alternative.

As their functions become better understood, intronic sequences are becoming of greater interest to scientists. In R looping, a technique used to identify introns, a fully processed mRNA strand is hybridized with its double-stranded DNA counterpart under conditions that favor formation of hybrids between DNA and RNA strands. In this process, the RNA strand displaces one DNA strand and binds to the other DNA strand along complementary sequences. The results can be visualized through electron microscopy, as shown in Figure 2.

Figure 2 R looping formed by hybridization between DNA and the resultant mRNA sequence

This passage was adapted from "Intronic Alus Influence Alternative Splicing". Lev-Maor G, Ram O, Kim E, Sela N, Goren A, et al. *PLoS Genetics*. 2008. 4(9) doi:10.1371/journal. pgen.1000204 for use under the terms of the Creative Commons CCBY 3.0 license (http:// creativecommons.org/licenses/by/3.0/legalcode).

Question 28

Which of the following would most strongly indicate that the poly-A tail is added after transcription rather than during transcription?

○ **A.** Evidence of an enzyme in the nucleus that catalyzes the synthesis of a sequence of multiple adenosine phosphate molecules

○ **B.** A sequence of multiple thymine nucleotides following each gene in eukaryotic DNA

○ **C.** A sequence of multiple uracil nucleotides following each gene in eukaryotic mRNA

○ **D.** A sequence of multiple adenosine nucleotides following each gene in eukaryotic DNA

Question 29

Small nuclear ribonucleoproteins (snRNPs) catalyze the splicing reaction in the post-transcriptional processing of RNA. Based upon the information in the passage, in which of the following locations would snRNPs most likely be found?

○ **A.** The cytosol of a prokaryotic cell

○ **B.** The cytosol of a eukaryotic cell

○ **C.** The lumen of the endoplasmic reticulum

○ **D.** The nucleus of the eukaryotic cell

Question 30

The loops in Figure 2 represent:

○ **A.** DNA introns.

○ **B.** DNA exons.

○ **C.** RNA introns.

○ **D.** RNA exons.

Question 31

If true, which of the following would cast the greatest doubt on the findings of the Alus experiment described in the passage?

○ **A.** Constitutive splicing evolved before alternative splicing.

○ **B.** Exons evolved before introns.

○ **C.** Alternative splicing evolved before introns.

○ **D.** Introns evolved before alternative splicing.

Question 32

All of the following are associated with the process of eukaryotic mRNA splicing EXCEPT:

○ **A.** snRNP.

○ **B.** snRNA.

○ **C.** rRNA.

○ **D.** the lariat.

Passage III (Questions 33-37)

Preterm birth, defined as birth before 37 weeks of gestation, accounts for an estimated 2 million annual deaths worldwide and is the major cause of serious morbidity in infants born preterm. Currently, approximately 12% of all births in the United States are premature. Most preterm births are due to spontaneous onset of labor without a known cause or effective prevention. Both maternal and fetal genomes influence the predisposition to spontaneous preterm birth (SPTB), but the susceptibility loci remain to be defined. A history of SPTB of a single fetus is a strong predictor of its recurrence in families. Approximately 20% of mothers with a preterm delivery have another baby born preterm, suggesting that factors that are stable over time, such as genetics, affect birth timing.

To detect novel regions of the genome associated with preterm birth, researchers performed linkage analysis on seven carefully selected large families in northern Finland with recurrent SPTB. They looked at 6377 DNA markers, or variable DNA sequences with a known chromosomal location. A study of the fetuses revealed linkage of a region on chromosome 15 with spontaneous preterm birth, with the highest linkage signals occurring within a single gene, *IGF1R*. The *IGF1R* gene encodes insulin-like growth factor receptor 1 (IGF-1R), an important protein that potentially regulates signaling cascades involved in the onset of labor.

Figure 1 shows the pedigree and chromosome 15 of preterm newborns in one of the seven families. The diagram denotes the haplotype, or set of DNA variations that are usually inherited together, with the highest linkage to SPTB within the outlined black box.

Next ▶

Figure 1 Pedigree and corresponding sequence of paternal (p) and maternal (m) chromosome 15

This passage was adapted from "Mapping a New Spontaneous Preterm Birth Susceptibility Gene, IGF1R, Using Linkage, Haplotype Sharing, and Association Analysis." Haataja R, Karjalainen MK, Luukkonen A, Teramo K, Puttonen H, et al. *PLoS Genetics.* 2011. 7(2) doi: 10.1371/journal.pgen.1001293 for use under the terms of the Creative Commons CC BY 3.0 license (http://creativecommons.org/licenses/by/3.0/legalcode).

Question 33

Researchers commonly use DNA markers to locate genes implicated in disease. Which of the following features of DNA markers allows this methodology to be possible?

○ **A.** DNA markers sort independently from the genes of interest.

○ **B.** DNA markers with a close chromosomal proximity to the diseased gene tend to be inherited with the diseased gene.

○ **C.** DNA markers frequently cross over during meiosis to join mutated genes.

○ **D.** DNA markers are uniform in all individuals.

Question 34

Haplotypes are likely less susceptible than other parts of the human genome to:

○ **A.** recombination.

○ **B.** mutation.

○ **C.** methylation.

○ **D.** segregation.

Question 35

In Figure 1, individual 7 has the haplotype that is associated with SPTB but was not born preterm. This may be explained by which of the following reasons?

○ **A.** The mutation is autosomal recessive.

○ **B.** The mutation in the *IGF1R* gene has variable expressivity.

○ **C.** The mutation in the *IGF1R* gene has a penetrance less than 100%.

○ **D.** The mutation is autosomal dominant.

Question 36

The researchers begin to notice that none of the individuals tested have the mutated *IGF1R* on both the paternal and maternal chromosome. Which of the following best explains this finding?

○ **A.** When an embryo inherits two copies of the mutation, DNA polymerase repairs one of the mutations.

○ **B.** Two people who both carry the mutated *IGF1R* gene have never conceived offspring.

○ **C.** Embryos with two mutated *IGF1R* genes are not viable.

○ **D.** *IGF1R* is located on the Y chromosome.

Question 37

Another group of researchers determine that some SPTB babies are less likely to be susceptible to diabetes mellitus. How can this group of researchers alter their experiment to determine if the *IGF1R* mutation is partially advantageous?

○ **A.** Trace the incidence of diabetes mellitus in SPTB babies with the *IGF1R* mutation

○ **B.** Compare the incidence of diabetes mellitus in SPTB babies with the *IGF1R* mutation to SPTB babies without the *IGF1R* mutation

○ **C.** Compare the incidence of SPTB in babies with the *IGF1R* mutation to babies without the *IGF1R* mutation

○ **D.** Trace the incidence of diabetes mellitus in babies with *IGF1R* mutation that were not born preterm

Passage IV (Questions 38-41)

Human papillomavirus (HPV) has been detected in primary lung carcinomas with frequent integration into the host genome, suggesting a causal association between lung cancer and HPV in a subset of patients. Previous research has reported that HPV-16 E6 and E7 oncoproteins and cigarette smoke condensate (CSC) cooperate, increasing the proliferative and tumor properties of lung epithelial cells. Tobacco smoke is a complex mixture of more than 4,000 compounds and more than sixty of them have a demonstrated carcinogenicity. Because the upper respiratory tract and aero-digestive epithelia are potentially exposed to both HPV and environmental contaminants such as tobacco smoke, an interaction between both carcinogenic agents is plausible.

Experiment 1

In order to determine if CSC and HPV cooperate to increase the risk for lung cancer, scientists tested whether tobacco smoke was able to activate the HPV-16 p97 promoter in SiHa, a lung cancer cell line. The full-length HPV-16 p97 promoter region was amplified by PCR from DNA extracted from SiHa cells and inserted upstream of a *luc2 reporter* gene that fluoresces when the promoter is active. The p97-luc2 plasmid was transfected into HPV-16 E6/E7 expressing SiHa cells and the transfected cells were exposed to CSC ranging from 0.1 to 50 µg/mL. The results of the experiment are presented in Figure 1.

$** \ p < 0.01$
$* \ p < 0.05$

Figure 1 Effect of cigarette smoke condensates (CSC) on the activation of the HPV-16 p97 promoter

This passage was adapted from "Tobacco smoke activates human papillomavirus 16 p97 promoter and cooperates with high-risk E6/E7 for oxidative DNA damage in lung cells." Pena N, Carrillo D, Munoz J, Chnaiderman J, Urzua U, et al. *PLoS One.* 2015. 10(3) doi:10.1371/journal.pone.0123029 for use under the terms of the Creative Commons CC BY 4.0 license (http://creativecommons.org/licenses/by/4.0/legalcode).

Question 38

Which additional experiment would most likely be performed to confirm the role of HPV-16 E6 and E7 oncogenes in inducing DNA damage in cooperation with CSC in lung cells?

- **A.** Use of anti-sense short hairpin non-coding RNA (shRNA) to silence E6 and E7 expression in SiHa cells.
- **B.** Use of anti-sense short hairpin non-coding RNA (shRNA) to silence E6 and E7 expression in control cells.
- **C.** Overexpression of E6 and E7 in SiHa cells not exposed to CSC.
- **D.** Overexpression of E6 and E7 in control cells not exposed to CSC.

Question 39

The transcription of the *luc2* gene most likely:

- **A.** decreases with increasing CSC concentration.
- **B.** increases with increasing CSC concentration.
- **C.** is independent of CSC concentration.
- **D.** cannot be inferred from the presented experiments.

Question 40

Upon microscopic examination of dividing cells, the scientists note SiHa cell chromosomes in a linear arrangement within the cell. Which phase of mitosis are the scientists most likely observing?

- **A.** Prophase
- **B.** Metaphase
- **C.** Telophase
- **D.** Cytokinesis

Question 41

The number of chromosomes present during prophase in SiHa cells is most likely:

- **A.** 46
- **B.** 23
- **C.** 12
- **D.** 92

Next ▶

Questions 42 through 46 are NOT based on a descriptive passage.

Question 42

Which of the following is true concerning the genetic code?

  ○ **A.** There are more amino acids than there are codons.

  ○ **B.** Any change in the nucleotide sequence of a codon must result in a new amino acid.

  ○ **C.** The genetic code varies from species to species.

  ○ **D.** There are 64 codons.

Question 43

Turner syndrome occurs due to nondisjunction at the sex chromosome resulting in an individual with one X and no Y chromosome. Color-blindness is a sex-linked recessive trait. A color-blind man marries a healthy woman. They have two children, both with Turner syndrome. One of the children is color-blind. Which of the following is true?

  ○ **A.** Nondisjunction occurred in the father for both children.

  ○ **B.** Nondisjunction occurred in the mother for both children.

  ○ **C.** Nondisjunction occurred in the mother for the colorblind child and in the father for the child with normal vision.

  ○ **D.** Nondisjunction occurred in the father for the colorblind child and in the mother for the child with normal vision.

Question 44

A primary spermatocyte is:

  ○ **A.** haploid and contains 23 chromosomes.

  ○ **B.** haploid and contains 46 chromosomes.

  ○ **C.** diploid and contains 23 chromosomes.

  ○ **D.** diploid and contains 46 chromosomes.

Question 45

Which of the following is true of X chromosomes in humans?

  ○ **A.** An X chromosome is randomly inactivated in all female human cells.

  ○ **B.** An X chromosome is randomly inactivated in all human cells.

  ○ **C.** The paternally-derived X chromosome is inactivated in all human female cells.

  ○ **D.** Alleles located on either X chromosome in females may be transmitted to offspring.

Question 46

Which of the following is true of the structure and function of the lac operon?

  ○ **A.** It is active unless it is repressed, and it controls the expression of one gene.

  ○ **B.** It is inactive unless it is activated, and it controls the expression of one gene.

  ○ **C.** It is active unless it is repressed, and it controls the expression of three genes.

  ○ **D.** It is inactive unless it is activated, and it controls the expression of three genes.

STOP. IF YOU FINISH BEFORE TIME IS CALLED, CHECK YOUR WORK. YOU MAY GO BACK TO ANY QUESTION IN THIS TEST BOOKLET.

30-MINUTE IN-CLASS EXAM FOR LECTURE 3

Passage I (Questions 47- 51)

Acute lung injury (ALI) is an inflammatory disease of the lungs that is characterized by hypoxemic respiratory failure with bilateral pulmonary infiltrates. Sites of acute inflammation are frequently characterized by considerable shifts in the supply and demand of metabolites.

In vivo analysis of ^{13}C-glucose metabolites utilizing liquid-chromatography tandem mass-spectrometry demonstrated that increases in glycolytic capacity, improvement of mitochondrial respiration, and concomitant attenuation of lung inflammation during ALI were specific for alveolar-epithelial expressed hypoxia-inducible factor 1A (HIF1A).

Scientists hypothesized that HIF1A in alveolar epithelial cells dampens lung inflammation by enhancing glycolysis and optimizing mitochondrial respiration during ALI.

Experiment 1

This experiment used $Hif1A^{ff}$ SurfactantCre[+] mice with induced deletion of HIF1A in their alveolar epithelial cells; mice lacking HIF1A were found to experience profound lung inflammation during ALI.

Some of the $Hif1A^{ff}$ SurfactantCre[+] mice were exposed to ventilator induced lung injury (VILI). Elevations of transcript levels of glycolytic enzymes were found to be attenuated in $Hif1A^{ff}$ SurfactantCre[+] mice compared to wild type mice.

Measured [[13]C6] Glucose and Glut1 transcript levels are shown in Figure 1.

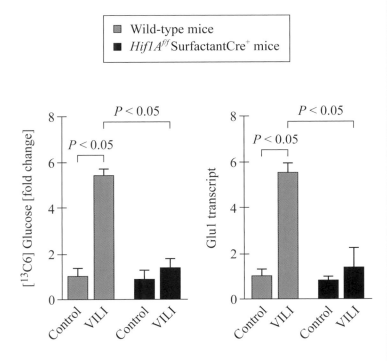

Figure 1 Effect of induced deletion of alveolar epithelial HIF1A on glycolysis during ALI

Experiment 2

Wild-type and $Hif1A^{ff}$ SurfactantCre[+] mice treated with the glycolysis inhibitor 2-deoxy-D-glucose (2-DG) were exposed to VILI. Survival times are shown in Figure 2.

Figure 2 Effect of inhibition of glycolysis on survival time during VILI

This passage was adapted from "HIF1A Reduces Acute Lung Injury by Optimizing Carbohydrate Metabolism in the Alveolar Epithelium." Eckle T, Brodsky K, Bonney M, Packard T, Han J, et al. *PLoS Biology*. 2013. 11(9) doi:10.1371/journal.pbio.1001665 for use under the terms of the Creative Commons CCBY 3.0 license (http://creativecommons.org/licenses/by/3.0/legalcode).

Question 47

The substrates of glycolysis include which of the following monomers?

    I. Monosaccharides

    II. Fatty acids

    III. Amino acids

  ○ **A.** I only

  ○ **B.** I and II only

  ○ **C.** I and III only

  ○ **D.** I, II and III

Next ▶

Question 48

Which of the following describes the most likely effect of an increased ratio of insulin to glucagon on glycolytic rate and overall metabolism?

- O **A.** Increased glycolytic rate and net anabolism
- O **B.** Increased glycolytic rate and net catabolism
- O **C.** Decreased glycolytic rate and net anabolism
- O **D.** Decreased glycolytic rate and net catabolism

Question 49

Based on passage information, which of the following is likely to have the highest glycolytic rate?

- O **A.** Wild type without VILI
- O **B.** Wild type with VILI
- O **C.** *Hif1A^{f/f}* SurfactantCre^+ without VILI
- O **D.** *Hif1A^{f/f}* SurfactantCre^+ with VILI

Question 50

Cancer cells are known to display increased expression of hypoxia-inducible transcription factor (HIF-1). Based on passage information, cancer cells are LEAST likely to exhibit increased expression of:

- O **A.** glycolytic enzymes.
- O **B.** glucose transporter GLUT1.
- O **C.** glucose transporter GLUT3.
- O **D.** gluconeogenic enzymes.

Question 51

Each reaction in the glycolytic pathway is governed by an enzyme. Phosphofructokinase, which catalyzes the conversion of fructose 6-phosphate to fructose 1,6-bisphosphate, is allosterically regulated. What is the most likely mechanism of regulation?

- O **A.** ADP activates the enzyme by decreasing its affinity for fructose 6-phosphate.
- O **B.** ADP inhibits the enzyme by increasing its affinity for fructose 6-phosphate.
- O **C.** ATP inhibits the enzyme by decreasing its affinity for fructose 6-phosphate.
- O **D.** ATP activates the enzyme by increasing its affinity for fructose 6-phosphate.

Passage II (Questions 52-55)

In the fed state, under the influence of insulin, white adipose tissue (WAT) stores excess energy as triacylglycerols. Lipolysis is the process by which stored triacylglycerols are released as nonesterified fatty acids.

Enzymatic breakdown of triacylglycerols is initiated by adipose triglyceride lipase (ATGL) and leads to the formation of diacylglycerols that are in turn hydrolyzed by hormone-sensitive lipase (HSL). The final step of this catabolic process is the hydrolysis of monoacylglycerols by monoglyceride lipase, leading to the release of one molecule of glycerol and three fatty acids.

Fatty acids have been postulated to play a critical role in the development of insulin resistance. In the two experiments below, researchers investigated the role of WAT lipolysis, including the specific contribution of HSL, in the control of insulin sensitivity and glucose metabolism.

Experiment 1

Researchers investigated the relationship between WAT lipolysis and insulin sensitivity in humans. As shown in Figure 1, a positive association was found between spontaneous glycerol release, measured ex vivo on WAT explants, and insulin resistance, as measured by the homeostasis model of indirect assessment of insulin resistance (HOMA-IR).

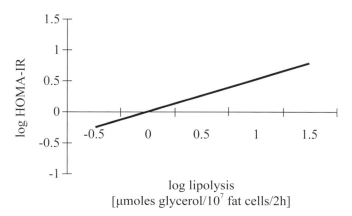

Figure 1 Relationship between WAT lipolysis and insulin resistance in human subjects

Experiment 2

Mice haploinsufficient for HSL were generated by mating wild type (WT) and *HSL*$^{-/-}$ mice. Resultant *HSL*$^{+/-}$ mice showed reduced lipolytic capacities without alteration of fat mass. Both WT and *HSL*$^{+/-}$ mice underwent insulin tolerance tests, where higher insulin tolerance corresponds to a greater decrease from basal glucose levels. The results are shown in Figure 2.

Figure 2 Results of insulin tolerance tests performed on wild type and *HSL*$^{+/-}$ mice fed a high fat diet for 12 weeks

This passage was adapted from "Partial Inhibition of Adipose Tissue Lipolysis Improves Glucose Metabolism and Insulin Sensitivity Without Alteration of Fat Mass." Girousse A, Tavernier G, Valle C, Moro C, Mejhert N, et al. *PLoS Biology*. 2013. 11(2) doi:10.1371/journal. pbio.1001485 for use under the terms of the Creative Commons CCBY 3.0 license (http://creativecommons.org/licenses/by/3.0/legalcode).

Question 52

Insulin activates enzymes involved in which of the following metabolic processes?

 I. Glycogenesis

 II. Gluconeogenesis

 III. Lipolysis

 ○ **A.** I only
 ○ **B.** I and II only
 ○ **C.** I and III only
 ○ **D.** I, II, and III

Question 53

What is the most likely reason that mice haploinsufficient for HSL were used in experiments designed to assess the role of WAT lipolysis in the control of insulin sensitivity?

 ○ **A.** HSL expression promotes insulin resistance.
 ○ **B.** HSL initiates enzyme breakdown of triacylglycerols.
 ○ **C.** HSL level is a determinant of lipolytic capacity in WAT.
 ○ **D.** HSL level is an indirect measure of glucose metabolism.

Question 54

Based on passage information, what would be the most likely effect of a drug designed to inhibit HSL expression on insulin resistant individuals?

 ○ **A.** Increased insulin sensitivity and increased fat mass
 ○ **B.** Decreased insulin sensitivity and increased fat mass
 ○ **C.** Increased insulin sensitivity and no change in fat mass
 ○ **D.** Decreased insulin sensitivity and no change in fat mass

Question 55

Which finding would provide the strongest support for the passage assertion that, compared to WT mice, *HSL*$^{+/-}$ mice exhibited diminished lipolytic capacities?

 ○ **A.** HSL mRNA expression was reduced by 50% in *HSL*$^{+/-}$ mice.
 ○ **B.** HSL protein expression was reduced by 50% in *HSL*$^{+/-}$ mice.
 ○ **C.** ATGL protein expression was not significantly altered in *HSL*$^{+/-}$ mice.
 ○ **D.** Adipocytes in *HSL*$^{+/-}$ mice had reduced in vitro response to stimulation by lipolytic agents.

Next ▶

Passage III (Questions 56-60)

Non-alcoholic fatty liver disease (NAFLD) has become the most frequent chronic liver disease in Western countries. Non-alcoholic steatohepatitis (NASH) is regarded as a subgroup of NAFLD defined by histological coexistence of inflammation and hepatic steatosis, the process of liver tissue converting to fat. NASH, but not NAFLD, carries the risk of disease progression and complications such as cirrhosis, liver failure or hepatocellular carcinoma (HCC). NAFLD and NASH are associated with obesity, insulin resistance (IR), and type 2 diabetes mellitus (T2DM). The main events in the pathophysiology of NAFLD/NASH are hepatic lipid accumulation, lipotoxicity, and inflammation.

Hepatic lipid accumulation is due to different mechanisms, mainly increased dietary intake, de-novo lipogenesis and influx of free fatty acids (FFA). A major risk factor is IR. IR induces lipolysis in adipose tissues, hereby increasing flux of FFA into the liver. The incretins, glucagon-like peptide-1 (GLP-1) and glucose-dependent insulinotropic polypeptide (GIP) are gastrointestinal peptide hormones regulating postprandial insulin release from pancreatic b-cells, the so-called "incretin effect." GLP-1 is released postprandially from endocrine L-cells into the splanchnic and portal circulation. It lowers plasma glucose and improves insulin sensitivity by increasing postprandial insulin release, decreasing glucagon secretion, and delaying gastric emptying. Additional effects include reduction in energy intake, increase in satiety, and weight loss.

Researchers hypothesized that deficiency in GLP-1 secretion might maintain hepatic steatosis. To test their idea, an oral glucose tolerance test (oGTT) was performed in 52 non-diabetic patients with NAFLD and NASH after an overnight fast according to a standardized protocol using 75 g of glucose in 300 ml tap water (300 kcal). GLP-1, glucose, insulin and glucagon levels were measured. The results are shown in Figure 1.

A.

Time (min.)

B.

Time (min.)

C.

Time (min.)

D.

Time (min.)

Figure 1 The levels of (A) GLP-1, (B) Glucose, (C) Glucagon and (D) Insulin in NAFLD patients, NASH patients and controls after the administration of an oGTT

This passage was adapted from "Glucose-Induced Glucagon-Like Peptide 1 Secretion Is Deficient in Patients with Non-Alcoholic Fatty Liver Disease." Bernsmeier C, Meyer-Gerspach AC, Blaser LS, Leker L, Steinert RE, et al. *PLoS ONE.* 2014. 9(1) doi: 10.1371/journal. pone.0087488 for use under the terms of the Creative Commons CC BY 4.0 license (https://creativecommons.org/licenses/by/4.0/legalcode).

Question 56

High incidence of NAFLD/NASH has led researchers to look for a possible genetic predisposition. A mutation leading to which of the following metabolic defects would promote the pathogenesis of NAFLD/NASH?

○ **A.** Over-activity of peripheral lipase

○ **B.** Constitutive activity of an enzyme in glycolysis

○ **C.** Decreased secretion of glucagon

○ **D.** Increased GLP-1 activity

Question 57

Based on the passage, how does GLP-1 deficiency contribute to the pathogenesis of NAFLD/NASH?

○ **A.** Decreased glucagon levels leading to increased insulin sensitivity

○ **B.** Increased insulin resistance leading to increased lipolysis

○ **C.** Decreased glucose levels after meals leading to inflammation

○ **D.** GLP-1 does not contribute to the pathogenesis of NAFLD/NASH

Question 58

The liver is a key regulator of glucose storage and release. During glycogenolysis in the liver:

○ **A.** ATP is used to break glycogen into glucose monomers.

○ **B.** phosphate is enzymatically added to free a glucose monomer from glycogen.

○ **C.** glucose is generated from non-carbohydrate carbon sources.

○ **D.** glucose is transformed into pyruvate.

Question 59

A separate group of researchers hypothesize that changes in diet and exercise habits can lead to reversal of NAFLD/NASH. How can this group of researchers alter their research design to provide further information on this hypothesis?

○ **A.** Measure GLP-1 levels in NAFLD/NASH patients after one week on an unsaturated fats only diet.

○ **B.** Compare GLP-1 levels between NAFLD/NASH patients and controls who have both been on an unsaturated fats only diet for several months.

○ **C.** Measure GLP-1 levels in NAFLD/NASH patients after several months on an unsaturated fats only diet.

○ **D.** Compare GLP-1 levels between NAFLD/NASH patients and controls who have both been on a saturated fats only diet for several months.

Question 60

Based on the passage, what is the most likely explanation for the discrepancy in glucagon levels between controls and NAFLD/NASH patients?

○ **A.** The controls have more insulin resistance than NAFLD/NASH patients.

○ **B.** The controls have more circulating GLP-1 leading to decreased suppression of glucagon secretion.

○ **C.** Prolonged insulin levels in NAFLD/NASH patients lead to decreased levels of glucagon.

○ **D.** Decreased levels of GLP-1 in NAFLD/NASH patients lead to decreased suppression of glucagon secretion.

Next ▶

Passage IV (Questions 61- 64)

Apoptosis of the insulin producing beta-cells is a major mechanism leading to the development of diabetes. The rapid loss of beta-cells, which secrete insulin, and the relative discrepancy between insulin demand and insulin secretion worsen a person's ability to maintain normal serum glucose levels.

Important metabolites that regulate insulin secretion are generated in the mitochondria. The beta-cell mitochondria are key regulators of glucose-stimulated insulin secretion, and several mitochondrial pathways are disabled in type 2 diabetes (T2DM). There is also increased UCP-2 expression, which uncouples mitochondrial oxidative phosphorylation. As a result, the energy inherent in the proton gradient across the mitochondrial membrane is wasted as heat. Mitochondria also play a prominent role in apoptosis. In beta-cells, elevated free fatty acids and the production of reactive oxygen species (ROS) have been shown to induce apoptosis through the release of cytochrome c from the inner mitochondrial membrane to the cytosol. Mitochondria are the principal source of ROS, which accumulate when the electron transport chain is defective.

The apoptosis-inducing factor (AIF) is a mitochondrial inter-membrane protein, which translocates to the cytoplasm and nucleus during apoptosis. In the nucleus, it binds to DNA, triggering DNA fragmentation and nuclear condensation.

Evidence that AIF serves as a superoxide scavenger to prevent apoptosis comes from studies on the Harlequin mutant mouse. These mice have an 80% reduction in AIF protein due to a proviral insertion in the first intron of the AIF gene. They exhibit reduced oxidative phosphorylation in the retina and in the brain, which entails increased oxidative stress and neuronal cell death. If cells are damaged by agents which induce oxidative stress, a cell checkpoint response is triggered. In the case of severe damage, cells may alternatively undergo apoptosis.

This passage was adapted from "Deletion of the Mitochondrial Flavoprotein Apoptosis Inducing Factor (AIF) Induces Beta-Cell Apoptosis and Impairs Beta-Cell Mass." Schulthess FT, Katz S, Ardestani A, Kawahira H, Georgia S, et al. *PLoS Medicine.* 2009. 4(2):e4394. doi:10.1371/journal.pone.0004394 for use under the terms of the Creative Commons CC BY 3.0 license (http://creativecommons.org/licenses/by/3.0/legalcode).

Question 61

In people with type 2 diabetes who have a severe decline in beta cell mass, the expected result of the low serum insulin is:

- ○ **A.** an increase in gluconeogenesis in skeletal muscle.
- ○ **B.** a decline in glycogenolysis in the liver.
- ○ **C.** an increase in lipolysis in adipocytes, or fat cells.
- ○ **D.** a buildup of lactic acid in skeletal muscle.

Question 62

The inner mitochondrial membrane protein associated with the initiation of apoptosis through a rise in reactive oxygen species is most closely related to which of the following biomolecules?

- ○ **A.** Ubiquinone
- ○ **B.** ATP synthase
- ○ **C.** Succinate dehydrogenase
- ○ **D.** Flavin adenine dinucleotide (FAD)

Question 63

In the absence of oxidative stress, an electrochemical gradient of protons is generated across the inner mitochondrial membrane through a series of steps involving:

- ○ **A.** the reduction of NADH to NAD^+.
- ○ **B.** the oxidation of molecular oxygen (O_2).
- ○ **C.** the reduction of water (H_2O).
- ○ **D.** the oxidation of cytochrome c.

Question 64

Researchers design an experiment to study the role of AIF in beta-cell apoptosis. Which of the following factors would be expected to affect their ability to study this relationship?

- ○ **A.** Apoptosis involves both mitochondria and lysosomes.
- ○ **B.** The role of AIF may overlap with that of cytochrome c
- ○ **C.** It is difficult to predict apoptosis in cells because it results from oxidative stress.
- ○ **D.** Only cells of the retina and brain contain AIF.

Questions 65 through 69 are NOT based on a descriptive passage.

Question 65

In aerobic respiration, the energy from the oxidation of NADH:

○ **A.** directly synthesizes ATP.

○ **B.** passively diffuses protons from the intermembrane space into the matrix.

○ **C.** establishes a proton gradient between the intermembrane space and the mitochondrial matrix.

○ **D.** pumps protons through ATP synthase.

Question 66

The process of synthesis of ATP in the glycolytic reaction governed by *phosphoglycerate kinase* is called:

○ **A.** oxidative phosphorylation.

○ **B.** substrate-level phosphorylation.

○ **C.** exergonic phosphate transfer.

○ **D.** electron transport.

Question 67

Glucose-6-phosphate can serve as an important precursor to nucleotides in rapidly dividing tissues as well as an important substrate in cells involved in lipid synthesis. Which pathway is responsible for this process?

○ **A.** Pentose phosphate pathway

○ **B.** Gluconeogenesis

○ **C.** Urea cycle

○ **D.** Glycolysis

Question 68

Dietary supplementation with which of the following macromolecules is LEAST likely to increase blood glucose levels?

○ **A.** Alanine

○ **B.** 3-phosphoglycerate

○ **C.** Palmitate

○ **D.** Triglyceride

Question 69

^{14}C-radiolabeled dietary triacylglyceride is most likely to be found in highest concentrations in:

○ **A.** chylomicrons.

○ **B.** very low density lipoproteins (VLDL).

○ **C.** low density lipoproteins (LDL).

○ **D.** high density lipoproteins (HDL).

STOP. IF YOU FINISH BEFORE TIME IS CALLED, CHECK YOUR WORK. YOU MAY GO BACK TO ANY QUESTION IN THIS TEST BOOKLET.

STOP

30-MINUTE IN-CLASS EXAM FOR LECTURE 4

Passage I (Questions 70- 73)

Stem cells incur DNA damage in both nuclear and mitochondrial DNA (mtDNA). Accumulation of unrepaired DNA lesions over a person's lifespan greatly increases the risk of cancer formation, with the types of mutations determining disease severity. Duplex Sequencing (DS) allows for accurate analysis of mtDNA because DS is >10,000-fold more accurate than conventional next generation sequencing (NGS). While NGS only sequences a single strand of DNA, DS sequences both strands to detect rare mutations that cause metastasis or drug resistance as the tumor continues to evolve.

In Duplex Sequencing, sequencing reads sharing unique experimentally-added barcodes to the sample DNA result in αβ or βα families that represent the sense and anti-sense strands of the same DNA molecule. Mutations are of three different types: sequencing mistakes (white dots), polymerase chain reaction (PCR) errors caused by erroneous base insertion by TAQ Polymerase (grey dots), and true mutations (black dots). Formation of the single strand consensus sequence (SSCS) removes the first type of error because the mutation is not found in all molecules of the same family. Comparing related αβ and βα families generates a double strand consensus sequence (DCS) that eliminates PCR errors because the mutation is not found in both strands of DNA. True mutations are present at the same position in both strands of DNA.

Using Duplex Sequencing, scientists detected that stem cells had significantly lower frequencies of rare mutations than non-stem cells. Of these mutations, about 75 to 75.5% were non-synonymous and likely contributed to the oncogenic potential of a small population of cells.

This passage is adapted from "Detection of ultra-rare mitochondrial mutations in breast stem cells by duplex sequencing." Ahn E, Hirohata K, Kohrn B, Fox E, Chang C-C, et al. *PLoS One*. 2015. 10(8) doi:10.1371/journal.pone.0136216 for use under the terms of the Creative Commons CC BY 4.0 license (http://creativecommons.org/licenses/by/4.0/legalcode).

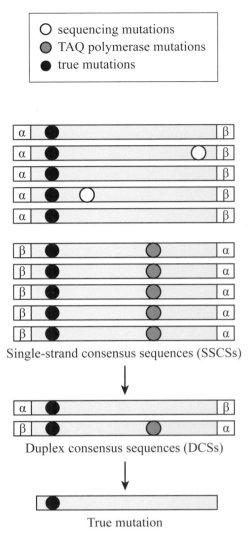

Figure 1 Theoretical framework of duplex sequencing

The figure is adapted from "Ultra-sensitive sequencing revels an age-related increase in somatic mitochondrial mutations that are inconsistent with oxidative damage." Kennedy S, Salk J, Schmitt M, and Loeb L. *PLos Genet*. 2013. 9(9) doi:10.1371/journal.pgen.1003794 for use under the terms of the Creative Commons CC BY 4.0 license (http://creativecommons.org/licenses/by/4.0/legalcode)

Question 70

When programming the PCR machine to amplify a 120 bp fragment of the *TP53* gene, a student failed to reduce the temperature from 95°C to 60°C after the first two minutes. Which of the following statements describes the most probable outcome?

- **A.** A Western blot fails to detect the presence of DNA polymerase in the PCR products.
- **B.** After running an agarose gel, the student observes migration of 250 bp fragments.
- **C.** After running an agarose gel, the student observes no bands.
- **D.** A Northern blot fails to detect the presence of RNA primers in the PCR products.

Question 71

Digestion of PCR products by restriction enzymes can confirm the presence of a desired PCR product. Which of the following sequences would be the most likely to serve as a restriction site?

- **A.** 5'-GA-3'
  3'-CT-5'
- **B.** 5'-GGATCC-3'
  3'-CCTAGG-5'
- **C.** 5'-TGCAA-3'
  3'-ACGTT-5'
- **D.** 5'-TCGTTAGCC-3'
  3'-AGCAATCGG-5'

Question 72

Scientists designed a separate experiment to test the specificity of Duplex PCR for quantifying post-transcriptional nucleotide substitutions in RNA from the *TP53* gene. Scientists would be LEAST likely to be able to detect variation in:

○ **A.** AT rich regions of DNA upstream of exon one.

○ **B.** transitions in exon three.

○ **C.** transversions in exon five.

○ **D.** single nucleotide polymorphisms in the 3' untranslated region.

Question 73

8 -oxo-2'-deoxyguanosine (8-oxo-dG) is produced by the oxidation of DNA under physiopathological conditions and has been shown to preferentially pair with dA, resulting in transversions. Which of the following bases would likely be read by Duplex Sequencing in place of 8-oxo-dG after three rounds of PCR?

○ **A.** A

○ **B.** G

○ **C.** T

○ **D.** C

Passage II (Questions 74-78)

Naturally occurring bioactive compounds can serve as chemotherapeutic agents against endometrial and other types of cancers. The present study focuses on whether or not steam distilled extract of ginger (SDGE) and its bioactive components have the potential to be developed as chemotherapeutic agents for endometrial cancer.

In this experiment, endometrial cancer cells were plated in a 96-well plate at a density of 5000 cells/well. Ginger roots were submerged in deionized water and steam distillation was carried out for 4–6 hours by heating the flask. The cancer cells were then treated with various concentrations of SDGE and DSMO, with the exception of several wells which were treated only with DSMO. After treatment of cells with SDGE, cells were lysed with RIPA buffer and loaded at 25 mg/well onto a 12% resolving polyacrylamide gel and separated by electrophoresis. Protein detection was performed using Horseradish peroxidase conjugated secondary antibodies.

Additionally, further separation and identification of compounds in SDGE was desired. To do this, a Shimadzu GC-17A gas chromatograph equipped with a mass analyzer was used. Three distinct preparations of SDGE, two from the US (termed Wisconsin 1 and 2) and one from India, were separated on a polar gas chromatography column (**Figure 1**). The compounds separating on this column were identified by mass spectrometry. Based on identification using the NIST Mass Spec Library, terpenes are the major components of SDGE identified by GC-MS analysis.

Figure 1 Gas chromatograph for compounds in SDGE

This passage was adapted from "Terpenoids from Zingiber officinale (Ginger) Induce Apoptosis in Endometrial Cancer Cells through the Activation of p53." Liu Y, Whelan RJ, Pattnaik BR, Ludwig K, Subudhi E, et al. *PLoS ONE*. 2012 7(12): e53178. doi:10.1371/journal. pone.0053178 for use under the terms of the Creative Commons CC BY 3.0 license (http://creativecommons.org/licenses/by/3.0/legalcode).

Question 74

Which of the following is true about the separation technique used in paragraph 2?

○ A. Larger DNA particles migrate towards the cathode faster than smaller particles.

○ B. RNA is uncharged and therefore cannot be separated by the electric field.

○ C. The isoelectric point of proteins is the only determinate of their migration.

○ D. Protein size requires agarose used for DNA to be replaced by another type of gel.

Question 75

Even without the application of an electric field, a property of polyacrylamide gel makes it a good candidate for the separation of proteins and peptides. This property is also utilized in:

○ A. ion-exchange chromatography.

○ B. affinity chromatography.

○ C. size exclusion chromatography.

○ D. paper chromatography.

Question 76

Another lab attempted to reproduce the results of this study, but did not have access to GC-MS. Which of the following techniques would be the most appropriate to replace the GC in order to isolate the terpene component from SDGE?

○ A. Extraction

○ B. Ion-exchange chromatography

○ C. Affinity chromatography

○ D. Crystallization

Question 77

Based on Figure 1, which of the following is true about the compounds that generated the spike at 12 minutes?

○ A. There was more terpene collected at min=12 in each individual study (Wisconsin 1, 2, and India) than at any other time during the collection phase.

○ B. The terpene at min=12 was likely more polar than the compound at min=10.

○ C. The peak at min=12 represents a compound that equilibrated less with the liquid phase than the compound at min=10.

○ D. The terpene at min=12 was likely more polar than the compound released at min=18.

Question 78

In previous experiments, investigators found that phenolic compounds in dry ginger extract were the chemotherapeutic agents. Assuming this finding is true, which of the following results would make SDGE a nonviable candidate for chemotherapeutic drugs?

○ A. An IR study with a broad peak at 3300 cm^{-1} for a compound with 1 oxygen species.

○ B. An IR study with a sharp dip at 1710 cm^{-1} for a compound with 2 oxygen species.

○ C. An IR study with a broad peak at 3300 cm^{-1} for a compound with 2 oxygen species.

○ D. An IR study with a sharp dip at 1710 cm^{-1} for a compound with 1 oxygen species.

Next ▶

Passage III (Questions 79-83)

Prion diseases are fatal neurodegenerative diseases of humans and animals which, in addition to sporadic and familial modes of manifestation, can be acquired via an infectious route of propagation. Extensive investigations have provided evidence for prion protein (PrP) related sequences in most species of the vertebrate lineage and revealed two mammalian paralog sequences encoding for the proteins Doppel (Dpl) and Shadoo (Sho), which together with PrP constitute the mammalian prion protein family. Investigations of PrP have revealed an unusual dichotomy of its structure, which consists of an extended, largely unstructured N-terminus and a globular and relatively stable C-terminal domain formed by two short beta-strands and three alpha-helices. Most proteins do not act in isolation but partner with other proteins to exert their biological roles. Surprisingly, a subset of the ZIP family of zinc transporters act as prion protein interactors, as well as evolutionary precursors to PrP, Sho, and Dpl proteins.

The length as well as the location of the PrP, Sho, Dpl, and ZIP proteins are represented in Table 1.

Alignment of a Sho sequence showed considerable sequence conservation to ZIP (34% identity, 41% similarity) and close examination revealed that (i) a group of basic residues, (ii) the position of a hydrophobic segment and (iii) a cluster of histidines are shared between these sequences.

This passage was adapted from "Evolutionary Descent of Prion Genes from the ZIP Family of Metal Ion Transporters." Schmitt-Ulms G, Ehsani S, Watts J, Westaway D, Wille H. *PLoS ONE*. 2009. 4(9): e7208. doi: 10.1371/journal.pone.0007208 for use under the terms of the Creative Commons CC BY 3.0 license (http://creativecommons.org/licenses/by/3.0/legalcode).

Name		Localization			Length	
Protein	Gene	Compartment	Mode of membrane attachment	N-terminus	Total	Extra-cellular domain
mZIP	*slc39a5*	Plasma membrane	Type-3 TM	Extracellular	535	~210
mPrP	*Prnp*	Plasma membrane	GPI-anchor	Extracellular	254	230
mSho	*SPrn*	Plasma membrane	GPI-anchor	Extracellular	147	122
mDpl	*Prnd*	Plasma membrane	GPI-anchor	Extracellular	179	157

Table 1   Length and location of specific proteins

Figure 1   Lineage of Sho, PrP, and Dpl proteins from ZIP

Question 79

Which resin used in an ion exchanger at a pH of 4 would cause Sho to be eluted last from a solution containing other proteins?

- ○ **A.** $RCOO^-$
- ○ **B.** RNH_3^+
- ○ **C.** RCH_3
- ○ **D.** Histidine

Question 80

A solution containing ZIP and Sho proteins was isolated after treating cells with a detergent that removes proteins from the plasma membrane. Experimenters should use which technique to collect a purified sample of ZIP from this solution?

- ○ **A.** Southern blotting
- ○ **B.** NMR spectroscopy
- ○ **C.** Size-exclusion chromatography
- ○ **D.** Ion-exchange chromatography

Question 81

According to Figure 2, the disulfide domain of the prion protein family is highly conserved throughout generations. How could researchers understand the functional significance of the disulfide bond on prion protein propagation?

- ○ **A.** Create a mutation that replaces a cysteine with a tryptophan.
- ○ **B.** Create a mutation that replaces cysteine with alanine.
- ○ **C.** Delete one of the cysteine codons from the DNA sequence.
- ○ **D.** Delete both of the cysteine codons from the DNA sequence.

Question 82

Bacteria were made to take up the PrP gene through transformation. How could scientists isolate a large quantity of bacteria that successfully incorporated the gene into their genome?

- ○ **A.** Lyse cells and conduct a western blot to detect PrP.
- ○ **B.** Link a penicillin resistance gene to the PrP gene and treat cells with penicillin.
- ○ **C.** Monitor cells for PrP activity.
- ○ **D.** Link a fluorescent tag to the PrP gene and monitor bacteria for fluorescence.

Question 83

Researchers isolated Dpl mRNA and treated it with reverse transcriptase in order to produce DNA. They then combined this DNA strand with a plasmid that was taken up by bacteria. Why did scientists begin with a mRNA strand rather than starting with Dpl DNA?

- ○ **A.** The Dpl gene is unique in that it is stored as mRNA and not DNA.
- ○ **B.** DNA is very difficult to isolate in large enough quantities.
- ○ **C.** Bacteria does not have a mechanism to eliminate introns from DNA.
- ○ **D.** mRNA is less likely to be affected by mutations of the genome.

Next ▶

Passage IV (Questions 84-87)

Current molecular diagnostic technologies for septicemia have primarily focused on pathogen identification as a means to optimize antimicrobial therapy for patients. Such developments have included multiplexed PCR, microarray platforms, and chemiluminescent RNA probes for the genetic detection of known bacterial and fungal organisms responsible for septicemia. Compounding the issue of genotyping for resistance is the fact that the number of potential resistance genes scale with each pathogen, straining the limits of current diagnostic technology and economic feasibility.

Direct susceptibility testing of such blood-borne pathogens may be of greater importance than species identification via genotyping as the selective pressures of broad-spectrum antibiotic use have contributed to the increased incidence and virulence of antimicrobial resistant septicemia. One such method may be Real-time colony PCR. Real-time colony PCR is performed using universal forward and reverse primers specific for the highly conserved region of the 16S ribosomal RNA gene sequence. Real-time PCR enables the comparison of bacterial load after antibiotic exposure by monitoring the amount of 16S DNA present. Variations in bacterial load post-exposure to an array of antibiotics are amplified by PCR, allowing pathogen detection and susceptibility to be obtained in much less time.

Primer	Sequence (5' → 3')
Forward	AGAGTTT
Reverse	CTGCTGC

Table 1 Primers for 16S rRNA PCR

This passage was adapted from "A Real-Time PCR Antibiogram for Drug-Resistant Sepsis." Waldeisen JR, Wang T, Mitra D and Lee LP. *PLoS ONE.* 2011. 6(12) doi:10.1371/journal. pone.0028528 for use under the terms of the Creative Commons CC BY 3.0 license (http://creativecommons.org/licenses/by/3.0/legalcode).

Question 84

What is the DNA segment that the forward 16S rRNA primer would bind to?

- A. 5'- CTCTGGG - 3'
- B. 5'- GGGTCTC - 3'
- C. 5'- TCTCAAA - 3'
- D. 5'- AAACTCT - 3'

Question 85

Which of the following would most strongly reduce the strength of a real-time colony PCR?

- A. 16S rRNA has minor SNPs between different species of bacteria.
- B. Consistently running the PCR amplification for one extra cycle.
- C. Different species of bacteria have different numbers of 16S rRNA gene copies.
- D. Different species of bacteria express 16S rRNA in different levels.

Question 86

What is the most likely application of microarrays to testing for antibiotic resistance?

- A. To determine the number of copies of specific genes in each species
- B. To determine the expression level of genes that confer antibiotic resistance
- C. To measure survival rates when exposed to certain antibiotics
- D. To distinguish between different strains of bacteria

Question 87

What would most strongly impact the performance of the PCR amplification?

- A. Missense mutation in primer binding site
- B. Deletion mutation in primer binding site
- C. Nonsense mutation in primer binding site
- D. Faulty processing of 16S rRNA following transcription

Next ▶

Questions 88 through 92 are NOT based on a descriptive passage.

Question 88

The chart below contains information regarding two non-polar compounds, compound A and compound B.

	Compound A	Compound B
Molar mass (g/mol)	92.14	78.16
Vapor pressure at 25° C (mm Hg)	38.95	101.24
Boiling point (°C)	110.63	80.12
$\Delta H°_{f,gas}$ (kJ/mol)	+50.00	+82.93

What is the most efficient way to separate these two compounds?

○ **A.** Extraction

○ **B.** Distillation

○ **C.** Column chromatography

○ **D.** Crystallization

Question 89

Using a nucleic acid hybridization technique, scientists created a double-stranded combination of DNA and RNA. Scientists most likely employed this technique in order to:

○ **A.** amplify a DNA sequence.

○ **B.** create a recombinant DNA sequence.

○ **C.** locate recognition nucleotide sequences known as restriction sites.

○ **D.** identify DNA or RNA molecules with sequences similar to those of a labeled probe.

Question 90

A chemist used paper chromatography in order to determine the relative polarities of four unknown compounds. His results are shown in the table below.

	R_f
Compound A	0.92
Compound B	0.76
Compound C	0.78
Compound D	0.54

Which of the four compounds is the most polar?

○ **A.** Compound A

○ **B.** Compound B

○ **C.** Compound C

○ **D.** Compound D

Question 91

Which of the following could be used to separate D- and L-glucose?

    I. Thin-layer chromatography (TLC)

    II. Column chromatography

    III. Chiral resolution

○ **A.** I only

○ **B.** II only

○ **C.** III only

○ **D.** I and II

Question 92

Scientists interested in observing the fat and tissue distribution of an experimental drug synthesized using ^{13}C would be LEAST likely to suggest characterizing:

○ **A.** the chemical field shifts of functional groups containing a mix of ^{12}C and ^{13}C.

○ **B.** the splitting pattern of neighboring ^{13}C.

○ **C.** the ratio of peak integral heights between adjacent ^{13}C.

○ **D.** the number of chemically nonequivalent ^{13}C contained in a molecule.

STOP. IF YOU FINISH BEFORE TIME IS CALLED, CHECK YOUR WORK. YOU MAY GO BACK TO ANY QUESTION IN THIS TEST BOOKLET.

STOP

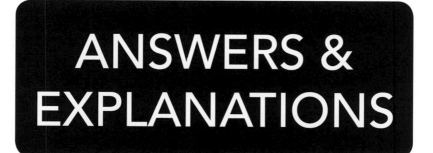

ANSWERS & EXPLANATIONS

FOR

30-MINUTE IN-CLASS EXAMINATIONS

ANSWERS FOR THE 30-MINUTE IN-CLASS EXAMS

Lecture 1	Lecture 2	Lecture 3	Lecture 4
1. C	24. C	47. A	70. C
2. C	25. B	48. A	71. B
3. B	26. B	49. B	72. A
4. A	27. D	50. D	73. C
5. B	28. A	51. C	74. D
6. B	29. D	52. A	75. C
7. A	30. A	53. C	76. A
8. B	31. C	54. C	77. B
9. D	32. C	55. D	78. D
10. A	33. B	56. A	79. A
11. B	34. A	57. B	80. C
12. C	35. C	58. B	81. B
13. B	36. C	59. B	82. B
14. C	37. B	60. D	83. C
15. A	38. A	61. C	84. D
16. B	39. B	62. A	85. C
17. A	40. B	63. D	86. B
18. C	41. A	64. B	87. B
19. C	42. D	65. C	88. B
20. A	43. C	66. B	89. D
21. C	44. D	67. A	90. D
22. C	45. D	68. C	91. C
23. D	46. D	69. A	92. B

SCORING

Any attempt we could make at score correlation to the MCAT® would mislead. Unlike the AAMC MCAT®, which includes easy questions, Examkrackers deliberately asks questions only of medium and high difficulty in order to optimize your practice time and maximize the increase to your MCAT® score. To accurately predict your MCAT® score, use an official AAMC MCAT® practice test.

Your goal is to see your raw score improve with each Examkrackers In-Class Exam and full-length EK-Test® you take. Look closely at each question you get wrong to find areas for review and to notice the habits that don't work. As you approach each new In-Class Exam or practice test, make commitments to replace what doesn't work with the approach you need to get questions right. Focus on the questions you get wrong to learn to think like the MCAT® and increase your score.

Toward your success!

EXPLANATIONS TO IN-CLASS EXAM FOR LECTURE 1

Passage I (Questions 1-5)

1. **C is the best answer.** Any answer choice that does not accurately describe the results of the experiment can be eliminated. Choice B can be eliminated because this result was part of the background research rather than being a result of the experiment. Choice A describes the results accurately but overstates the evidence; the results described show that the Unc45b^{Flag}/Hsp90 complex binds selectively to the myosin motor domain, which in turn supports the co-chaperone function, but is not conclusive. Choice C is a better answer because it points out an experimental setup and result that would provide stronger support for a co-chaperone function. Choice D is not the best answer because it describes the results accurately but does not answer the question. The result indicated actually provides support (but not conclusive evidence) for the co-chaperone function, since a chaperone should not bind to the native protein, which is already fully folded.

2. **C is the best answer.** Process of elimination is the best technique for this question. To help clarify a question, it is sometimes helpful to reword the question as a statement with "because," and then add the answer choices. For example, "Attempts at predicting protein configuration based upon amino acid sequence have been unsuccessful because:..." Even if choice A were true, it does not answer the question. Choice B is false because chaperones do not determine the product; they only stabilize intermediates. Choice D is generally false except in rare cases of neutral mutation. Choice C is a direct response to the question and is also true.

3. **B is the best answer.** This question requires an understanding of the experimental methodology. The Anti-Flag antibody is used to visualize the binding of Unc45b^{Flag} or the Unc45b^{Flag}/Hsp90 complex to the protein subfragments. If the antibody itself bound to any of the subfragments, it would be impossible to address the hypothesis that Unc45b^{Flag} will selectively bind to the non-native myosin motor domain. Choice A is not the best answer because it is not implied in the passage and is not the purpose of this experimental step. Choice C is not the best answer because the Anti-Flag antibody is already bound to the Unc45b^{Flag} in each other trial; even if this were a concern of the researchers, it could not be addressed when only the Anti-Flag antibody is present. Choice D is true but does not answer the question that was asked.

4. **A is the best answer.** Choice A describes the role of chaperones as explained in the passage. A cell with more chaperones can synthesize proteins more easily, giving it a selective advantage. Choice B is not the best answer because chaperones do not slow the process of protein folding. C is not the best answer for a number of reasons. For one, the energy for protein synthesis comes from ATP, not heat. As for choice D, chaperones do not affect the rate of polypeptide synthesis; they affect polypeptide folding.

5. **B is the best answer.** Why does a protein denature in the presence of heat? The hydrogen bonds and other non-covalent interactions in the secondary and tertiary structure are disrupted. Another way to answer this question is to notice that all the bonds are covalent except hydrogen bonds. Although hydrogen bonds are the strongest type of intermolecular bond, they are much weaker than covalent bonds, and will be disrupted before covalent bonds when heat is applied.

Passage II (Questions 6-10)

6. **B is the best answer.** An enzyme (like any type of catalyst) lowers the energy of activation of both the forward and reverse reactions, as stated in answer choice B. This means that choices A and C can be eliminated. Choice D is not the best answer because a catalyst does NOT alter the equilibrium mix of reactants and products. The reason that lowering the energy of activation for both the forward and reverse reactions can cause a buildup of the product is that in the absence of the enzyme, the forward rate would be so low that no significant amount of product would be formed.

7. **A is the best answer.** The correct answer to this question has to accurately describe the effects of the type of inhibition named and describe an effect that would decrease the specificity constant. Recall from the passage that the specificity constant is found by dividing the turnover number, k_{cat}, by K_m. A decrease in turnover number or an increase in K_m would decrease the specificity constant. Also notice that turnover number must be proportional to V_{max}. Replacing "turnover number" in each answer stem with "V_{max}" makes it possible to answer the question based on background knowledge of the types of inhibition. Competitive inhibition increases K_m but does not change V_{max}. Choices C and D do not accurately describe competitive inhibition and can be eliminated. The effect of the scenario described in choice D on the specificity constant also cannot be predicted; it would depend on the exact amount of change in each parameter. Choice B is not the best answer because noncompetitive inhibition does not change K_m. Choice A is the best answer because it describes the effect of noncompetitive inhibition and contains a scenario that would lead the specificity constant to decrease.

8. **B is the best answer.** This question requires reasoning about the equation given for the specificity constant in the passage. If the turnover number (the numerator) decreases, K_m (the denominator) must decrease by the same amount for the overall value of the fraction to stay the same. Choice A can be eliminated - as described in the passage and demonstrated in Figure 1, E43G does show some enzymatic activity, although the catalytic efficiency is reduced. Choice C is true but does not answer the question. (Choice C also probably goes beyond the knowledge of amino acids required for the MCAT®. Glutamate is the name for the amino acid glutamic acid in its anion form.) Finally, choice D is a tempting answer, since increased K_m reflects decreased enzymatic affinity for the substrate. Notice that according to the equation given in the passage, however, an increase in K_m along with the decrease in turnover number would cause the specificity constant to decrease, not stay the same.

9. **D is the best answer.** It is the only answer choice that describes the effect of an uncompetitive inhibitor on K_m and V_{max}. Choice A describes a mixed inhibitor (recall that some mixed inhibitors preferentially bind to the enzyme prior to formation of the enzyme-substrate complex and therefore raise K_m, while others preferentially bind to the enzyme-substrate complex and therefore lower K_m). Choice B describes a competitive inhibitor. Choice C describes a noncompetitive inhibitor, which has no preference between the enzyme alone or enzyme-substrate complex and therefore does not change K_m.

10. **A is the best answer.** One of the key characteristics of proteins is that they can have a huge variety of structures due to the multitude of possible combinations of R groups with differing chemical properties. As a result, the active site of each type of enzyme can be precisely fitted to a particular substrate (enzyme specificity). In contrast, choice D describes the characteristics of proteins inaccurately. Choice B describes a characteristic feature of lipids, not proteins. Choice C is not the best answer, since extremes of pH and temperature can denature proteins.

Passage III (Questions 11-14)

11. **B is the best answer.** This question is a straightforward test of knowledge of the structures of various types of fats. It is important to be familiar with the general structure of triglycerides, phospholipids (described by A), waxes (described by C), and steroids (described by D). Even without remembering the structure of a triglyceride, it would be possible to find the answer to this question by reasoning from the name: "tri-" means 3, and "glyceride" refers to the glycerol backbone.

12. **C is the best answer.** The MCAT® is likely to ask questions asking for the interpretation of additional findings, but this is a particularly difficult example. It is best answered by process of elimination. Choice A can be eliminated because it does not refer to lipoviro-particles at all. This answer might be chosen by a test-taker who was reading too quickly and thought it referred to lipoviro-particles rather than VLDL. Choice B contradicts the conclusion: if a cell line with no apoB lipoproteins was able to secrete the HCV envelope proteins, an alternative mechanism would have to be considered. Choice C directly relates to the experimental design described in the passage. If MTP inhibition reduced the secretion of multiple proteins other than apoB, it would be possible that the effect on E1 and E2 secretion was due to one of those other proteins. The fact that only apoB was reduced supports the conclusion that apoB is involved in the secretion of these glycoproteins and ultimately lipoviro-particle formation. The finding described in D does not provide firm support for or against the conclusion described in the question stem. Choice C is a better answer.

13. **B is the best answer.** This question requires interpretation of the graphical data and the findings described in the passage. Choice B is the best answer because Figure 2 shows a significant decrease in secreted apoB in the presence of Cp 346086, and Figure 1 shows that Cp 346086 did in fact inhibit MTP. Therefore, apoB secretion decreases when MTP activity decreases, a direct correlation. If choice A were true, Figure 1 would show no difference between the two doses of MTP inhibitor, but the data indicate a difference at both 24h and 48h. Choice C can be eliminated because the passage states that the secretion of these glycoproteins was greatly decreased when MTP was inhibited. This finding suggests a direct correlation rather than an inverse correlation. Choice D is not the best answer: as shown in Figure 1, MTP activity was significantly lower in the presence of Cp 346086.

14. **C is the best answer.** The passage says that a glycoprotein is composed of a protein and a short chain of monosaccharides. Choices A, B, and D are all polysaccharides used for long-term energy storage or structural material; only glucose is a monosaccharide.

Passage IV (Questions 15-18)

15. **A is the best answer.** The carbonyl of the four-membered ring in the penicillin derivatives is an electrophile that can be attacked by a nucleophile with electron density. The side chains, or R groups, of the amino acids facilitate the chemistry that happens in the active site of an enzyme. Only side chains with valence shell electrons that can act as nucleophiles would be able to attack the carbon of the carbonyl to open the ring. Serine has a hydroxyl on the end of the R group, with an oxygen with free electrons. Hydroxyls can act as nucleophiles, eliminating choice B. Similar to serine, cysteine has a thiol group, -SH, at the end of its side chain. Sulfur also has free electrons that could attack the carbonyl, eliminating choice C. Glutamate is an acidic amino acid with a carboxylic acid at the end of its side chain. The terminal oxygen has significant electron density and can also act as a nucleophile, eliminating choice D. Isoleucine is a nonpolar amino acid with methyl groups at the end of its side chain. It has no free electron density to serve as a nucleophile, making it the LEAST likely to facilitate the reaction. Choice A is the best answer choice.

16. **B is the best answer.** The last sentence of paragraph two describes how penicillin-derivative antibiotics function by competing with the pentapeptide in the active site of the PBPs, which makes the antibiotics competitive inhibitors. In the Lineweaver-Burk plot presented above, a competitive inhibitor would raise K_m and maintain V_{max}. The x-intercept represents $1/K_m$, so the best answer will show an intercept with a value closer to zero, or the origin on the graph provided. With a competitive inhibitor, the K_m would increase, meaning that the value of $1/K_m$ would decrease and become closer to zero. The y-intercept represents $1/V_{max}$, so it should be the same. Choice A represents a non-competitive inhibitor that decreases V_{max} and keeps K_m constant. Choice A can be eliminated because the y-intercept is higher in A versus the no competition, meaning that the value of $1/V_{max}$ is larger, making V_{max} smaller. Choice A can be eliminated. Choices C and D represent allosteric activators of the protein, as V_{max} is increased and K_m is maintained. V_{max} in increased in both of these choices because the value of the y-intercept, $1/V_{max}$, is reduced, meaning that V_{max} is higher. Choices C and D can be eliminated. Additionally, there is no way to distinguish between choices C and D from the information provided in the passage, so the answer choices may also be eliminated this way. Choice B is the best answer because it shows the same y-intercept, maintaining V_{max}, while showing an increased K_m.

17. **A is the best answer.** Paragraph two describes penicillin and penicillin derivatives as competitive inhibitors of PBPs, as the molecules compete for the pentapeptide in the enzyme active site. The passage does not describe the role of glycoproteins in maintaining the fidelity of the bacterial cell wall. While it is possible that differences in glycoprotein concentration could occur in antibiotic-resistant bacteria, choice B is unlikely to be the best answer because no information is provided. Antibiotic-resistant bacteria are more likely to have increased expression of β-lactamase, based on the second paragraph, eliminating choice C. Nonsense mutations truncate a protein, rendering it non-functional. The passage notes that transpeptidase is responsible for catalyzing reactions that maintain the fidelity of the bacterial cell wall. Nonsense mutations would greatly decrease the concentration of functional transpeptidase, weakening the stability of the wall. This would make bacteria more likely to be killed, eliminating choice D. A competitive inhibitor, such as penicillin, can be overcome by increasing the concentration of the normal substrate. In this case, the normal substrate is the D-Ala-D-Ala component of peptidoglycan. Increasing the concentration of peptidoglycan would make it more likely that the transpeptidase would catalyze the reaction that maintains the bacterial cell wall, providing a selective advantage against antibacterial treatment. Choice A is the best answer.

18. **C is the best answer.** Paragraph three describes how a –COOH group of the derivative is condensed with an –NH$_2$ group of the 6-APA penicillin precursor molecule to generate the penicillin-derivative antibiotic. While this question appears to test specific knowledge of any pathways, it really tests the types of enzyme reactions. A lyase is responsible for reactions where functional groups are added to double bonds, or conversely when a double bond is formed by removal of a functional group. Because this is a condensation reaction, where one group is added to another, a lyase is unlikely to be the best answer, eliminating choice A. A DNA ligase joins the phosphodiester backbone of DNA, eliminating choice B. An isomerase catalyzes the transfer of groups within a molecule. Because two molecules are being added together, choice D is unlikely to be the best answer. A ribosome is a type of ribozyme, meaning an RNA molecule that catalyzes a reaction. In the ribosome, the protein components serve to orient and secure the RNA molecules that actually catalyze the reaction. A ribosome catalyzes the formation of peptide bonds between the –COOH of one amino acid and the –NH$_2$ of another. This reaction is nearly identical to the formation of the penicillin derivatives, making choice C the best answer choice.

Stand-alones

19. **C is the best answer.** Recall that hydrogen bonds are critical to the structure of DNA. Purine-pyrimidine base pairs from complementary DNA strands are held together by hydrogen bonds. Choices A and B can be eliminated because covalent bonds are not involved in holding together complementary DNA strands; although hydrogen bonds are the strongest of the intermolecular bonds, they are not as strong as covalent bonds. Van der Waals forces exist between all molecules, but they are not the major forces behind complementary base pairing. Choice C is a better answer.

20. **A is the best answer.** This question is a good example of one that appears much more difficult than it actually is. The MCAT® probably would not require knowledge of Lineweaver-Burk plots; the question simply requires application of knowledge about the types of inhibition. Choices B and C can be eliminated because they both demonstrate a change in V$_{max}$, whereas competitive inhibition does not change V$_{max}$. Choice D can be eliminated because it does not show a change in K$_m$, unlike in competitive inhibition.

21. **C is the best answer.** This answer choice describes a difference between the two types of nucleic acids but switches RNA and DNA. It is RNA that contains the hydroxyl group and DNA that contains only a hydrogen at the same carbon. This difference can be remembered by thinking of the full names of RNA and DNA: ribonucleic acid and *deoxygenated* ribonucleic acid. The other answer choices describe key differences between RNA and DNA that must be known for the MCAT®.

22. **C is the best answer.** The phospholipid elements exposed to the outside of the cell will be most likely to bind to the protein that reacts with antiphospholipid antibodies. Sphingosine does not contain phosphate although some sphingolipids do. This makes choice D a possible answer but likely not the best answer. Fatty acid chains are nonpolar and remain localized to the hydrophobic region of the phospholipid bilayer, which makes choice A unlikely. Similarly, the glycerol backbone is composed of a three-carbon chain that is nonpolar and unlikely to be exposed to the aqueous environment outside the cell, eliminating choice B and making choice C, the polar phosphate head group, the best answer.

23. **D is the best answer.** Notice that the table provides K$_m$ and V$_{max}$ values, indicating that the three compounds interact with the GLUT2 protein in different ways. Compound C shows relatively no change in K$_m$ from the no inhibition state but a decrease in V$_{max}$. A competitive inhibitor increases K$_m$ and does not change V$_{max}$, eliminating choice A. An uncompetitive inhibitor decreases K$_m$ and decreases V$_{max}$. Because compound C does not decrease K$_m$, it is most likely not the best answer choice, eliminating choice B. Keep in mind, if there was an answer choice that was 9×10^{-7}, that is the same as 0.9×10^{-6} which is relatively similar to 1×10^{-6} as well. A mixed inhibitor can increase or decrease K$_m$ and decrease V$_{max}$. Because the K$_m$ value does not change, choice C can be eliminated. A noncompetitive inhibitor maintains the K$_m$ but decreases the V$_{max}$, as is seen in choice D. Choice D is the most likely type of inhibition seen by compound C.

EXPLANATIONS TO IN-CLASS EXAM FOR LECTURE 2

Passage I (Questions 24-27)

24. **C is the best answer.** The passage states that there was no specific enrichment of DNA methylation on chromosome 21, eliminating choices A and B. It also states that enrichment occurred on various autosomes, so the effects are not sex-linked; D can be eliminated.

25. **B is the best answer.** Aneuploidy is the term used to describe the condition of having one or more extra or missing chromosomes, such as trisomy 21 (DS). Aneuploidy is a major chromosomal mutation that generally results from nondisjunction during meiosis. The results of Experiment 1 suggest that altered DNA methylation may be a response to trisomy 21. The results of Experiment 2 indicate that altered DNA methylation affects gene expression. Also recall that the background prior to the experiments describes the hypothesis that DNA methylation is altered in response to changes in gene dosage, which must occur due to an alteration of ploidy. According to this hypothesis, which is supported by the results of the experiments, aneuploidy would have to precede DNA methylation, which means choices A and D can be immediately eliminated. The results of Experiment 2 indicate that DNA methylation precedes differential gene expression, so choice C is not the best answer.

26. **B is the best answer.** The graph from Experiment I shows that DS individuals have DECREASED methylation compared to the control group, so choice I is false. Choices A and C can be eliminated. Option II appears in both of the remaining answer choices, so it is only necessary to determine whether III is true to answer the question. The graph from Experiment I shows that methylation of *TMEM131* DECREASES with age, so gene expression should INCREASE with age in control individuals. Option III can be eliminated, making B the best answer. It is also possible to determine that option II is true. The passage states that the drug 5aza-dC causes decreased methylation. The graph from Experiment 2 shows that increased doses of the drug (decreased methylation) cause gene expression of *TMEM131* in control cells to mimic that of DS individuals. Based on this information, DNA methylation inhibits *TMEM131* gene expression, making option II true.

27. **D is the best answer.** If it is true that increased methylation in repressor regions increases gene expression, decreasing the methylation of repressor regions on *CD3Z* with 5aza-dC could decrease gene expression. Choice A is not the best answer because 5aza-dC DECREASES methylation rather than increasing it. Choice B is not the best answer because if most methylation sites were located on the promoter region, demethylation would cause INCREASED gene expression. Choice C is irrelevant since all of the genes explored were autosomal.

Passage II (Questions 28-32)

28. **A is the best answer.** Choice A indicates that the poly-A tail is not coded for by DNA, but is synthesized separately. It offers a mechanism by which synthesis may take place other than transcription. Choice B indicates that the poly-A tail is transcribed from DNA at the end of the gene. Even if choices C and D made sense, they would indicate that the poly-A tail was transcribed from a gene.

29. **D is the best answer.** The question is really asking, "Where does post-transcriptional processing take place?" The answer is in the nucleus. Post-transcriptional processing of rRNA and tRNA commonly takes place in prokaryotes, but the post-transcriptional processing of mRNA described in the passage takes place in eukaryotes. Furthermore, snRNPs are not found in prokaryotes. The "sn" stands for "small nuclear" and prokaryotes do not have nuclei.

30. **A is the best answer.** Figure 2 is an electron micrograph of R looping. The passage explains that R looping is a technique where DNA and mature RNA are hybridized. Mature RNA has no introns, so choice C is not the best answer. The loops are parts of the DNA that correspond to the removed sections of the RNA and therefore have no complementary RNA sequence; the loops are DNA introns.

31. **C is the best answer.** The outcome of the experiment described indicates that intronic sequences (the inserted Alus) control the changeover of splicing from constitutive to alternative. If alternative splicing existed before introns evolved, factors other than intronic sequence would have had to be controlling alternative splicing mechanisms, contradicting the study's findings of intronic control.

32. **C is the best answer.** Splicing in eukaryotes is carried out by the spliceosome complex. A spliceosome is composed of snRNPs which, in turn, are made up of snRNA and a variety of proteins. The spliceosome brings the ends of an intron together to form a loop known as a lariat, excises the intron, and joins the ends of the two exons together. Splicing takes place in the nucleus. By contrast, rRNA is located in the cytoplasm of the cell and is involved in translation, not splicing.

Passage III (Questions 33-37)

33. **B is the best answer.** As stated in the passage, DNA markers are variable DNA sequences with a known location on a chromosome. Researchers track which version of each marker is present in the DNA of a given person and try to find correlations with a specific phenotype, in this case preterm birth. If a DNA marker is close to the gene of interest it will have a high probability of being inherited with that particular gene. This phenomenon is called gene linkage. Choice A describes the opposite of what occurs in gene linkage. If the genes and DNA markers were independently assorted, there would be no correlation between DNA markers and specific genes in the pattern of inheritance. Choice B describes the gene linkage phenomenon and allows for the linkage studies described in the question stem. The mechanism of crossing over does not specifically move DNA markers from one place on a chromosome to another, but rather switches chucks of chromosomes between homologous pairs. This makes choice C not the best answer. In the passage, DNA markers are described as variable DNA sequences. Choice D describes them as uniform, which is in opposition to what is stated in the passage. Because choice B is the only answer choice that explains why markers can locate genes, it is the best answer.

34. **A is the best answer.** As stated in the passage, a haplotype is a set of DNA variations that are usually inherited together. This is similar to the concept of gene linkage and opposite to the concept of independent assortment. Recombination would separate the DNA variations and make it less likely for the variations to be inherited together. This makes choice A a strong answer choice. No evidence is given in the passage that haplotypes are more or less likely than other DNA to be prone to methylation or mutation, which makes choice B and choice C unlikely answers. Segregation is the process during meiosis when chromosomes separate into daughter cells. All genetic material is segregated, and there is no reason to suggest that haplotypes would not segregate. Choice D can be eliminated.

35. **C is the best answer.** Figure 1 shows that several individuals have the mutation in *IGF1R* on only one chromosome, paternal or maternal, and have SPTB. This eliminates choice A because the individual would need the mutation on both the maternal and paternal chromosome to have a phenotypic outcome if the mutation was autosomal recessive. Expressivity is how much of a genotype is expressed as a phenotype. In this case, the passage only gives us information on whether the individual was born preterm or not. There is not a spectrum of phenotypic outcomes. Figure 1 does not give the reader enough information to determine whether choice B is true. Choice D can be eliminated because the fact that individual 7 has one copy of the gene but does not have the phenotype means that it cannot be an autosomal dominant mutation. Penetrance is the probability of a gene being expressed if it is present. In other words, will the phenotype appear if the individual has the genotype? Choice C is the best answer because it explains why individual 7 could have the mutation and not be born preterm, without assuming anything about the pattern of inheritance.

36. **C is the best answer.** Recall that DNA polymerase can repair errors during DNA replication. However once meiosis is complete, the DNA polymerase cannot make repairs to the DNA. When the embryo is formed by the two gametes, there is no mechanism to detect that the *IGF1R* mutation has been inherited twice. While the *IGF1R* gene may have poor outcomes for the fetus, there is nothing intrinsically wrong with the DNA for DNA polymerase to fix. This makes choice A a weak answer choice. While it is possible that two people who have the mutated *IGF1R* gene have never had a child, this is an unlikely scenario, especially since preterm birth has a high prevalence according to the passage. Choice B is possible, but it is not the most plausible answer choice. Students should always be wary of answer choices that use absolute terms like never. When an individual has a deleterious gene like *IGF1R*, the normal copy of the gene may be able to compensate and allow the individual to survive if the individual is a hybrid. If there are two copies of a deleterious gene, the consequences may be so severe on the embryo that it is no longer viable and the mother will have a miscarriage. Choice C is the best answer because it accounts for the fact that hybridization allows for the viability of the embryo. Choice D directly contradicts the information stated in the passage: the *IGF1R* gene is located on chromosome 15.

37. **B is the best answer.** Choice A is not the best way to alter the experiment because it does not include a control variable for the researchers to compare the experimental variable to. Choice B is the better answer because it does include a baseline to compare to. Choice C is not a strong answer choice because it would not give any information on the relationship of IGF1R to the incidence of diabetes mellitus, instead of building upon what the researchers were already exploring. The question stem specifies that SPTB babies were identified to be less likely to be susceptible to diabetes mellitus. Exploring the mutation in non-SPTB babies would not allow the researchers to discover its relationship to the individual's susceptibility to diabetes mellitus. This makes choice D not the best answer.

Passage IV (Questions 38-41)

38. **A is the best answer.** The scientists that performed the experiments in the passage used plasmids encoding HPV-16 E6 and E7. These plasmids already allowed overexpression of the E6 and E7 oncoproteins, making choices C and D less likely to be the answer because further overexpression of the proteins would not confirm their ability to induce DNA damage in cooperation with CSC. Given that the scientists overexpressed the proteins in their presented experiments, the most likely next step would be to reduce the expression of these proteins and observe if the oncogenic potential decreased. A reduction of expression should occur in the SiHa lung cancer cells in order to compare these results to the control and overexpression studies, making choice A the best answer choice. Because choice B uses control instead of SiHa cells, it is unlikely to be the best answer.

39. **B is the best answer.** The implied transcription of the *luc2* gene can be determined by the relative production of luc2 protein. Figure 1 shows the levels of the luc2 protein produced with varying CSC concentrations. According to Figure 1, as the concentration of CSC increases from 0 to 50 μg/mL CSC, the luc2 fluorescence increases, meaning more protein is produced, making choice B the most likely answer choice. Figure 1 does not show a decrease with increasing concentration, making choice A unlikely to be the best answer. Given that a positive correlation is observed, luc2 transcription is likely dependent upon CSC concentration, making choice C unlikely to be the answer. Figure 1 also provides the data that determine the relationship between transcription and CSC concentration, making choice D unlikely to be the best answer.

40. **B is the best answer.** In metaphase, the chromosomes of the cell line up on the equator of the cell in a linear arrangement, making choice B the most likely answer choice. Mitosis begins with prophase, which is characterized by the breakdown of the nuclear membrane and the condensation of chromosomes. However, these chromosomes are not yet aligned on the cell equator, making choice A less likely. Telophase and cytokinesis occur at the end of mitosis and are characterized by reforming the nuclear membrane and separation of the two halves of the cell into two separate cells. Because the sister chromosomes have already been split apart and are not aligned at the equator, choices C and D are less likely to be the best answers.

41. **A is the best answer.** Prophase is the first step of mitosis, which is the phase of the cell cycle that is directly after the G2 growth phase. During mitosis, two identical daughter cells are produced from one parent cell. The DNA has been replicated into two copies during S (Synthesis) phase prior to G2 and will be separated during metaphase of mitosis. There are two copies of the genome at the beginning of prophase. One copy of the genome consists of 23 pairs of chromosomes, or 46 chromosomes. The chromosomes have been replicated, but not separated, and each chromosome consists of 2 chromatids. There are a total of 92 chromatids but still 46 chromosomes, eliminating choice D and making choice A the most likely answer choice. There would be 92 chromosomes in the cell only during anaphase when the chromatids have been separated but the cell has not yet fully separated. Cells undergoing meiosis would be expected to have 23 chromosomes at the end of meiosis I, eliminating choice B. A cell that has only 12 chromosomes would be considered an aneuploid cell and would likely not undergo mitosis but instead undergo apoptosis, making choice C unlikely.

Stand-alones

42. **D is the best answer.** There are 4^3 possible codons. There are more codons than there are amino acids used to produce proteins. This means that an amino acid could be coded for by several codons. The genetic code is evolutionarily very old, and is almost universal.

43. **C is the best answer.** Both children are female because the genotype of Turner syndrome, according to the information provided, must be XO. The O reflects the lack of a chromosome from the parent within whom nondisjunction occurred; the X came from the other parent. In the scenario described in the question stem, the mother only has healthy X chromosomes to pass on, while the father has only one colorblind X chromosome to pass on. Therefore, the colorblind child got her X chromosome from the father and no chromosome from the mother, and the healthy child got her X chromosome from the mother and no chromosome from the father.

44. **D is the best answer.** The primary spermatocyte is the spermatogonium just after DNA replication. Humans never have more than 46 chromosomes. The primary spermatocyte has 92 chromatids but only 46 chromosomes.

45. **D is the best answer.** An X chromosome is randomly inactivated in only female somatic cells, eliminating choices A and C. Human males have only one X chromosome and do not undergo X chromosome inactivation, eliminating choice C. X chromosomes do not become inactivated in female germ cells, allowing either X chromosome to be transmitted to offspring, making choice D the best answer.

46. **D is the best answer.** The lac operon is a common example of a bacterial operon. It contains an operator, promoter, and the genes transcribed. These units frequently contain multiple genes controlled by the operon unit, and this is referred to as polycistronic. The *E. coli* that have this operon generally use glucose for energy but can break down lactose when it is present and when glucose is absent. In such a situation, an activator binds the promoter region to turn it on to its active form. Choice D is the best answer because it accurately describes the structure and function of the lac operon: it contains three genes and is inactive unless activated externally. The other answer choices misidentify one or both of these points. It is easy to become confused by redundant two-part answer choices, but one strategy that helps is to try to think of the best answer and then find the answer that most closely matches..

EXPLANATIONS TO IN-CLASS EXAM FOR LECTURE 3

Passage I (Questions 47-51)

47. **A is the best answer.** The substrates of glycolysis are monosaccharides—including glucose, fructose, and galactose—and the glycerol backbones of triglycerides, which are converted into intermediates of the glycolysis pathway. Glycolysis produces pyruvate, which is converted into acetyl-CoA, a substrate of the citric acid cycle. Fatty acids are broken down into acetyl-CoA via beta-oxidation. They enter the citric acid cycle but do not undergo glycolysis. The carbon chains of amino acids also serve as substrates for the citric acid cycle, but not glycolysis.

48. **A is the best answer.** Insulin promotes cellular uptake and use of glucose. An increased ratio of insulin to glucagon is most likely to lead to an increased glycolytic rate. The choices can be narrowed down to A or B. Insulin also promotes storage of glucose and inhibits breakdown of glycogen and fats, so an increased insulin to glucagon ratio is most likely to lead to net anabolism.

49. **B is the best answer.** According to Figure 1, wild type mice exposed to VILI have the highest glucose and Glut1 transcript levels. Wild-type with VILI would have the highest glycolytic rate. Given that "elevations of transcript levels of glycolytic enzymes were found to be attenuated in *Hif1A^ff* SurfactantCre⁺ mice," it is unlikely that *Hif1A^ff* SurfactantCre⁺ mice would have the highest glycolytic rate.

50. **D is the best answer.** The hypoxia-inducible factor described in the passage promotes glucose uptake and usage, so it can be inferred that hypoxia-inducible transcription factor (HIF-1) does the same. Increased expression of HIF-1 should lead to increased expression of transporters and glycolytic enzymes. Choices A, B, and C can be eliminated, leaving D as the best answer. Glycolysis and gluconeogenesis are reciprocally regulated, meaning that when one is occurring relatively frequently, the other is occurring relatively infrequently. For this reason, cancer cells, which display increased expression of HIF-1 and therefore increased expression of glycolytic enzymes, would be least likely to exhibit increased expression of gluconeogenic enzymes.

51. **C is the best answer.** Decreasing an enzyme's affinity for its substrate inhibits that enzyme, so choice A can be eliminated. Conversely, increasing an enzyme's affinity for its substrate activates that enzyme, so choice B can be eliminated. Because glycolysis produces ATP, it makes sense that ATP would inhibit and ADP would activate phosphofructokinase. Choice D can be eliminated, and choice C is the best answer.

Passage II (Questions 52-55)

52. **A is the best answer.** Insulin promotes use and storage of glucose, and therefore activates enzymes for glycogenesis (glycogen synthesis). It concurrently inhibits enzymes for gluconeogenesis (glucose synthesis) and lipolysis (fat breakdown).

53. **C is the best answer.** According to the passage, HSL hydrolyzes diacylglycerols, so HSL level is a determinant of lipolytic capacity. HSL promotes lipolysis, which is positively associated with insulin resistance, but HSL does not directly promote insulin resistance; choice C is a better answer. It is ATGL that initiates enzymatic breakdown of triacylglycerols, not HSL, so choice B is not the best answer. While it may be the case that higher levels of HSL tend to be associated with lesser metabolism of glucose, HSL level is more appropriately a measure of lipid metabolism rather than glucose metabolism, making choice D not the best answer.

54. **C is the best answer.** As shown in Figure 2, reduced HSL activity is associated with increased insulin sensitivity; that is, $HSL^{+/-}$ mice had lower percentages of basal glucose in their plasma. Choices B and D, which suggest that reduced HSL activity would decrease insulin sensitivity, can be eliminated. The passage states that $HSL^{+/-}$ mice did not experience a change in fat mass, so a drug that inhibits HSL would not be expected to increase fat mass. Choice A can be eliminated. The most likely outcome would be an increase in insulin sensitivity and no change in fat mass, making C the best answer.

55. **D is the best answer.** Choices A, B, C and D all provide support for the assertion that $HSL^{+/-}$ mice exhibited diminished lipolytic capacities. Choice D, however, provides the strongest support. The findings presented in choices A and B confirm that $HSL^{+/-}$ mice are haploinsufficient for hormone sensitive lipase, but they do not rule out the existence of a compensatory mechanism occurring as a result of the reduction in HSL expression. The finding presented in answer choice C does rule out one potential compensatory mechanism, but it does not, in and of itself, suggest diminished lipolytic capabilities. Only answer choice D confirms that reduced lipolytic response was actually observed in $HSL^{+/-}$ mice.

Passage III (Questions 56-60)

56. **A is the best answer.** To answer this question, the reader should refer to the passage to review the main causes and risk factors of NAFLD/NASH. Mutations that promote any of these processes would promote NAFLD/NASH. Lipase is an enzyme that breaks down triglycerides and releases free fatty acids into the blood stream. As stated in the passage, hepatic lipid accumulation can be a result of an influx in free fatty acids. Overactive lipase in the cells of the body would cause increased free fatty acids. This makes choice A consistent with NAFLD/NASH pathogenesis. Because insulin resistance is a major risk factor for NAFLD/NASH, mutations that impaired the effect of insulin would be consistent with NAFLD/NASH pathogenesis. Normally, insulin speeds up glycolysis. Choice B, a constitutively active enzyme of glycolysis, would not slow down glycolysis but would more likely speed it up. This would enhance the effect of insulin and act in opposition to insulin resistance, eliminating choice B. Choice C, decreased secretion of glucagon, is not consistent with the findings in Figure 1, which shows that patients with NAFLD/NASH have increased glucagon levels compared to the controls. Additionally, the passage states that GLP-1 decreases glucagon secretion and that GLP-1 deficiency contributes to the diseases. A mutation leading to decreased glucagon secretion would most likely not contribute to disease progression. Choice D is in direct opposition to the researchers' findings in Figure 1. NAFLD/NASH patients are found to have decreased levels of GLP-1 and this likely contributes to insulin resistance and disease development.

57. **B is the best answer.** According to the passage, GLP-1 improves insulin sensitivity. A deficiency in GLP-1 would contribute to insulin resistance, which results in increased lipolysis and free fatty acids. Free fatty acids accumulate in the liver and lead to NAFLD/NASH. Choice B accurately describes the series of events leading to NAFLD/NASH. Figure 1 demonstrates that a deficiency in GLP-1 would lead to increased glucagon levels. Choice A describes the opposite effect that a GLP-1 deficiency would have on glucagon levels. Choice C is not the best choice because a GLP-1 deficiency would lead to decreased efficiency of insulin and result in increased glucose levels not decreased levels of glucose. Decreased glucose levels would also not result in inflammation. Choice D is not the best answer because Figure 1 A shows that patients with NAFLD/NASH do have a decreased GLP-1 level compared to controls. This makes choice B the best answer.

58. **B is the best answer.** Glycogenolysis is the process of breaking glycogen down into glucose monomers. Choice C and choice D can quickly be ruled out because they describe gluconeogenesis and glycolysis respectively. Glycogen is broken down to form glucose, which can then be used to generate ATP. Glycogenolysis occurs via addition of a free phosphate to create glucose-1-phosphate which is then converted to glucose-6-phosphate for glycolysis. Choice A can be eliminated because ATP is not used to cleave glucose from the glycogen molecule.

59. **B is the best answer.** A sound experimental design would include both patients and controls. Choice A and choice C propose only measuring GLP-1 levels in patients. Because unsaturated fats have less reducing potential than saturated fats, they store less energy, or calories, in the body. It is more likely that unsaturated fats will be burned and used than saturated fats. Choice B and D propose similar experimental designs. Choice B is the better answer because unsaturated fats are less likely to be stored in the body and contribute to the pathogenesis of NAFLD/NASH.

60. **D is the best answer.** According to the passage, GLP-1 decreases glucagon secretion after a meal. Glucagon opposes the effects of insulin and insulin resistance is a major risk for NAFLD/NASH. Choice A can be eliminated because the controls are meant to be healthy individuals to compare to patients and the results of the oGTT shown in Figure 1 do not show insulin resistance. Choice B is partially true because the controls do have more circulating GLP-1. However this would lead to increased suppression of glucagon secretion, not decreased suppression. In normal physiology, insulin release suppresses glucagon secretion. In NAFLD/NASH patients, Figure 1 shows that while insulin remains high for a longer time than in control patients, the NAFLD/NASH patients still exhibit more glucagon secretion than control patients. This eliminates choice C. Choice D is the best answer because decreased levels of GLP-1 would lead to decreased suppression of glucagon secretion and this is supported by the data in Figure 1.

Passage IV (Questions 61-64)

61. **C is the best answer.** Insulin is a major regulator of many metabolic processes. In general, it is best to think of insulin as supporting processes that build larger molecules such as glycogen and triglycerides. Glucagon does the opposite and increases the breakdown of these larger compounds for energy in the fasting state. Since people with low β cell mass have impaired insulin secretion, cells in the body may continue to function as if they are under fasting conditions at all times. Insulin inhibits gluconeogenesis, since insulin is present at high levels after a meal where glucose is already abundant. The lack of insulin is expected to lead to an increase in gluconeogenesis, though this process only occurs in the liver and in some cells in the kidney, so choice A is misleading. Because a lack of insulin leads to an increase and not a decrease in the breakdown of glycogen, choice B can be eliminated. Choice C is the best answer, since it identifies a process associated with a low serum insulin. Lipolysis is the breakdown of triglycerides, and this process is supported by a lack of insulin. Choice D is tricky, since issues of metabolism in diabetes can lead to ketoacidosis from ketone bodies, though not from lactic acid. The increase in ketogenesis is also the result of a lack of insulin where the increase in the breakdown of lipids leads to the overproduction of ketone bodies.

62. **A is the best answer.** The passage explains that following an increase in reactive oxygen species in the cell, cytochrome c is released from the inner mitochondrial membrane to the cytosol to induce apoptosis. Cytochrome c is a major constituent of the electron transport chain and along with ubiquinone, it functions as an intermediate electron carrier to shuttle electrons between the complexes of the chain, so choice A is the best answer. ATP synthase is the major enzyme at the end of the electron transport chain responsible for creating ATP from ADP. This is not the best answer because cytochrome c is more similar to ubiquinone, since they are both intermediate electron carriers, whereas ATP synthase is an enzyme complex with a fixed position in the chain. Succinate dehydrogenase is the name for the second enzyme complex of the electron transport chain and is also an enzyme involved with the citric acid cycle. It is not necessary to know the name of this enzyme, and this answer choice can be ruled out using the knowledge that cytochrome c is an electron carrier and not a stable enzyme complex. FAD and NADH are electron carriers and can be considered similar to cytochrome c. These electron carriers bring electrons to the chain, whereas ubiquinone and cytochrome c move electrons within the chain, so choice D is not the best answer.

63. **D is the best answer.** This question can be tricky in light of the details about oxidation and reduction. For the purpose of this question it is best to think about reduction as a gain in electrons, while oxidation is a loss of electrons. NADH is the reduced form of NAD⁺ and carries electrons to the electron transport chain. At that point, it donates the electrons and is oxidized. Choice A is inaccurate because it substitutes reduction for oxidation. Oxygen is the final electron acceptor, though as an acceptor, it is reduced and not oxidized, so choice B can be eliminated. Choice C is also misleading, since while it is true that water is formed from the reduction of oxygen, water itself is not reduced. Choice D is the best answer, since as a component of the electron transport chain, cytochrome c is both oxidized and reduced.

64. **B is the best answer.** This is a research question asking for the factor that would make it difficult to study the role of AIF in beta-cell apoptosis. The passage discusses previous research about the role of AIF in apoptosis in neuronal and retinal cells. Choice A is true, but is not a true barrier to the study. Many cellular processes involve complex signaling in cells, but they can be studied by inhibiting different steps along the pathway to determine the effects of upstream molecules. The passage explains that both AIF and cytochrome c are mitochondrial proteins that can trigger apoptosis through migrating from the mitochondria to the cytosol. This means that there may be considerable overlap between these two proteins, and this may make it difficult to isolate the role of one from the other. It is still possible to study the role of one independently, as the previous studies indicate. Of all the answer choices, however, this is the only one that presents a logical issue that should be addressed. Choice C is not supported from the passage, since apoptosis predictably follows oxidative stress. Choice D is not supported by the passage, since there is no indication that AIF is only present in these cells. AIF is found in mitochondria, and mitochondria are found in cells throughout the body.

Stand-alones

65. **C is the best answer.** The high-energy electrons from NADH drive protons outward across the inner mitochondrial membrane. Even without remembering the role that NADH plays in aerobic respiration, it would be possible to eliminate choice B because energy is not required for passive diffusion.

66. **B is the best answer.** Substrate-level phosphorylation is a reaction through which an energy-rich intermediate transfers its phosphate group to ADP, forming ATP. Glycolysis produces ATP through substrate-level phosphorylation. A glycolytic reaction that produces ATP would do so through substrate-level phosphorylation. Note that the reference to phosphoglycerate kinase is not relevant to answering the question. Substrate-level phosphorylation should be distinguished from oxidative phosphorylation, which is the production of ATP via the electron transport chain and ATP synthase.

67. **A is the best answer.** Glucose-6-phosphate can serve as an important molecule in both glycolysis as well as the pentose phosphate pathway. The pentose phosphate pathway produces ribose-5-phosphate, glyceraldehyde-3-phosphate, and fructose-6-phosphate. The question stem indicates that glucose-6-phosphate is a precursor for nucleotides. One of the most important roles of the pentose phosphate pathway is to produce ribose-5-phosphate, which is a precursor for the production of nucleotides. The pentose phosphate pathway also produces NADPH, which is essential for fatty acid synthesis. Choice B and D both make use of glucose-6-phosphate, but neither process produces nucleotides. Choice C is inaccurate because the urea cycle does not make use of glucose-6-phosphate.

68. **C is the best answer.** Blood glucose levels are increased when the liver exports glucose that it has broken down from glycogen or synthesized through gluconeogenesis. Amino acids, glycolysis intermediates, and triglycerides can all feed into the gluconeogenic pathway, helping to synthesize new glucose. In contrast, even numbered carbon chain fatty acids are broken down into acetyl-CoA, which is unable to be turned into glucose because it directly enters the citric acid cycle. Therefore, the macromolecule least likely to increase blood glucose levels is palmitate, a 16-carbon fatty acid, making choice C the best answer choice. Alanine is converted into pyruvate and feeds into gluconeogenesis, eliminating choices A. 3-phosphoglycerate is a glycolysis/gluconeogenesis intermediate and could contribute to gluconeogenesis, eliminating choice B. The glycerol of the triglyceride feeds into gluconeogenesis as DHAP, eliminating choice D.

69. **A is the best answer.** Dietary fatty acids, of which triacylglyceride is an example, are absorbed in the small intestine and repackaged into chylomicrons by enterocytes. Chylomicrons then travel through the lymphatic system into the venous blood supply. Chylomicrons are then picked up by the liver and repackaged into VLDL. Radiolabeled free fatty acids would be found in highest concentration in chylomicrons because they would be directly packaged by enterocytes, making choice A the best answer choice. VLDL, LDL, and HDL would all contain some amount of radiolabeled carbon that would decrease each time the lipoprotein was processed by the liver. While memorizing the triglyceride content of chylomicrons, VLDL, LDL, and HDL is not necessary for the MCAT®, they contain 90%, 70%, 10%, and 5% triglyceride, respectively. Choices B, C, and D are unlikely to contain as much radiolabeled carbon as chylomicrons and can be eliminated as the best answer choice.

EXPLANATIONS TO IN-CLASS EXAM FOR LECTURE 4

Passage I (Questions 70-73)

70. **C is the best answer.** PCR is characterized by three phases: denaturation, annealing, and extension. During the denaturation phase, the PCR reaction is heated to a high temperature, where the double stranded DNA denatures into two single strands. During annealing, the temperature is lowered, allowing the primers to bind the complementary sequence of DNA, marking the region for amplification. During extension, the DNA polymerase extends the sequence from the annealed primer, creating a new copy of a gene. The temperature must be lowered during the annealing phase in order to allow the primer to hydrogen bond to its complementary DNA sequence. The DNA polymerase used in PCR is designed to withstand high temperatures and was unlikely to be degraded during the reaction, eliminating choice A. If the temperature were maintained too high, no fragments would be observed because the primers did not have an opportunity to anneal to mark the region of amplification, eliminating choice B. The RNA primers would not be destroyed by high temperatures, much like the DNA polymerase. They would, however, be unable to bind their complementary sequence on DNA, eliminating choice D and making choice C the best answer.

71. **B is the best answer.** A restriction site is cut by an enzyme that cleaves the double stranded DNA, typically in an asymmetric fashion. This cleavage produces a short fragment of DNA that can be run on a Northern blot to check for a specific sequence or on an agarose gel to check for a specific size. Restriction enzyme sites are typically 4-6 bases long in order to provide specificity. Choice A is less likely to be the best answer because it is only 2 bases long. Restriction enzyme sites also have a tendency to be palindromic, meaning that the sequences are read the same forward and backwards. Comparing choices B and C, choice B is palindromic because it is read 5′-GGATCC-3′ on both the sense and antisense strands, making choice C less likely than choice B to be the best answer. Choice D is 9 bases long, which would be less likely than choice B, which is 6 bases long and palindromic to be the best answer choice. Choice B fits the criteria to be a candidate restriction enzyme site because it is 6 bases long and palindromic, making it the best answer.

72. **A is the best answer.** In order to use duplex PCR to look at nucleotide substitutions in RNA, scientists would first need to create a sequencing library of cDNA. cDNA is the complementary DNA copy of an RNA transcript, produced by reverse transcription. The AT rich region upstream of exon one is most likely the TATA Box of the promoter. The promoter sequence is not transcribed into RNA and would not be included in a cDNA library. Variations in the sequences described in choice A would be the LEAST likely to be discovered by duplex PCR, making choice A the best answer choice. Transitions are base changes that occur between similarly structured bases, such as between purines, which include A and G, and between pyrimidines, which would include C and T. Exons are included in the cDNA and transitions could be detected, eliminating choice B. Transversions are between dissimilar bases, such as A and C. Transversions in exon five could be detected as well in cDNA, eliminating choice C. The 3′ untranslated region is part of an RNA template and would be reverse transcribed, along with the exons of a given gene. The untranslated region follows the stop codon in the RNA. The portion of the RNA is not translated to protein but would be transcribed by reverse transcriptase since reverse transcriptase is not halted by stop codons. Single nucleotide polymorphisms (SNPs) are common variants that can occur between individuals. These SNPs would be detected in cDNA as well and could be sequenced, eliminating choice D.

73. **C is the best answer.** According to the question stem, the 8-oxo-dG preferentially pairs with dA, leading to a transversion of the DNA sequence. In PCR, the polymerase creates a complementary copy of the DNA strand it is reading. If 8-oxo-dG is present in an oxidized strand and the polymerase inserts dA across from the oxidized base, the next round of replication would lead to the insertion of a T. Additionally, the question stem describes that a transversion occurs, which is a substitution of bases of dissimilar type, such as a purine to a pyrimidine. Insertion of an adenine would be on the complementary strand during PCR, not on the original strand, eliminating choice A. The polymerase inserts a complementary base across from the oxidized base. 8-oxo-dG would not pair with its identical guanine base, G, eliminating choice B. Cytosine incorporation would be found on the complementary strand if the original G were not oxidized. Choice D can be eliminated because it does not describe the original strand containing 8-oxo-dG. A transversion would describe a G to a T change and a T would be inserted opposite A. Choice C is the best answer choice.

Passage II (Questions 74-78)

74. **D is the best answer.** This question is testing the principles of gel electrophoresis. Gel electrophoresis is used to separate mixtures of DNA, RNA, or protein on the basis of size and charge. Fragments are loaded into wells at the top of the gel and electrical charge is applied. The gel used for DNA and RNA is typically agarose gel. The smaller the fragment, the more easily it can move down the gel through the pores in the agarose. Larger fragments tend to get stuck and move more slowly. In gel electrophoresis, the anode is the positively charged terminal while the cathode is the negatively charged terminal. Choice A seems to address movement of fragments based on charge, but really the question does not require knowledge of which terminal is positively or negatively charged. The answer choice states that the larger particles would move faster, which is untrue, so choice A can be eliminated without knowing the charge of the cathode. Gel electrophoresis relies on charge for separation of particles, and because DNA and RNA are both charged molecules, they are good candidates for separation. Choice B is false and can be eliminated because it claims that RNA is uncharged. Gel electrophoresis for proteins, like DNA and RNA, relies on both size and charge for separation, so choice C can be eliminated because the isoelectric point is not the only determinant for separation. The MCAT® will often use language like "always" and "only" in answer choices. It is rare that things are so clear cut, and these are usually not the best answers. Proteins are much larger than fragments of DNA or RNA so agarose gel is not the best medium for gel electrophoresis because few, if any, of the proteins will be able to migrate. This gel is typically replaced with another type of gel, so choice D is true and should be selected as the best answer.

75. **C is the best answer.** Gel electrophoresis relies on both the charge and size of proteins and peptides in order to achieve separation. The charge of a given protein or peptide will cause it to migrate toward the oppositely charged pole when an electric field is applied to the gel. The type of gel used also aids in the separation because different gels have different sized pores. These pores are rate determining in the migration of proteins, because smaller proteins can more easily wind through the pores while the larger ones become stuck. The question stem states that the property of interest is independent of the electric field, so the question must be asking about size. Different types of chromatography utilize similar principles, so the best answer choice will be the one related to separation based on size. Ion-exchange chromatography relies on net surface charge to separate molecules. Based on the question stem, it is known that the property referred to does not rely on charge, so choice A is not the best answer. Affinity chromatography takes advantage of highly specific interactions to select molecules. Affinity chromatography does not separate molecules based on a particular property, like size, so choice B is not the best answer. Size exclusion chromatography allows for the separation of molecules based on size or molecular weight, so choice C is consistent with the question stem. Paper chromatography relies on the polarity of different compounds to achieve separation. Since paper chromatography does not rely on the principle of size, choice D can be eliminated, leaving choice C as the best answer.

76. **A is the best answer.** This question is asking which method would be the most appropriate to separate a group of compounds, terpenes, from an SDGE. When considering separation techniques, think about what these compounds have in common. This will usually point to one technique over the others. Terpenes are a subset of lipids, meaning that they have *hydrophobic* hydrocarbon backbones. Choice A, extraction, allows for the separation of a mixture using solubility – remember "like dissolves like." So extracting the terpene layer of solution using various solvents is a reasonable way to achieve this separation. Ion-exchange relies on the charge and size to separate various compounds, usually via gel filtration. Since the passage does not indicate anything about the size or charge of the molecules, choice B is not the best answer. Affinity chromatography uses highly specific interactions to slow down select molecules. Because investigators want to separate out an entire group of terpenes with potentially variable properties, choice C is not the best answer. Crystallization is not a very strong method of separation, so choice D is not the best answer and can be eliminated, leaving choice A as the best answer.

77. **B is the best answer.** A signal is generated on the gas chromatograph when a compound is released from the column. Compounds are released based on their ability to equilibrate with the stationary liquid phase inside the column; the more they equilibrate, the slower they are released. The passage indicates that the liquid phase is polar, so the compounds that are released most quickly should be non-polar. Considering Figure 1, choice A is not the best answer because in the India study, more compound was collected at min=5 than min=12. Choice B states that the compound released at min=12 was more polar than the compound at min=10, and this is true based on the above logic; if the compound at min=10 is less polar, it should be released first. Choice C is not the best answer because the compound at min=12 represents a compound that equilibrated more with the stationary liquid phase than the compound at min=10, which is why it was released after more time. Choice D states that the more polar compound would have been released first. This is inconsistent with this study because the liquid phase was polar, so choice D can be eliminated, leaving choice B as the best answer.

78. **D is the best answer.** Infrared spectroscopy relies on the presence of functional groups to generate signals. Some of the most important functional groups for the MCAT® include the alcohol/phenol and the carbonyl, their signals can typically be seen as a broad peak between 3200-3600 cm^{-1} and a sharp dip at 1710 cm^{-1}, respectively. The question is asking which IR study results would indicate that there is not a therapeutic phenol in the compound. An IR study of a compound with its only oxygen generating a broad peak in the phenolic area, as described in choice A, suggests the presence of a phenol and can be eliminated. Choices B and C are tricky because there are two oxygen species which means that either of these compounds could contain a carboxylic acid rather than a carbonyl and phenol separately. In choice D, there is a sharp dip in the carbonyl range and this is the only oxygen in the compound, so there could not possibly be a phenol present. Choice D is the best answer because there is no scenario in which this compound contains a phenol. For both choices B and C, it is possible that these compounds contain phenols so these answers should be eliminated, and choice D should be selected.

Passage III (Questions 79-83)

79. **A is the best answer.** Ion exchangers function by forming ion pairs with the protein or molecule of interest. Ion pairs form when there is both a positive and negative charge present. When choosing which resin to use, the charge on the protein of interest should be considered. An oppositely charged resin will attract the protein and cause it to be eluted last from the solution. The passage states that Sho contains histidine residues as well as a basic patch. At a pH of 4, both of these segments of the protein will be positively charged because in an acidic solution basic residues pick up protons. The positively charged Sho protein will be attracted to a negatively charged anionic resin. Choice A is the best answer because it is the only resin that is negatively charged. Choice B can be eliminated because the positive charge on RNH_3^+ will repel the positive charge on Sho and would cause the protein to be eluted quickly from the ion-exchange column. Choice C can be eliminated because the passage states that there are charges present. RCH_3 is a hydrophobic resin and would only be effective for a mostly nonpolar protein. The hydrophobicity of RCH_3 would not attract the positively charged Sho, and the protein would be eluted quickly from solution. Choice D can be eliminated because Sho contains histidine residues. A histidine resin would have the same charge as Sho and would result in Sho being repelled and eluted from the solution.

80. **C is the best answer.** This question is asking which purification technique would be best suited to separate a solution containing ZIP and Sho. Information pertaining to these two proteins can be found in Figure 1. Southern blotting is a purification technique that is used to isolate a piece of DNA from a large sample of DNA. Since ZIP and Sho are proteins, Southern blotting cannot be used to separate them, so choice A can be eliminated. NMR spectroscopy is an imaging technique that is useful for predicting the structure of an unknown protein based on the arrangement of protons in the molecule; however, it cannot separate proteins in a solution. Choice B can therefore be eliminated. Size-exclusion chromatography is a protein purification technique that separates proteins based on size. Figure 1 contains the length of both Sho and ZIP and it shows that ZIP is more than three times larger than Sho. As a general rule, proteins need to differ in size by at least 10% in order to be separated by size-exclusion chromatography. The difference in size of these two proteins is significant enough that size-exclusion chromatography would efficiently separate them, so choice C is the best answer. Ion-exchange chromatography separates proteins based on differing charges due to the amino acid residues present. The passage states that there are many conserved amino acid residues between Sho and ZIP and no information in the passage indicates that these proteins have different charges. Therefore, choice D is not the best answer.

81. **B is the best answer.** A disulfide bond is the covalent linkage of two sulfur atoms that are part of cysteine residues. This bond can also be called a cystine bond. When doing any type of protein manipulation, it is important to replace amino acids with other residues that will have the least impact on the structure of the protein but will still allow for information about function to be gather. Choice A can be eliminated because a tryptophan amino acid is large and hydrophobic whereas cysteine residues are small and polar. By using a tryptophan residue, the structure of the prion proteins will be largely disrupted and little information about the role of the cystine bond will be obtained. Using an alanine residue to replace a cysteine amino acid is a good option. Alanine residues are similarly sized to cysteine residues and will only disrupt the structure of the protein by eliminating the disulfide bond so choice B is the best answer. Choice C can be eliminated because deleting the cysteine residue completely from the protein will cause a larger structural impact than replacing it with an alanine residue. Similarly, choice D can be eliminated because by deleting both cysteine residues from the protein structure, the protein structure would deviate significantly compared to replacing the cysteine residue with an alanine residue.

82. **B is the best answer.** When creating a transgenic bacteria, it is important to efficiently identify the bacteria that successfully incorporated the gene into their genome. Choice A can be eliminated because each individually lysed bacteria would not produce enough PrP protein to be detected by Western blotting. Western blotting is most useful for detecting the presence of proteins in a larger sample. Additionally, lysing each individual bacteria in the colony and conducting a Western blot is not practical. The best way to identify the bacteria that successfully incorporated the DNA into their genome is to link the gene of interest to a penicillin resistance gene and then treat the bacteria colony with penicillin. Only the bacteria that successfully took up the DNA will survive after being treated with penicillin so choice B is the best answer. Choice C can be eliminated because there is no efficient way to directly see PrP activity within the bacteria. Even if a method did exist, it is easier to eliminate all of the non-transgenic bacteria from the population so choice B is better than choice C. Choice D can be eliminated because it would require researchers to examine every bacteria in the population and look for the fluorescent tag. It would be more effective to apply penicillin and remove the bacteria that did not incorporate the gene so choice B is better than choice D.

83. **C is the best answer.** In all species, genes are always stored as DNA and not RNA so choice A can be eliminated. Choice B can be eliminated because many different methods exist for isolating DNA from eukaryotes. After a eukaryotic cell has been lysed, its DNA can be collected fairly easily using different purification techniques. The benefit of isolating the eukaryotic mRNA is that the introns have already been removed. Bacteria do not contain enzymes that eliminate introns. If the DNA was directly incorporated into the plasmid, it would also contain introns and the Dpl protein would be nonfunctional so choice C is the best answer. Choice D can be eliminated because mRNA is based on the DNA. A mutation in the DNA will always be transcribed into the mRNA because DNA serves as the template for mRNA production.

Passage IV (Questions 84-87)

84. **D is the best answer.** Choices A and B are not the best answers because they contain mispairings of A to C and G to T. The last two choices both contain the same sequences but are in opposite order to each other. When complementary strands bind, the order is reversed. $5' \rightarrow 3'$ binds to $3' \rightarrow 5'$. The complementary segment is 3'-TCTCAAA-5', which is choice D.

85. **C is the best answer.** Consider each answer individually. Minor SNPs, unless they are in the primer binding site, would not affect the experiment much. Choice A is unlikely because of the degree of change that the SNPs cause. Choice B would double the quantitative result of each experiment, but the relative values would remain unchanged. If strains have different numbers of gene copies, then this experiment that uses 16S DNA to measure bacterial survival is confounded. A bacteria with twice as many gene copies in this test would misleadingly seem to have its population doubled based on the PCR results, making choice C the best answer. In this experiment, rRNA expression is not measured. It is the 16S DNA that is measured, so choice D is unlikely.

86. **B is the best answer.** Microarrays are used to measure the level of gene expression. RNA is converted to DNA, and this DNA is quantified on the microarray. There is no way for a microarray to determine survival rate, so choice C is unlikely. A better test for this would be a proliferation assay. The number of gene copies is not directly reflective of gene expression, so choice A does not describe what a microarray is able to do. Choice D can be eliminated because distinguishing bacterial strains does not specifically help to determine antibiotic resistance. Measuring the expression of genes that are known to give antibiotic resistance directly tackles the goal in the question, making choice B the best answer.

87. **B is the best answer.** Nonsense and missense mutations are single replacements. While these mutations could slightly reduce primer binding, it should not be totally disrupted since the other bases are still complementary and in the right position, eliminating choices A and C. A deletion mutation removes one base from the sequence, shifting the remainder of the DNA sequence by one base. This will greatly interfere with the primer binding sequence, making choice B the best answer. Choice D can be eliminated because the passage states that Real-time PCR quantifies the level of DNA, not transcribed rRNA.

Stand-alones

88. **B is the best answer.** Compounds with boiling points differing by more than 20°C can be separated by distillation, a separation technique made possible by differences in vapor pressure. Compound A has a boiling point of 110.63° whereas compound B has a boiling point of 80.12°. Both extraction and column chromatography rely on difference in polarity. The question stem states that both compounds are non-polar. Crystallization is a very inefficient method of separation.

89. **D is the best answer.** Nucleic acid hybridization techniques are used to identify DNA or RNA molecules with sequences similar to those of a labeled probe. For example, a fluorescently or radioactively labeled complementary RNA sequence (called a probe) might be used to identify a target DNA sequence among a library of DNA sequences.

90. **D is the best answer.** R_f = length traveled by the component divided by length traveled by the mobile phase. Because polar compounds are attracted to the polar paper on which they travel, their movement is slowed, giving them R_f values lower than those of nonpolar compounds. The most polar compound is the compound with the lowest R_f value.

91. **C is the best answer.** Most types of chromatography separate substances based on differences in polarity, including the two listed in options I and II. There is no significant difference in polarity between the two chiral partners of glucose. Chiral resolution, on the other hand, is a technique specifically designed to separate racemic mixtures, or mixtures consisting of two chiral compounds. Choice C is the best answer.

92. **B is the best answer.** In contrast to ^{1}H-NMR, ^{13}C-NMR does not contain splitting patterns due to neighboring radioactive carbons. Remember that ^{13}C is the only isotope of carbon that might appear in an NMR spectrum and can be treated the same way as ^{1}H-NMR, with the exception that ^{13}C-NMR does not contain splitting, making choice B the best answer. The other aspects of NMR, such as shifting chemical fields due to neighboring electron-withdrawing and electron-donating groups, the ratio of peak heights, indicating the number of chemically equivalent carbons giving rise to a peak, and the number of chemically nonequivalent carbons should all be recorded to characterize a molecule. Choices A, C, and D can be eliminated.

ANSWERS & EXPLANATIONS

FOR

QUESTIONS IN THE LECTURES

ANSWERS TO THE LECTURE QUESTIONS

Lecture 1	Lecture 2	Lecture 3	Lecture 4
1. B	25. B	49. C	73. C
2. B	26. D	50. C	74. A
3. C	27. A	51. C	75. D
4. D	28. D	52. A	76. A
5. C	29. B	53. C	77. B
6. A	30. A	54. D	78. B
7. C	31. C	55. C	79. B
8. C	32. C	56. D	80. D
9. B	33. D	57. D	81. C
10. C	34. C	58. D	82. C
11. D	35. C	59. B	83. B
12. C	36. B	60. A	84. C
13. C	37. C	61. D	85. A
14. B	38. A	62. C	86. D
15. D	39. B	63. D	87. A
16. B	40. A	64. A	88. B
17. C	41. D	65. A	89. D
18. B	42. B	66. A	90. D
19. A	43. A	67. C	91. A
20. D	44. A	68. A	92. B
21. C	45. B	69. D	93. C
22. C	46. A	70. B	94. A
23. B	47. A	71. B	95. B
24. B	48. D	72. A	96. D

EXPLANATIONS TO QUESTIONS IN LECTURE 1

1. **B is the best answer.** Fundamentally, catabolic reactions break down molecules while anabolic reactions build up molecules. Hydrolysis is used to break down triglycerides, proteins, and carbohydrates, and is involved in nucleotide catabolism, making choice B the best answer. For the MCAT®, choices A and C are synonymous and both describe anabolic reactions: dehydration and condensation reactions link together two monomers, releasing a water molecule in the process. Choice D is a distracter: elimination describes a class of reactions within organic chemistry, but this question is written from a biological/biochemical perspective. Given the presence of choice B, which answers the question on a biochemical level, choice D can be eliminated.

2. **B is the best answer.** DNA is a nucleotide polymer. A nucleotide is comprised of a ribose sugar, a phosphate group, and a nitrogenous base. The nucleotides in DNA are held together by phosphodiester bonds, eliminating choices A, C, and D. Peptide bonds link amino acids together to make polypeptides or proteins, making choice B the best answer.

3. **C is the best answer.** Van der Waals forces are the sum of the attractive and repulsive forces, not including covalent and electrostatic interactions between molecules making statement I true and eliminating choice B. Hydrogen bonds may occur between amino acids, and they also occur between complementary DNA bases, making statement III true and eliminating choice A. Disulfide bonds can stabilize proteins but are not seen in the DNA double helix, eliminating statement II and making choice C the best answer.

4. **D is the best answer.** Fats are a more efficient form of energy storage than carbohydrates and proteins, making choice C unlikely to be the best answer choice and choice D the best answer choice. The phospholipid bilayer membrane is a component of cell structure that is made up of fat, eliminating choice A. Fats, such as prostaglandins, behave as hormones, eliminating choice B.

5. **C is the best answer.** DNA is double-stranded with A, C, G, and T, while RNA is single stranded with uracil (U) replacing T. The 'D' in DNA stands for deoxy-, meaning that DNA lacks a hydroxyl group possessed by RNA at its second pentose carbon atom. RNA contains an additional hydroxyl group, making choice C the best answer choice. Thymine is found in DNA, but not RNA, ruling out choice A. A double helix is the characteristic shape of DNA, not RNA, making choice B unlikely to be the best answer choice. Both DNA and RNA are capable of hydrogen bonding, eliminating choice D.

6. **A is the best answer.** Though this question presents with a lot of distracting information, it is merely asking what reactant is necessary to break a glycoside linkage. Both alpha and beta linkages in polysaccharides are hydrolyzed by adding water, making choice A the best answer. The question asks for a reactant; choices C and D are enzyme catalysts which are never reactants, eliminating them as possible answer choices. Choice B can also be eliminated.

7. **C is the best answer.** Since A always binds with T and G always binds with C, both the ratio of A/T and the ratio of G/C equal one, making choice C the best answer. In a single strand of DNA, there is no pairing between adenine and thiamine and guanine and cytosine. Therefore it cannot be expected that the number of adenine residues equals the number of thymine residues (in biochemistry, residues refer to monomers), making choice A unlikely to be the best answer choice. Likewise, there is no reason to believe that the number of adenine residues should equal the number of guanine residues, eliminating choice B. While the ratio of A/T and G/C both equal one because there is one purine for every pyrimidine in double stranded DNA, there is no reason to believe that the sum of adenine and thymine residues equals the sum of cytosine and guanine residues, eliminating choice D.

8. **C is the best answer.** Prostaglandins are lipids that act as hormones, and hormones are secreted into the circulatory system and allow for communication with various organs or tissues. Hydrophobic hormones bind with receptors intracellularly. As such, prostaglandins would not be able to achieve their end effect if they were embedded in membranes, making choice C the best answer. Glycolipids, sphingolipids, and steroids are all major components of the cell membrane.

Lecture Question Expls.

9. **B is the best answer.** Proteins are the only major nutrient containing nitrogen. The body begins breaking down its proteins during times of fasting and starvation. Glycogenolysis is the breakdown of glycogen which does not contain nitrogen so choice A can be eliminated. Similarly, lipolysis is the breakdown of lipids; lipids do not contain nitrogen, choice C can be eliminated. Excess ADH secretion would result in decreased urine production. Though this may increase the concentration of nitrogenous waste products because they will be dissolved in less water, this would not result in excessive amounts of nitrogen. Also note that the question asks what the most likely cause is. It is far more likely that one has a breakdown in bodily proteins rather than a tumor in that specific location. Choice D can be eliminated.

10. **C is the best answer.** The bending of the polypeptide chain is the tertiary structure of a protein, so choice C is the best answer. The primary structure describes only the amino acid sequence of the protein, ruling out A. Secondary protein structure refers to the formation of α-helices and β-pleated sheets. As the question states that proline cannot participate in the α-helices, it does not participate in secondary structure, eliminating choice B. Quaternary structure describes the union of multiple peptide chains, which is not described in this question, eliminating choice D.

11. **D is the best answer.** Prosthetic groups are molecules that remain covalently bound to enzymes during a reaction. They are often necessary for moving molecules between multiple active sites within a single enzyme. Co-factors are the broad class of molecules that are required for proper enzyme function. Prosthetic groups function most similarly to co-factors, making choice D the best answer. The holoenzyme itself, not the prosthetic group, would function like a catalyst, making choice A less likely to be the best answer . Reactants and intermediates are also part of a chemical reaction that would use prosthetic groups, not act like them, making choices B and C unlikely to be the best answer.

12. **C is the best answer.** Decreasing the temperature always decreases the rate of any reaction, and has the ability to bring the enzyme either closer or farther from its optimal temperature, eliminating choice B. Lowering the concentration of a substrate will only lower the rate of an enzymatic reaction if the enzyme is not saturated, making choice C the best answer. Adding a noncompetitive inhibitor will definitely lower the rate of a reaction because it lowers V_{max}, eliminating choice D. Changing the pH will increase or decrease the rate of an enzymatic reaction depending upon the optimal pH for that enzyme, eliminating choice A.

13. **C is the best answer.** A high temperature would denature the enzyme, rendering it ineffective. This precludes all other answers from being true: without a functioning enzyme, an enzyme-catalyzed reaction would not proceed to completion, eliminating choices A, B, and D.

14. **B is the best answer.** The amino acid bias and shapes of the secondary structures (α-helices and β-pleated sheets) are partially explained by the rigid structure of the peptide bond, whose double bond character prevents rotation and makes the amide group planar. This rigidity provides steric constraints on hydrogen bond formation for some amino acids that prevents them from participating in some secondary structural elements. This structural feature does not affect the sequence of amino acids, eliminating choice A. Secondary structure is a better answer than tertiary structure: secondary structure is defined by hydrogen bonding along the protein's backbone, while tertiary structure is defined by interactions between side groups. The partial double bond character of the peptide bond is a characteristic of the backbone, so it more logically affects secondary structure, eliminating choice C. For the same reasoning, choice B is a better answer than D, which can be eliminated.

15. **D is the best answer.** This question expects the reader to gather enough information from the question stem to classify both thrombin and fibrinogen. The question states that fibrinogen is cleaved to fibrin. The cleavage of "fibrinogen to the active fibrin enzyme" is a buzz phrase for a zymogen, which is a precursor protein that needs to be cleaved in order to form the active enzyme. Zymogens often end with the suffix -ogen. A protease is an enzyme that cleaves peptide bonds and a restriction enzyme cleaves DNA. Based on the question stem, there is not sufficient evidence to suggest that fibrinogen acts as a cleavage enzyme, so choices B and C can be eliminated, leaving choices A and D. The question then states that thrombin catalyzes the reaction that cleaves fibrinogen. The two remaining answer choices are restriction enzyme and protease. As discussed above, a restriction enzyme cleaves DNA and a protease cleaves peptide bonds. Most enzymes are proteins, so thrombin is most likely a protease and choice D is the best answer.

16. **B is the best answer.** Enzymes function by aiding in the breaking of bonds in the substrate and making the bonds in the product, eliminating choice A. Choice C is true: this is a description of the induced-fit model, eliminating it. Enzymes are more effective catalysts than non-biological catalysts, eliminating D. Choice B is a false statement: at equilibrium there is no net change in the concentration of products and reactants, making it the right answer.

17. **C is the best answer.** Feedback inhibition works by inhibiting enzyme activity and preventing the buildup and waste of excess nutrients, making both I and II true and eliminating choices A and B. Non-enzymatic feedback mechanisms also exist, like the action potential in the neuron. This makes III false, eliminating choice D and making choice C the best answer.

18. **B is the best answer.** Noncompetitive inhibition changes the configuration of the enzyme. In competitive inhibition, an inhibitor binds to the active site, preventing the substrate from binding. The shape of the enzyme is not altered, eliminating A. Both positive inhibition and feedback inhibition can occur via competitive or noncompetitive means, eliminating choices C and D.

19. **A is the best answer.** The implanted, fertilized embryo produces human chorionic gonadotropin (HCG), which stimulates the corpus luteum to continue producing progesterone in a positive feedback mechanism. Negative feedback would result in stable, rather than increasing levels of progesterone, eliminating choice B. Feedback inhibition describes the process by which a molecule binds to an enzyme, decreasing its activity, eliminating choice C. Feedback enhancement is a made up term and a distractor, eliminating choice D.

20. **D is the best answer.** The small intestine is more basic than the stomach, meaning that there is a decreased hydrogen ion concentration, eliminating choices A and B. Peptidases that function in the stomach must work at a low pH. Because enzymes are only active across a narrow pH range, the movement from a high pH environment to a low pH environment would decrease the enzymes' activity, eliminating C and making D the best answer.

21. **C is the best answer.** A competitive inhibitor may be overcome by increasing the concentration of substrate. With a sufficiently large concentration of substrate, the substrate will outnumber the competitive inhibitor and outcompete it. Choices A and D can be eliminated. Increasing temperature would not allow the substrate to outcompete the inhibitor, eliminating choice B.

22. **C is the best answer.** Noncompetitive inhibitors lower V_{max} and have no effect on K_m. V_{max} is a measure of the velocity, or speed at which the enzyme can catalyze the reaction. Because there is less enzyme available as it becomes unable to bind to the substrate once it binds to the inhibitor, V_{max} decreases. Noncompetitive inhibitors have no effect on K_m, which indicates the concentration of substrate needed to saturate the enzyme. This is generally used as a measure of the enzyme's affinity for the substrate. In this case, the active sites of uninhibited enzymes are unaffected, resulting in no effect on K_m. Uncompetitive inhibitors decrease both V_{max} and K_m, eliminating choice A. Proteolytic enzymes are those that catalyzes the hydrolysis of peptide bonds, eliminating choice B. Mixed inhibitors share characteristics of both noncompetitive and competitive inhibitors. They decrease V_{max} and have the ability to either increase or decrease K_m, eliminating choice D.

23. **B is the best answer.** Cooperativity occurs in enzymes when the binding of one substrate either increases or decreases the affinity of the enzyme for the binding of another substrate. Cooperativity requires multiple binding sites on the enzyme, making choice B the best answer. A mixed inhibitor binds to both the substrate and enzyme-substrate complex. This is unrelated to cooperativity, eliminating choice A. Likewise, a high concentration of substrate and positive or negative feedback are not necessary for cooperativity, eliminating choices C and D.

24. **B is the best answer.** K_m indicates the concentration of substrate needed to saturate the enzyme. Uncompetitive inhibitors only bind to the enzyme-substrate complex but do not bind to free enzyme. K_m is decreased because the binding of the uncompetitive inhibitor prevents the enzyme and substrate from dissociating. Because the substrate cannot dissociate from the enzyme, it takes a lower concentration of substrate to saturate the enzyme, lowering the K_m. This makes choice B the best answer and eliminates choices A and D. C is not likely to be the best answer because uncompetitive inhibitors bind to the enzyme-substrate complex; this complex does not exist until the enzyme binds substrate.

EXPLANATIONS TO QUESTIONS IN LECTURE 2

25. **B is the best answer.** This question involves a few parts and can be somewhat confusing. It is asking for a logical setup for an experiment that would test the effects of a compound on repair pathways during replication. In the absence of repair pathways, changes to the DNA sequence go uncorrected and lead to mutations. The experiment requires an effective control that differs from the test sample in only one variable. Choice A is lacking because the control differs in two ways: the cells are non-dividing, making them less prone to mutation, and there is no compound in the sample. Choice B is the best answer, since the control is only differs in terms of the absence of the compound. The researchers could then evaluate for the number of new mutations that arise in one replication cycle in the presence or absence of the compound. Choices C and D are misleading but difficult because they focus on heterochromatin and euchromatin. Euchromatin is DNA that is loosely-packed around histone proteins and is easy to uncoil during transcription, whereas heterochromatin is very tightly-packed, making the DNA less accessible to the enzymes carrying out replication or transcription. Heterochromatin is highly methylated, allowing for increased DNA to histone binding and a tighter configuration. These ratios would not help to determine the effects on repair pathways because they do not indicate the presence of mutations arising from a lack of repair pathways.

26. **D is the best answer.** Choice A is not the best choice because environmental factors can play a role in gene regulation at nearly every step of the process of expression. Gene expression is often regulated by environmental factors at the level of transcription, for example, through epigenetic changes. In choice B, environmental effects select for certain phenotypic differences, but do not produce them. Additionally, even though living organisms share many of the same gene sequences necessary for supporting life, it is inaccurate to say that genetic differences are negligible. Choice C is true but does not directly address the question of the interplay between genes and the environment. Choice D is the best answer because environmental factors affect where and how a genome is read, which can result in differing products or differing amounts of products.

27. **A is the best answer.** Epigenetic alterations change the way the genome is read by the cellular machinery, but they do not change the genome itself, making choice A false and the best answer. Choice C is true but not the best answer because, while most organisms have DNA genomes, some viruses do contain genomes made from RNA. For choices B and D, it is true that the genome can be read differently depending on the circumstance. Notice that choices B and D are essentially saying the same thing – that it is possible for the genome to be read differently. The repetitiveness of these two choices prevents either from being the best answer.

28. **D is the best answer.** Epigenetic changes help control gene expression by regulating the access of cellular machinery to certain areas of the genome through their effects on chromatin structure. Choices A, B, and C all affect chromatin structure and are examples of epigenetic changes. Epigenetic changes do NOT change the sequence of the genome's nucleotides (only the way the genome is read), making choice D the best answer.

29. **B is the best answer.** Increased DNA methylation generally blocks cellular machinery from transcribing the highly methylated area. This results in inactivation of Section X. Without the up-regulation from Section X, Gene Y will produce fewer products which will result in decreased disease symptoms. This chain of logic makes B the best answer. Choices A and D can be eliminated because activation of Section X would not result in decreased symptoms and inactivation of Section X will not result in increased symptoms.

30. **A is the best answer.** In order to fit large amounts of genetic material into a small volume, the genome is tightly wound around a series of proteins. The DNA is wrapped around histone proteins. Eight wrapped histones in conjunction form a nucleosome. The nucleosomes wind into complexes to form chromatin. When cellular division takes place, chromatin is further condensed into chromosomes that can be split between the two daughter cells.

31. **C is the best answer.** Nucleosomes are the structural level that allows the DNA/protein complex to form tightly organized spirals called solenoids and supercoils, eliminating choice A. Choice B is true but not the best answer choice. Histone proteins do contain basic functional groups that give them a net positive charge at normal body pH, which encourages interaction with the negatively charged phosphates groups on DNA. By mass, chromatin is approximately one-third DNA and two-thirds protein, eliminating choice D. Choice C is untrue because heterochromatin is too tightly wound to be accessed by cellular machinery. Before transcription can take place, heterochromatin must first be unwound, but constitutive heterochromatin is permanently wound and therefore is not transcribed.

32. **C is the best answer.** Homologous chromosomes contain information coding for the same traits, but each chromosome may contain multiple alleles coding for distinct phenotypes for each trait, making choice C the best answer. Choice A is false because the number of chromosomes in a human cell prior to replication is 46 (23 homologous pairs) and the number following replication is also 46 (with sister chromatids). Choice B is also false. Diploid cells have homologous chromosomes; haploid chromosomes lack homologues. Choice D is not the best answer choice because the tightly wound structure of chromosomes inhibits the process of transcription which can only take place on relatively unwound genetic material.

33. **D is the best answer.** This question is asking about factors that may affect transposition. This can occur in eukaryotic cells when pieces of DNA containing a gene or multiple genes flanked by nucleotide sequences are able to move between chromosomes. In order to evaluate the mechanism of this process, one would have to consider other ways that DNA may move between chromosomes and changes to the transposon element that may affect its ability to function. Choice A is a valid consideration, since bacteria may also have transposons, and in order to evaluate eukaryotic transposition, it is necessary to exclude transposition that may occur from bacteria. Choice B is also a valid concern, since these cells undergo meiosis and crossing over, and this involves other methods of genetic alterations. Choice C is a consideration, since the ends of the transposons have specific sequences that allow for excision and reentry, and a substitution in this critical region may affect that ability. Choice D is not a valid concern, since a transposon with several genes would be expected to have stop codons for every one of those genes to indicate the end of the coding region that will be translated. The presence of stop codons is not an unusual variable that would alter the results, since it is expected that transposons have stop codons. Choice D is the best answer for this reason.

34. **C is the best answer.** In eukaryotes, transcribed mRNA leaves the nucleus prior to translation and the processes of transcription and translation are spatially separated by the nuclear membrane. No translation takes place within the nucleus, making C the best answer. The other organelles mentioned are associated with translation. Mitochondria contain their own ribosomes which create proteins through translation. Other ribosomes are responsible for translation of mRNA products from the nuclear genome and are present in the cytosol and at the rough endoplasmic reticulum.

35. **C is the best answer.** It is important to notice that both sickle cell anemia and malaria are life threatening, causing decreased life expectancies. Because the population still exists in the region, there must be some mitigating factor that prevents the lethal conditions from eliminating everyone. Choice A cannot be the best answer for this reason. Choice B is completely contradicted by the information in the question and nothing suggests that the two disorders affect unique populations. Choice D is eliminated because there is unlikely to be a genetic predisposition towards an external threat such as a parasitic infection. The best answer identifies the phenomenon of heterozygous advantage. The sickle cell anemia which creates a sickling of the RBCs actually prevents the virulent spread of malaria, because the malarial parasites cannot reproduce within these malformed RBCs. While this information is beyond the scope of the MCAT®, it is important nonetheless to remember how heterozygous advantage can be used to explain atypical genetic phenomena.

36. **B is the best answer.** Only choice B is both true and concerns translation. Choice A is not the best answer because eukaryotic cells contain some ribosomes that are larger than those of prokaryotes. Prokaryotes do contain ribosomes, so choice C can be eliminated. Translation does not concern DNA, so choice D can be eliminated.

37. **C is the best answer.** Choice A would be a reasonable explanation for the reduced length of mRNAs, but it does not take place. The production of multiple copies of an mRNA discussed in choice B does not address the questions stem and can be eliminated. Choice D is likewise irrelevant to the difference in length between a gene and its associated mRNA. Introns make up a large component of gene sequences. During posttranscriptional modification, the introns (intervening sequences) are removed from a pre-mRNA sequence, which makes the mRNA shorter than the corresponding gene.

38. **A is the best answer.** Introns are removed from the primary transcript during posttranscriptional processing. The number of nucleotides in the mature mRNA would have to be less than the number of base pairs of the gene. Choices B, C, and D all have an equal or greater number of nucleotides than the original gene. Only choice A contains a decreased number of nucleotides to allow for the removal of the introns.

39. **B is the best answer.** To accomplish gene expression, transcription always occurs before translation; choices C and D can be eliminated. To choose between choices A and B, recall that a gene is transcribed into mRNA in the nucleus. The mRNA then leaves the nucleus in its finished form and can be transcribed into protein in the cytoplasm.

40. **A is the best answer.** Both the mRNA produced through transcription and the coding strand are complementary to the template strand, making choice A false and the best answer. Choices B, C, and D are all true. Activators and repressors bind to the DNA close to the promoter region and either activate or repress the transcription activities of RNA polymerase. The nucleotide sequence of the promoter region affects the likelihood and frequency of transcription – sequences which more exactly estimate the consensus sequence are more likely bind RNA polymerase and are more likely to be transcribed. During the elongation phase of transcription, the RNA polymerase moves along reading the antisense DNA strand in the $3' \rightarrow 5'$ direction and synthesizes the new mRNA strand in the $5' \rightarrow 3'$ direction.

41. **D is the best answer.** This is a calculation question where the Hardy-Weinberg equilibrium formulas must be applied. The first formula $p + q = 1$ will help us get started. In this formula, p represents the frequency of dominant alleles and q represents the frequency of recessive alleles in the population. The question states the population incidence of affected is 81/10000. This is q^2 because the disease is autosomal recessive and is only expressed in homozygous recessive individuals, so q = 9/100. Plugging this into the first formula, we find that p = 91/100. With the p and q values, the second formula $p^2 + 2pq + q^2 = 1$ will be used to find the heterozygous carriers. Since 2pq is the heterozygous incidence, $2 \times 91/100 \times 9/100 = 1638/10000$. This is the carrier incidence, which is closest to choice D.

42. **B is the best answer.** The point of this question is to choose the phase of the life cycle in which all three processes (replication, transcription, and translation) take place. Transcription and translation can take place throughout most of the lifecycle. Replication only takes place only during the synthesis (S) phase, making B the best answer.

43. **A is the best answer.** In normal meiosis, the only change in the nucleotide sequence of the third chromosome will occur during crossing over. Crossing over occurs in prophase I. Even though the cells remain diploid with sister chromatids at this point in meiosis, by the end of prophase I, crossing over has finished and the genetic sequence of each future gamete should be established with certainty, making choice A the best answer.

44. **A is the best answer.** Choice A gives the most logical explanation. Often, DNA damage is not permanent if it is repaired before replication. The time between S phases (when replication takes place) is shorter for rapidly reproducing cells. Cancer cells reproduce rapidly and cannot repair the damage as thoroughly as normal cells. Choices B and C are not true. Choice D is very unlikely as normal cells are necessary for proper functioning and the continuation of life. Choice A is best supported by the information presented in the book about the cellular life cycle.

45. **B is the best answer.** It is worth memorizing that in humans, the life cycle of all oocytes is arrested at the primary oocyte stage (prophase I) until puberty. Choice B is the best answer. Even without knowledge of the oocyte life cycle, be aware that oocytes are gametes and therefore produced through meiosis, not mitosis. Choice A can be readily eliminated.

46. **A is the best answer.** Choice D has a Y chromosome and is a male, so it can be eliminated. For female A, since her mother had hemophilia, the mother must have been homozygous recessive for the disease. The father could not have been a carrier. Female A received an X^h from her mother and an X^H from her father and is heterozygous for the disease. Since she is only a carrier, it is possible that she passed on only her good X and that all her children are healthy.

47. **A is the best answer.** If the father is homozygous recessive and the mother is heterozygous, their daughters MUST carry at least one recessive allele. The offspring of this couple could either be homozygous recessive and develop sickle cell anemia or be heterozygous carriers for the disease. Both girls must at least be carriers for the trait because definitely they receive their father's recessive chromosome.

48. **D is the best answer.** This is an application of the binomial theorem under Hardy Weinberg Equilibrium. $p^2 + 2pq + q^2 = 1$ and $p + q = 1$. The question stem states that $p^2 = 0.36$. Therefore, p = 0.6. Using subtraction, q = 0.4. Therefore the number of heterozygotes, 2pq = 0.48, makes choice D the best answer.

EXPLANATIONS TO QUESTIONS IN LECTURE 3

49. **C is the best answer.** For this question, it is best to consider the answer before approaching the choices so as not to get confused with the language of the answer choices. Saturated fat has a maximal number of bonds with hydrogen where the carbons have more surrounding electrons per carbon. In unsaturated fat, the carbons have two fewer electrons for each double bond. In the reduced state, each carbon atom essentially owns more electrons. Electrons signify energy as they will ultimately be exchanged for ATP in the electron transport chain. Oxidation occurs when there are more bonds between carbon and oxygen or when there are fewer carbon to hydrogen bonds, and each carbon owns fewer of the surrounding electrons. Unsaturated fat has fewer electrons to donate to the electron transport chain in exchange for energy in the form of ATP. Choice A can be eliminated because saturated fat stores more energy than unsaturated fat. Choice B can be eliminated because saturated fat is more reduced than unsaturated fat. Choice D can be eliminated because unsaturated fat stores less energy than saturated fat. Only Choice C pairs unsaturated fat with storing less energy as a result of its oxidized state.

50. **C is the best answer.** Small, nonpolar molecules are most easily able to cross the cell membrane through simple diffusion because of the hydrophobic interior of the membrane. For example, oxygen is a small and nonpolar molecule. It can diffuse across the cell membrane without the assistance of an accessory protein. Glucose and glycine are too polar to cross unassisted. Triglycerides, while nonpolar, are too large to cross the cell membrane without being broken down first.

51. **C is the best answer.** When oxygen intake is not sufficient, the body transitions to anaerobic respiration. In humans, this process leads to fermentation and produces lactic acid. Situations that can cause insufficient oxygen levels include vigorous exercise and asthma attacks. The question stem describes a patient running intensely, which would likely result in not enough oxygen intake. Choice A and choice C both describe insufficient oxygen intake. Choice A is not the best answer because gluconeogenesis is not triggered by low oxygenation. Gluconeogenesis is the process of generating glucose from non-carbohydrate carbon substrates. It is triggered by low glucose levels, which is described in choice D. Low glucose levels leading to gluconeogenesis would not cause low blood pH. Choice B is not the best answer because fermentation cannot occur without the products of glycolysis, which needs glucose as a substrate. Choice C is the best answer because it describes low oxygen levels, which is most consistent with the question stem, and low oxygen levels would lead to anaerobic respiration, increased levels of lactic acid, and a lower blood pH.

52. **A is the best answer.** Fatty acids, as the least oxidized of the macronutrients, contain greater reducing potential per unit mass than carbohydrates, which are glucose polymers, and proteins. The double bonds in unsaturated fats lowers their reducing potential compared to saturated fats of similar mass.

53. **C is the best answer.** Glycolysis is the first step of both aerobic and anaerobic respiration. The Krebs cycle, oxidative phosphorylation, and the electron transport chain only occur under aerobic conditions.

54. **D is the best answer.** ATP is a product. Two ATPs enter the reaction to "prime the pump," and four ATPs are produced. Glucose is a reactant and pyruvate is a product. Oxygen plays no role in glycolysis.

55. **C is the best answer.** This answer can most easily be found by process of elimination. Choice A is unlikely to be the best answer choice because ATP synthase is on the *inner* mitochondrial membrane. Choice B and D are poor answers because they mention the specific processes, glycolysis and Krebs cycle, with which you should be familiar. A change in these processes would indicate a completely separate process. Choice C, on the other hand, refers to membrane transport in a more general way allowing for the possibility that a specific mechanism of transport may differ in heart and liver cells.

56. **D is the best answer.** Substrate-level phosphorylation reactions are characterized by the direct transfer of a phosphate group from a reactive intermediate onto an ADP or GDP molecule. The addition of an inorganic phosphate to ADP, facilitated by pyruvate kinase, is an example of this. Glucokinase catalyzes the phosphorylation of glucose, not ADP. Triosephosphate dehydrogenase catalyzes an oxidation-reduction reaction, not a phosphorylation. Glucose-6-phosphatase catalyzes a dephosphorylation, not a phosphorylation.

57. **D is the best answer.** The pentose phosphate pathway is used to generate NADPH, which will be used to reduce glutathione in red blood cells. In the fasting state, red blood cells rely upon liver gluconeogenesis for their glucose supply. They do not have the enzymes necessary to produce glucose themselves. Red blood cells do not store glycogen, so they cannot have glyocogenolytic pathways active. The citric acid cycle occurs in mitochondria, which red blood cells do not possess.

58. **D is the best answer.** Glucose 6-phosphatase catalyzes the conversion of glucose-6-phosphate to glucose. Glucose 6-phosphate cannot easily cross cell membranes because of its charged phosphate group. Without glucose-6-phosphatase, there would be a buildup of glucose-6-phosphate at the site of gluconeogenesis: the liver. Gluconeogenesis occurs during the fasting state. At this time, the liver is the primary supplier of blood glucose. If it cannot export glucose, blood glucose levels will be low. Choices A and B can be eliminated because loss of this enzyme should not affect glycolysis or glycogenesis. Choice C is not the best answer because muscle tissue is not a major source of blood glucose even when this enzyme is functional.

59. **B is the best answer.** Gluconeogenesis occurs in the liver, not in muscle. The activation of hormone-sensitive lipase indicates that glucose produced by the liver will be preferentially used by the brain and red blood cells, but muscle has its own store of glycogen which it can use. This glycogen will be broken down into glucose, which can then enter glycolysis. Both the pyruvate produced by glycolysis and the acetyl-CoA from fatty acids can enter aerobic respiration.

60. **A is the best answer.** Carbon dioxide is produced by oxidative decarboxylation of pyruvate and by the citric acid cycle. Both of these processes occur in the mitochondria. Red blood cells do not contain mitochondria. All of the other cell types do.

61. **D is the best answer.** The precursor for gluconeogenesis that is derived from fatty acids, propionyl-CoA, contains a three-carbon backbone. Since beta-oxidation occurs in two carbon steps, only odd-numbered fatty acids can produce this molecule. When even-chain fatty acids are broken down, they only produce acetyl-CoA. Propionyl-CoA participates in gluconeogenesis by first being converted to pyruvate. Lactate can also undergo this conversion. Glycerol, which also has a three-carbon backbone, can enter gluconeogenesis by being converted to glyceraldehyde 3-phosphate.

62. **C is the best answer.** The brain cannot directly use fatty acids for energy; they must first be converted to ketone bodies.

63. **D is the best answer.** Enzymes can be either activated or inactivated by phosphorylation. Both insulin and glucagon control metabolic enzymes by phosphorylation. ATP slows down glycolysis by phosphorylating fructose-6-phosphate, which allosterically regulates phosphofructokinase. Epinephrine works by utilizing a cAMP cascade. This can result in enzymes being inactivated through phosphorylation, but it does not destroy them.

64. **A is the best answer.** One hour after a meal, the primary source of energy is the intestines. In the fed state, blood glucose levels are high. Hormones respond to environmental conditions. Insulin levels would rise in response to high blood glucose levels. Glucagon and epinephrine promote glycogenolysis and cortisol promotes gluconeogenesis. They are all catabolic hormones. Their levels should be low while blood glucose is high.

65. **A is the best answer.** The conversion of one mole of glucose into glucose-6-phosphate requires the breakdown of one mole of ATP into ADP + P_i and the addition of these phosphate groups onto glucose. $\Delta G = -48.1$ kJ/mol for the breakdown of ATP and $\Delta G = 20.9$ kJ/mol for the addition of phosphate onto glucose. Adding these numbers together gives $\Delta G = -27.2$ kJ/mol.

66. **A is the best answer.** In order to be an electron acceptor, the molecule must itself be reduced. Among the choices, only NAD+ can accept an electron and be reduced, so choice A is the best answer. The other molecules bear the maximum number of hydrogen atoms so they are unable to accept electrons and be reduced. They are electron donors, eliminating choices B, C, and D.

67. **C is the best answer.** NAD$^+$ is an oxidizing agent and will get reduced during conversion of NAD$^+$ to NADH. Protons do not have an available electron pair to donate in order to reduce NAD$^+$. The hydride ion has an electron pair which can be used to reduce NAD$^+$. Since the product of this reaction is NADH, the hydride ion must be transferred onto the NAD$^+$ ring.

68. **A is the best answer.** ATP stores energy to be used at a later time. This means that producing it must require energy and be an endergonic process. The energy input that is required to produce ATP is provided by dietary intake.

69. **D is the best answer.** Oxygen accepts the electrons (along with protons) to form water. ATP and NADH are not electron acceptors. H_2O is the product of the electron transport chain.

70. **B is the best answer.** The Krebs cycle occurs within the mitochondrial matrix in all eukaryotic cells. Glycolysis occurs in the cytosol and the electron transport chain occurs in the inner mitochondrial membrane of eukaryotes. The intermembrane space is located on the opposite side of the inner mitochondrial membrane from the mitochondrial matrix. Protons are pumped into the intermembrane space from the matrix during oxidative phosphorylation. The specific location of the cell is extraneous information.

71. **B is the best answer.** As electrons flow, the carriers pass along one or two electrons, and are reduced (gain electrons) then oxidized (lose electrons) until the last carrier donates electrons to oxygen.

72. **A is the best answer.** Electron carriers in the electron transport chain allow the electrons taken from NADH and FADH$_2$ to be transported through Complex I, III, and IV to generate a proton gradient that drives ATP synthesis. Ubiquinone is a lipid that moves two electrons between Complex II and Complex III, making choice A the best answer. Choice B is a component of the electron transport chain but removes an electron from FADH$_2$ and passes it to ubiquinone to carry, making choice B less likely to be the correct answer compared to choice A. The pyruvate dehydrogenase complex, choice C, is not a member of the electron transport chain and can be eliminated. ATP synthase generates ATP from the proton gradient and does not carry soluble electrons. Choice D is unlikely to be the best answer.

EXPLANATIONS TO QUESTIONS IN LECTURE 4

73. **C is the best answer.** Gel electrophoresis is a process that uses an electric field to separate nucleic acids or peptides based on size or charge. Since nucleic acid phosphate groups give each nucleotide a uniform negative charge, all strands of nucleic acid would migrate the same distance in an electric field if they encountered no resistance; this makes choice B true and unlikely to be the best answer. During electrophoresis, however, the strands must migrate through a porous agarose gel, which impedes the progress of larger segments and separates the strands by size. For this reason, choice A is true and can be eliminated. Proteins are large enough that they cannot be separated using pores, making choice C untrue and the best answer. Proteins are also unique in that they can be separated by isoelectric point, often in the same gel that was used to separate them based on size; choice D can be eliminated.

74. **A is the best answer.** The question stem describes the separation technique of extraction. Carbonic acid, H_2CO_3, is a weak acid and would be mixed with a strong base, such as NaOH. The aqueous layer would then be drained, leaving behind elemental (uncharged) calcium in the organic layer. Choice A is the best answer. Phosphoric acid, choice B, is a strong acid and would remove weak bases, eliminating it as a possible answer. A weak acid such as ethanol would remove strong bases, eliminating choice C. Ammonia is a weak base and would remove a strong acid, making choice D less likely to be the best answer compared with choice A.

75. **D is the best answer.** There are several types of chromatography that could be tested on the MCAT®. High performance liquid chromatography (sometimes called HPLC) involves using high pressure to force the elution mixture through a column. There is no indication in the question stem that this experiment is being done under pressure, eliminating answer choice A. Both ion exchange and size exclusion chromatography are effective at separating proteins and peptides, but neither of these methods utilize an antibody-antigen interaction – choices B and C can be eliminated. Using an antibody to separate some antigen from a mixture is an example of affinity chromatography, making choice D the best answer. This type of experiment can also utilize the high affinity binding between receptors and their ligands or enzymes and their substrates.

76. **A is the best answer.** Thin layer chromatography (TLC) uses a silica gel, which is highly polar. Polar compounds are strongly attracted to the polar silica, and have a more difficult time moving up the gel. Nonpolar substances, which are not attracted to the gel, will move further. This makes choice A the best answer and choice B can be eliminated. There is no lateral movement in TLC, making choices C and D distracter answers that can be eliminated.

77. **B is the best answer.** Crystallization is a very inefficient method for separating compounds, and it is extremely difficult to arrive at a pure substance with only this method, so II is false, which makes answer choice D not the best answer choice. Distillation, while generally an effective method, cannot completely separate two compounds. At some level of purity, an azeotrope will form which has a boiling point higher or lower than either of the pure compounds being separated. This makes I false, eliminating choices A and C. Only choice B remains. Distillation is more effective when done slowly, as this gives the compound with a lower boiling point time to completely boil off.

78. **B is the best answer.** It is important to know what each of the blotting techniques discussed in the lecture are used for. Southern blots use hybridization of small probes to identify specific segments of DNA. Northern blots are similar, but are used to detect RNA. Western blots are used to identify specific proteins or protein fragments, usually using antibodies. Only answer choice B, which includes both Northern and Southern blots, can be the best answer.

79. **B is the best answer.** Chiral resolution, which separates racemic mixtures, is a difficult task that can performed in three ways. The first involves differences in crystals formed by enantiomers. Through visualization of crystals, researchers can sometimes identify specific stereoisomers, making choice A unlikely to be the best answer. The second method uses stereospecific enzymes to modify only one enantiomer in a way that makes it susceptible to physical separation techniques; choice C can be eliminated. Finally, chemists can use reactions that convert enantiomers into diastereomers, which can be separated based on physical properties. They can be converted back into their enantiomeric forms. Choice D can also be eliminated. Enantiomers have identical physical properties, including solubility, meaning an extraction would be not be effective in separating them.

80. **D is the best answer.** This is a question whose answer choices have two parts – a common MCAT® occurrence. It can be helpful to focus on one portion of each answer at a time when answering these questions. The first part of each answer choice here calls DNA either positively or negatively charged. Because of its phosphate groups, DNA always has a negative charge. This eliminates choices A and B. The second part of each answer choice describes the direction DNA migrates during gel electrophoresis. Answering this portion requires some physics and inorganic chemistry knowledge. Anions are the source of electrons in an electrically charged device, which means they are the point that positive electrical charge enters the device. This flow of positive charge makes them attractive to anions, which have a negative charge. Negatively charged DNA will migrate toward the positively charged anode, making choice D the best answer and eliminating choice C. It is easiest to remember this simply as "*anions* flow toward the *anode*."

81. **C is the best answer.** NMR spectroscopy identifies unique atoms with odd mass numbers (usually protons) by measuring their spin states when different external magnetic field strengths are applied. The technique does not identify whole functional groups. This makes choice A true – it can be eliminated – and choice C untrue. The field strength is measured in parts per million (ppm) and displayed along the x-axis of an NMR readout. Peaks that occur farther right on the x-axis are considered more "upfield" whereas peaks farther to the left are "downfield." Answer choice B can also be eliminated. Although it is not necessary to know many of the specifics of NMR spectroscopy, it is helpful to know that delocalized electrons can shield or deshield nearby protons from the external magnetic field, shifting their peaks upfield or downfield. Choice D is true for this reason, and can be eliminated.

82. **C is the best answer.** The first thing worth noting in this spectrum is the sharp peak at roughly 1,700 cm^{-1}, which is indicative of one or more carbonyl groups. Unfortunately, every answer choice involves a carbonyl group, so none can be eliminated using this peak. The next region of interest occurs between 3,000 and 3,500 cm^{-1}. The peak here indicates the presence of an –OH or –NH group. Neither answer choices A nor B have these groups, so both can be eliminated. The –OH peak from the carboxylic acid in choice D would be very broad and span the region from 3,300 to 2,500 cm^{-1}. The question stem spectrum, however, shows a strong, sharp peak at 3,300 cm^{-1}, which is indicative of an amide. For this reason, answer choice C is the best answer.

83. **B is the best answer.** Although questions requiring memorization of spectroscopy peaks are not common on the MCAT®, they do sometimes occur. The two most commonly asked about are those that occur in IR spectroscopy at 1700 cm^{-1} for a carbonyl group and the broad dip at 3200-3600 cm^{-1} that represents an alcohol. This question asks about the peak that results from a carbonyl group, making the answer choice closest to 1700 cm^{-1} most likely to be the best answer. Choice B is therefore a better answer than choices A, C, or D.

84. **C is the best answer.** Note that this question is asking about C^{13} NMR spectroscopy. While less common, it is conceptually no different from proton NMR. In order to determine how many peaks would appear, it is necessary to identify how many unique carbons there are in each molecule. In methylcyclopentane, the methyl group carbon is unique, as is the carbon it is bonded to. The other four carbons, however, only constitute two pairs of unique atoms, since the molecule is perfectly symmetrical. This gives a total of four carbon peaks, meaning choice C is the only possible best answer. Since a plane of symmetry can be drawn through 1,2-dimethylbenzene that separates its eight carbons, the number of unique peaks will equal the number of unique carbons on one side of that plane. This number is also four. In other words, 1,2-dimethylbenzene has four unique pairs of two carbons each.

85. **A is the best answer.** The peak at 3.6 ppm is the furthest downfield in this NMR readout, meaning the protons represented by this peak are the most deshielded in the molecule. The question stem does not indicate this is a 13C NMR, nor is NMR used to detect oxygen atoms, so choices B and C can be eliminated. The remaining answer choices involve protons attached to a β-carbon of a carbonyl or the carbon in a methoxy group. Both groups of protons are going to experience some deshielding due to electron withdrawal, but the methoxy protons should be more deshielded due to their closer proximity to an electron withdrawing oxygen. This means the 3.6 ppm peak likely represents the "D" hydrogens, making choice A the best answer and eliminating choice D.

86. **D is the best answer.** The parent peak, which occurs farthest to the right in a mass spectroscopy result, represents the mass of the molecular ion. In other words, it represents the mass of the molecule being studied. This makes choice C unlikely to be false. If the molecular mass of the molecule is 134 g/mol, the mass of its most abundant isotope cannot be 160 g/mol – choice D is false. Without more information it is impossible to say what the base peak of the molecule is, although 15 m/z is entirely possible. This means that although there is no way of knowing whether answer choice B is true nor false, it is plausible and not more likely to be false than true. Mass spectroscopy does not give the information necessary to determine whether the normal molecule carries a net charge, meaning there is also no way of determining choice A's velocity. For this reason, answer choice D is the only choice that must be false, and should be chosen.

87. **A is the best answer.** An IR spectroscopy peak at 3400 cm^{-1} should immediately trigger thoughts of a hydroxyl group. In this case, a hydroxyl group that was present in the reactants but not in the products. Hydroxyl groups are lost during elimination reactions, making choice A the best answer. An addition reaction would add a new peak rather than removing an existing one, so choice B is not the best answer. Hydration of an alkene is a type of addition reaction. Remember that any time one answer being true would mean another must be true, both choices can be eliminated. Reduction of an aldehyde would yield a new alcohol with a peak at 3400 cm^{-1} in the product, not the reactant, so choice D can be eliminated.

88. **B is the best answer.** UV absorbance occurs in molecules with conjugated systems, which are double bonds separated by single bonds. The longer the conjugated system, the higher the wavelength of UV light absorbed by the molecule. Whereas answer choices A, C, and D depict unconjugated molecules, choice B is fully conjugated, and it is the best answer.

89. **D is the best answer.** This question requires no knowledge of PCR. It requires only the knowledge that a DNA polymerase replicates in the 5' to 3' direction, and that this replication occurs in the opposite direction (3' to 5') of the template strand. In other words, the DNA polymerase can only read from 3' to 5', so it must start at the 3' end of the template DNA fragment. The complement of the 3' end of the DNA fragment in the question stem is 5'-AGC-3', making answer choice D the best answer. Choices A and C are not complementary to any portion of the depicted DNA strand, so both can be eliminated. Choice B would be reverse complementary to the template strand if it was written in reverse – but at the 5' end of the template. A DNA polymerase could not work with this primer, eliminating choice B as well.

90. **D is the best answer.** Restriction enzymes are proteins produced by bacteria that recognize and cut specific sequences of viral DNA, protecting the bacterium from the virus; Choice A is true and can be eliminated. Since these molecules are prokaryotic proteins, they are produced in the cytosol, making B true. It is important to remember that prokaryotes do not have membrane-bound organelles, including the endoplasmic reticulum. Restriction enzymes are typically targeted to palindromic sequences, which read the same forward and backward, so C is also true. While strands of DNA cut by the same restriction enzyme can be joined together, the same is not true of strands cut by different enzymes, which will form non-complementary ends due to their distinct target sequences. For this reason, answer choice D is false, and should be chosen.

91. **A is the best answer.** The illustration depicts a dideoxynucleotide (ddNTP), which is used during Sanger sequencing to terminate DNA replication. ddNTPs contain phosphate groups, as illustrated in the question stem, so answer choices C and D can be eliminated. What distinguishes a ddNTP from a regular nucleotide is its lack of a 3' hydroxyl group. This makes it impossible to form a new phosphodiester bond and continue adding to the DNA strand, terminating replication; Choice B can be eliminated and A is the best answer.

92. **B is the best answer.** The question stem indicates that cystic fibrosis is caused by a loss of function mutation in a specific transporter protein. In order to best study this phenomenon, a model should involve the complete loss of function of the protein or its mouse homologue. Since both RNA interference and substituting a weaker promoter will cause a partial loss of function, these methods would not be the best methods for making a model; Choices C and D can be eliminated. While choice A might initially sound appealing, it does not involve any practical loss of function. Expressing the human protein in mice might cause it to stop functioning normally, but the mouse homologue of the chloride transporter would not be affected, meaning the mice would be essentially wild type. A much more effective method for generating a model would be to generate a knockout for the homologous mouse gene. For this reason, choice B is the best answer and choice A can be eliminated.

93. **C is the best answer.** The polymerase chain reaction (PCR) relies on the power of exponential growth to multiply copies of a DNA. Every time the reaction occurs, each copy of the gene is duplicated, meaning the total number of copies doubles. In a reaction starting with two copies of a particular gene, for example, one round of PCR should yield four copies (a gain of two), two rounds yields eight copies (a gain of four from round one and six overall), three rounds yields 16 copies, and four rounds yields 32 copies. Using a simple simulation like this can help to eliminate equations that do not accurately relate the number of reaction rounds to the number of gene copies. Choice A gives the equation n^x. Substituting 2 for n and 4 for x (an initial value of two, after four rounds) gives a value of $2^4 = 16$. Since four rounds yields 32 copies, choice A cannot be the best answer. If n^{2x} was the best answer, four rounds of PCR should yield $2^{2(4)} = 2^8 = 256$ copies. Since this is not consistent with the expected yield after four rounds of replication, choice B can be eliminated. Choice D offers x^n, which would yield $4^2 = 16$ copies after four rounds of replication rather than 32, eliminating this answer choice. Only answer choice C, with the equation $n(2^x)$, would give the proper value of $2(2^4) = 32$ copies after four rounds of PCR.

94. **A is the best answer.** The lecture states that a gene that is up-regulated after some treatment will appear green on a gene chip, whereas a gene that is down-regulated will appear red. After eating, insulin levels generally rise (recall that insulin is necessary to help remove nutrients like glucose from the bloodstream for intracellular use and storage), likely corresponding with a rise in expression of the gene that codes for insulin. The spot on the chip specific to insulin mRNA, then, should appear green rather than red, making choice A the best answer and eliminating choice C. A yellow spot would indicate a gene that was neither up-regulated nor down-regulated, eliminating choice B as well. There is no reason to suspect that no labeling would occur, so choice D can be disregarded.

95. **B is the best answer.** The most useful evidence for proving that an individual was at a crime scene is evidence that eliminates as many other suspects as possible, leaving only the individual in question. Evidence that the perpetrator has a rare blood disorder would be fairly useful, if not perfect, in this regard. Since the disorder is rare, it is likely that most other suspects can be eliminated based on this piece of evidence. RFLP or SNP analysis would be even more useful, since these techniques can be used to identify a single individual's genetic "fingerprint." For these reasons, answer choices A, C, and D can be eliminated. Blood type, on the other hand, would not be a very powerful piece of evidence. In a large population there will be many people with each blood type, making it a much less useful identification technique than the other three described. This makes choice B the best answer.

96. **D is the best answer.** One of the main disadvantages of standard knockout models is that they cannot be used to study genes that are essential for survival during development. Knocking out these genes is lethal to the embryonic mouse, making breeding (and continuation of the knockout line) impossible. For this reason, a *Hox* gene necessary for neurulation could only be studied using conditional knockouts or a similar method like RNA interference. This makes choice D the best answer. Although both the genes named in choices B and C could be studied using a conditional knockout, they are also accessible via traditional knockout technology, so conditional knockout technology would not be *most* helpful for their study. *LacZ* is a prokaryotic gene that is not expressed normally in mice, so choice A can also be eliminated.

Photo Credits

Covers

Front cover, Comparative DNA analysis: © zmeel/ iStockphoto.com; DNA: Computational results obtained using Discovery Studio Visualizer 3.5 from Accelrys Software Inc.

Lecture 1

Pg. 1, Phospholipid, collagen, amylose, ATP: Computational results obtained using Discovery Studio Visualizer 3.5 from Accelrys Software Inc.

Pg. 1, Cellular micrograph, TEM: © Steve Gschmeissner / Science Source

Pg. 2, Dolomedes fimbriatus on Black Water: © Alasdair James/ iStockphoto.com

Pg. 3, Overhead shot of food containing Omega 3: © Tooga/Getty Images

Pgs. 3-5, Fatty acids, triacylglycerols, phospholipids, glycolipids, sphingolipids, steriods, terpenes, waxes, phosphoglyceride: Computational results obtained using Discovery Studio Visualizer 3.5 from Accelrys Software Inc.

Pg. 4, Fat cells, TEM: © Steve Gschmeissner/Photo Researchers, Inc.

Pg. 5, Vitamin supplements: © Sarah Lee/iStockphoto.com

Pg. 6, Plant Cells (SEM): © Alice J. Belling, colorization by Meredith Carlson/Photo Researchers, Inc.

Pg. 6, Colored SEM of a liver cell (hepatocyte): © Professors Pietro M. Motta & Tomonori Naguro/Photo Researchers, Inc.

Pg. 7, The big graze: © Ken Banks/Flickr, adapted for use under the terms of the Creative Commons CC BY 2.0 license (http://creativecommons.org/licenses/by/2.0/legalcode)

Pg. 8, The discoverers of the structure of DNA: © A. Barrington Brown/Science Source

Pg. 10, DNA molecule: © Sci-Comm Studios/Science Source

Pg. 12, Peanuts: © RedHelga/iStockphoto.com

Pg. 15, Picture symbolizing high-protein diet (meat, fish, vegetables): © Ulrich Kerth/Getty Images

Pg. 18, Human Bone, Microscopic View: © David Scharf/Getty Images

Pg. 18, Small child: © Jaroslaw Wojcik/iStockphoto.com

Pg. 19, Hexokinase: Computational results obtained using Discovery Studio Visualizer 3.5 from Accelrys Software Inc.

Pg. 23, Pancreas cell, SEM: © Steve Gschmeissner/Photo Researchers, Inc.

Lecture 2

Pg. 31, Conceptual computer illustration of the DNA double helix: © David Parker/Science Photo Library

Pg. 34, Human female mitotic chromosomes: Hans Rins/Cell Image Library

Pg. 36, Cell nucleus and chromosomes stained by Spectral karytyping (SKY): National Human Genome Research, NIH

Pg. 47, Col TEM of structural gene operon from E. coli: © Professor Oscar Mille/Photo Researchers, Inc.

Pg. 50, 46 human chromosomes with telomeres: Hesed Padilla-Nash and Thomas Ried, the National Cancer Institute, NIH

Pg. 56, Cancer cell: © Quest/Photo Researchers, Inc.

Pg. 57, Human egg cell and sperm cells: © Thierry Berrod, Mona Lisa Production/Science Source

Pg. 57, Sperm: © Juergen Berger/Science Source

Lecture 3

Pg. 69, Basketball © Amanda Mills/CDC Public Health Image Library

Pg. 87, Mitochondrion, SEM: © Dr. David Furness, Keele University/ Photo Researchers, Inc.

Pg. 90, Shopping Woman © Amanda Mills /CDC Public Health Image Library

Lecture 4

Pg. 95, Western Blot: Maggie Bartlett/National Human Genome Research, NIH

Pg. 97, Iceburg: © Paul Souders/The Image Bank/Gettyimages.com

Pg. 99, GCMS sample: © Tek Image/Photo Researchers, Inc.

Pg. 101, Southern Blotting: © James King-Holmes/Photo Researchers Inc.

Pg. 110, Mass Spectrometer: Pacific Northwest National Laboratory/ Office of Biological and Environmental Research Information System of the U.S. Department of Energy Office of Science

Pg. 117, Well-plates in PCR thermal cycler: Maggie Bartlett/National Human Genome Research, NIH

Pg. 118, Purified DNA: Mike Mitchell, National Cancer Institute Visuals Online

Index

Symbols

5' cap 50, 52
½ V$_{max}$ 25
α-helix 14, 22
β-carotene 110
β-pleated sheet 14

A

abundance 110
acetyl-CoA 69-71, 74, 76-78, 82, 87-88, 90-91, 168, 186
activator 24, 40-41, 163
active site 1, 12, 14, 19-20, 22, 24-28, 127, 130, 162-163
adenine (A) 8
adenosine triphosphate (ATP) 85
adipocyte 70, 73, 76-78, 81, 83, 149
aerobic 71, 80, 87-88, 90, 150, 171, 185-186
affinity chromatography 102, 154, 187
allele 63-66, 121, 184
allosteric activator 24, 163
allosteric inhibitor 24
allosteric regulation 24
alternative splicing 33, 42, 138, 165
amide 12, 79, 180, 188
amino acid 12-14, 16, 24, 33, 38, 43, 44-46, 65, 70, 74, 77, 79, 88, 126, 132, 141, 162-163, 168, 175, 179, 180
amphipathic 4, 128
amylopectin 6
amylose 6, 191
anabolism 79, 145, 168
anaerobic 71, 73, 80, 88-89, 185
anaphase 51, 57-59, 167
anaphase I 58-59
anaphase II 59
aneuploidy 55, 136, 165
anneal 117, 172
anticodon 44-45
antiparallel 8, 34
antisense strand 39
apoenzyme 21
apoproteins 5
apoptosis 73, 88, 149, 167, 170-171
A site 45-46
adenosine triphosphate (ATP) 10, 85
ATP synthase 27, 73, 80, 86, 89, 90, 92-93, 149-150, 170-171, 185

B

Barr body 64
base-pairing 8, 137
base-pairs (bp) 8
base peak 110-111, 189
base substitution mutation 53
beta-oxidation 70, 76, 77-79, 81, 83, 87, 168, 186
biometry 121

C

carbohydrate 1, 3, 4, 6, 11, 17, 23, 27, 69-70, 74, 78, 179
carboxypeptidase 79, 130
carcinogen 56
carrier of a gas 99
carrier of a trait 52-53, 64-65, 184
catabolism 79, 145, 179
catabolite activator protein (CAP) 40
catalase 21
catalyst 19, 22, 161
cellulose 6, 7, 11
centriole 51
centromere 51
centrosome 51
chain-termination method 118
chaperones 46, 126, 161
chemically equivalent hydrogens 105
chemical shift 105
chemiosmotic coupling 89
chiasma 58
chromatids 36, 51, 57-61, 167-168, 184
chromatin 34-37, 51, 182
chromatography 96, 98-99, 102, 144, 153-154, 156, 158, 173-174, 176, 187-188
chromosomal mutation 53, 165
chromosome 34, 36-37, 48, 50-51, 55, 57-61, 63-64, 140-141, 165-168, 182-183, 191
chymotrypsin 79
clone 115-116
clone library 115
coding strand 39, 52, 184
co-dominant 63
codon 44-46, 53-54, 141, 172
coenzyme 10, 21
cofactor 21
collagen 18, 191
column chromatography 98, 176
competitive inhibitor 26, 163, 181

R

racemic mixture 101-102

reading frame 54

real-time PCR 117

recognition sequence 114

recombinant DNA 114-115, 117, 158

replication unit 49

replicon 49

replisome 48-49

restriction enzyme 114, 122, 152

restriction fragment length polymorphism (RFLP) 120-122

restriction site 114, 152, 172

reversible covalent modification 23

Rf factor 99

Rho proteins 40

RNA interference (RNAi) 120

ribonucleic acid (RNA) 10

S

safety and ethics of DNA technology 121

Sanger method 118

saturated fats 76, 148, 170, 185

saturated fatty acids 4

saturation kinetics 20

secondary antibody-enzyme 101

secondary oocytes 58

secondary spermatocytes 58, 60-61

secondary structure 14, 45, 180

sedimentation coefficients 45

sense strand 39

separation of enantiomers 101

separations 96-102

side chain 12, 127-128, 130, 163

single nucleotide polymorphisms (SNPs) 120

single strand binding (SSB) tetramer proteins 49

single stranded RNA 10

six carbon phase 71, 73

size-exclusion chromatography 99, 174

soluble electron carrier 86

solvation layer 15,

somatic mutation 53

southern blotting 100, 101, 120

spermatids 61

sphingolipid 4, 11, 164, 179, 191

sphingomyelin 4

spin-spin splitting 105

spontaneous 53, 71, 85, 138, 145

starch 6

stem cells 120-121, 152

steroids 3-5, 11, 75, 162, 179

sticky ends 114

structural 3, 5-6, 11, 16-17, 27, 45, 47, 63, 73, 95, 130, 163, 175, 180, 182, 191

substrate-level phosphorylation 72-73, 80, 86-87, 90, 150, 171

substrates 12, 19-21, 24, 70, 73-74, 77, 79, 86, 128, 144, 168, 185, 187

sugar-phosphate backbone 8

sulfanilamide 26

Svedberg units (S) 45

synthase 27

T

telomerase 50, 123

template strand 39, 184, 189

terpenes 3, 153, 173, 191

tertiary structure 12, 14-15, 126, 161, 180

tetramethylsilane 104-105

thin-layer chromatography 99

three carbon phase 73

thymine (T) 8

transcription bubble 39

transcription initiation complex 39

transferase 27, 45

transition mutation 53

transversion mutation 53

triacylglycerols 3-5, 145-146, 169, 191

triglycerides 2, 4, 70, 76-79, 81, 83, 129, 162, 168-169, 170-171, 179

trypsin 21, 79

U

ubiquinone 88, 170, 187

ultraviolet region 108

ultraviolet (UV) spectroscopy 108

uncompetitive inhibitors 26, 28, 181

unsaturated fats 4, 76, 80, 148, 170, 185

unsaturated fatty acids 4

upfield 104, 188

uracil (U) 10, 179

urea cycle 79, 171

V

vector 115-116, 121, 129

very low density lipoproteins (VLDL) 5, 77, 150

visible region 110

vitamin A 5, 110

vitamin D 5

vitamins 3, 5, 21, 196

V_{max} 20, 24-28, 128, 130, 133, 162-164, 180-181

W

water 1-3, 5-6, 14-15, 21, 46, 88, 97, 113, 147, 149, 153, 171, 179-180, 187
water-soluble vitamins 21
Watson-Crick model 8
waxes 3, 162, 191
western blot 101, 156, 175

Z

zymogen 22-23

About the Author

Jonathan Orsay is uniquely qualified to write an MCAT® preparation book. He graduated on the Dean's list with a B.A. in History from Columbia University. While considering medical school, he sat for the real MCAT® three times from 1989 to 1996. He scored above the 95th percentile on all sections before becoming an MCAT® instructor. He has lectured in MCAT® test preparation for thousands of hours and across the country. He has taught premeds from such prestigious universities as Harvard and Columbia. He has written and published the following books and audio products in MCAT® preparation: "Examkrackers MCAT® Physics", "Examkrackers MCAT® Chemistry", "Examkrackers MCAT® Organic Chemistry", "Examkrackers MCAT® Biology", "Examkrackers MCAT® Verbal Reasoning & Math", "Examkrackers 1001 questions in MCAT® Physics", "Examkrackers MCAT® Audio Osmosis with Jordan and Jon", all of which have evolved when the MCAT® has changed, and which continue to be the number one bestselling MCAT® materials available.

A Student Review of This Book

The following review of this book was written by Teri from New York.

"The Examkrackers MCAT® books are the best MCAT® prep materials I've seen-and I looked at many before deciding. The worst part about studying for the MCAT® is figuring out what you need to cover and getting the material organized. These books do all that for you so that you can spend your time learning. The books are well and carefully written, with great diagrams and really useful mnemonic tricks, so you don't waste time trying to figure out what the book is saying. They are concise enough that you can get through all of the subjects without cramming unnecessary details, and they really give you a strategy for the exam. The study questions in each section cover all the important concepts, and let you check your learning after each section. Alternating between reading and answering questions in MCAT® format really helps make the material stick, and means there are no surprises on the day of the exam-the exam format seems really familiar and this helps enormously with the anxiety. Basically, these books make it clear what you need to do to be completely prepared for the MCAT® and deliver it to you in a straightforward and easy-to-follow form. The mass of material you could study is overwhelming, so I decided to trust these books—I used nothing but the Examkrackers books in all subjects and scored in the 99th percentile in all sections. Thanks to Jonathan Orsay and Examkrackers, I was admitted to all of my top-choice schools (Columbia, Cornell, Stanford, and UCSF). I will always be grateful. I could not recommend the Examkrackers books more strongly. Please contact me if you have any questions."